CHALLENGII
RURAL
PRACTICE
HUMAN SERVICES IN
AUSTRALIA

Linda Briskman & Margaret Lynn
with
Helen La Nauze

Deakin University Press

Published by Deakin University Press, Geelong,
Victoria 3217, Australia
First published 1999

Graphic design by Graphic Design Services,
Learning Resources Services, Deakin University.
Edited by Bet Moore.
Printed by Deakin Print Services, Learning Resources Services,
Deakin University

Lynn, Margaret L. (Margaret Lilian).
Challenging rural practice: human services in Australia.

   Bibliography.
   ISBN 0 949823 80 5.

   1. Human services–Australia. 2. Social service, Rural–
   Australia. 3. Rural population–Services for–Australia.
   4. Australia–Rural conditions. I. Briskman, Linda.
   II. Title.

361.994

Acknowledgment
We wish to thank the following copyright holder for
permission to include its works in this book: map on page
209 and organisational chart on page 212, reproduced by
permission of the Nganampa Health Council.

Contents

Section 2: Creative practice

Section 3: Affirming diversity

Preface

This book is targeted at human services practitioners and students throughout rural Australia, including social workers, welfare workers, educationalists, community developers and health professionals. In highlighting the challenges of working in a rural environment, it aims to offer support and direction to rural practitioners, many of whom live in isolation from such professional input: new theoretical leads, practice examples and strategies intended to encourage rural practitioners, and prospective practitioners, to reflect on their own practice and to gain confidence in their skills and abilities.

We know that no two rural areas are the same, but assert that there are common themes that extend across rural and remote Australia, and across professional boundaries. One only has to attend the increasing number of rural conferences to forge the links of shared experiences, both in Australia and in other countries.

The authors have lived and worked in rural areas, in 'hands on' work as well as in academic positions. Together with other professional groups and academics, we have continually reflected on our practice as part of a striving for excellence in a responsive, empowering and effective way. This book is an amalgam of our 'practice wisdom' and that of the chapter contributors.

Contributors to this book draw upon their own creative responses to rural practice in a changing environment. Recurring themes include community partnerships, diversity/homogeneity debates, 'bottom-up' policy development and emancipatory practice approaches. The case studies demonstrate creative expertise throughout Australia. While not claiming to explore all fields of rural practice, the selections highlight a range of critical issues.

We hope that the enthusiasm of the written words will encourage others to venture into rural areas, to enhance their own experience, both professional and personal, and to contribute to affirming rural practice.

Linda Briskman
Margaret Lynn
May 1999

This book is dedicated to the memory of Helen La Nauze, who was the inspiration behind the project. In dedicating the book to Helen, we fondly remember the lively discussions, the laughter and the many cups of coffee which were part of its birth.

Helen was born in Launceston, Tasmania on 22 December 1948, married 9 December 1972 and died at home, as she wanted, with family and friends on 25 February 1998.

Her struggle with cancer and her untimely death prevented Helen from contributing to the book as she wanted, but we have incorporated her work where possible. We will miss her friendship, humour and the intellectual contribution she made to rural scholarship.

Contributors

Linda Briskman is a senior lecturer in Social Work at Deakin University. Her career has spanned academic appointments, and public sector employment in the field of family and children's services in rural areas. Current research interests focus on Indigenous issues, rural policy and practice, youth welfare and 'new managerialism' and professional ethics. She is completing a doctorate on the history of the Secretariat of National Aboriginal and Islander Child Care (SNAICC).

Hurriyet Babacan is a lecturer in Community Work at the Sunshine Coast University College. Prior to this appointment, Hurriyet lectured in Multicultural Studies at Queensland University of Technology. Hurriyet has had many years of experience in multicultural issues in a range of positions, including academic, social work and policy development and has undertaken research into ethnic and multicultural issues. She is well connected to ethnic communities and maintains networks and involvement with a wide range of community organisations.

David Barlow moved from the UK to Australia to take up a position as lecturer in Welfare Studies at the Gippsland Institute of Advanced Education (now Monash University) at Churchill in Victoria. From there he moved to Wodonga to help establish human service programs at the newly established Wodonga Institute of Tertiary Education shortly before its incorporation into the wider La Trobe University. At La Trobe's Albury-Wodonga campus, David helped establish the Department of Community Social Science and Rural Social Work and completed a period of secondment as Director of Studies. He left La Trobe in December 1996 to finish a PhD. David's current research interests are in the area of community communications, and centre on non-profit community media as sites of social, community and cultural development. He is also interested in electronic service delivery in rural communities.

Jan Brand is a Women's Health social worker, a counsellor and case manager, working in a rural setting. She is also an experienced community development worker. Jan was a late starter as a social worker, after leaving the computer industry to work initially with young people in Melbourne. She has since worked in several country locations in Victoria and in remote parts of South Australia. She developed a strong affinity with rural areas and great respect for the people of the outback. Working in women's health has provided her with the opportunity to bring together her fifteen years of rural experience, and her appreciation of the strengths and lifestyle of rural and remote women.

Garry Brian is an ophthalmic surgeon who has worked in Aboriginal and Torres Strait Islander communities since 1987. This has been predominantly in the Torres Strait, which he continues to visit. For three years from 1995, he provided services on Cape York Peninsula and at Aboriginal Medical Services in Cairns and Innisfail. Recently, he has also worked in North West Queensland, based at Mt Isa. Since 1995, this type of work has been his sole Australian clinical practice. From 1988, Garry has also been involved in eye service delivery projects and cataract surgery training, including that of non-medical personnel, in the developing world. He has worked in such places as Nepal, Sikkim and Eritrea. Garry is currently the medical director of the Fred Hollows Foundation, and an associate professor at the Mount Isa Centre for Rural and Remote Health.

Michael Brown resides in Northern New South Wales, and holds tertiary qualifications in Science, Education and Educational Administration. He has been an educator for twenty years, and a school principal for the past nine years. He states that he is 'passionate about youth leadership and building positive communities'.

Brian Cheers lives in a small remote community on Eyre Peninsula, and is a social worker and rural sociologist. He is a senior lecturer, and director of the Centre for Rural and Remote Area Studies at the Whyalla Campus of the University of South Australia. Brian's career has included social work in government departments and non-government organisations, human services management, counselling, therapy, private practice, community development, social planning, education, research and consultancy in rural and urban environments. Brian has published widely in international and national journals over a long period. Research and writing interests include rural social issues, social policy, human services, community development and social care practice, rural sociology and rural poverty. He is particularly interested in integrating creative writing with research and scholarship in recording the stories of small rural communities through participant observation. His latest book, *Welfare Bushed: Social Care in Rural Australia*, was published recently by Ashgate (UK).

Fran Crawford of the School of Social Work at Curtin University of Technology in Perth has a long-standing interest in rural social work. It is the field in which she gained most of her own practice knowledge but it also fits with her research focus on interpretive issues of context and culture in the practice of social work.

Judy Cue's mother's family come from Lake Condah in the Western District of Victoria. She states that her family 'has faced many hurdles through their journey of life and have survived many restrictions and constraints along with many Aboriginal families throughout Australia'. Judy has been involved with the community in the Wodonga area since 1991, when she moved from Ballarat. From this time, she has been actively involved in Aboriginal affairs in the Wodonga area and was involved in the formation of the Mungabareena Aboriginal Corporation. Judy is a qualified social worker, currently employed at the Child and Adolescent Mental Health Service in the Upper Hume Region.

Heidi Green lives in Kyogle, in Northern New South Wales. She describes herself 'as a high school drop-out' who has experienced the welfare system and also the suicide of a close friend. She was a founding member of Kyogle Youth Action and became its president in 1995. In 1996, at the age of 21, she was convinced to return to school to gain her Higher School Certificate. After finishing school, Heidi worked in a voluntary capacity for Project X, as its executive officer/ project officer. In 1998, she obtained paid work with Kyogle Youth Action under the Healthy Country Communities Competition. She also gained a position on the New South Wales Premier's Youth Advisory Council. She is working extensively on helping the community in developing a greater understanding of the needs of young people.

Lyn Harrison has recently been employed as a lecturer in Health & Physical Education at Deakin University. Previous to this she was a research fellow at the Australian Research Centre in Sex, Health & Society/National Centre in HIV Social Research, La Trobe University, Melbourne, Australia. She was also the postgraduate co-ordinator for the Australian Research Centre in 1997 and 1998. She obtained her BA (Ed) (Hons) in 1991 and her PhD in Health Education, which investigated young women and issues around identity, in 1995. For the last four years she has been involved in research on adolescent risk-taking and HIV/ AIDS, and community and school-based sexuality education. Her interests include gender, identity formation, sexuality education, and the social construction of sexualities. She is currently involved in a research project with school-based homeless young people in Victoria and a national project with same sex attracted young people. Her research has contributed to policy development in school-based STD/AIDS prevention education at the state and national level.

Lynne Hillier is a social psychologist who completed her PhD on the social construction of wife assault at La Trobe University in 1996. Since 1995 she has worked as a Research Fellow at The Australian Research Centre in Sex, Health and Society, La Trobe University, Melbourne on various projects concerning the sexuality and sexual health and well-being of marginalised youth. Young people included in this work have been those living in rural and remote areas, those who are homeless and those who are sexually attracted to people of their own sex. Her work is informed by feminist and post-modern theories and methodologies. She is interested in the social production of sexualities, gender and violence, discourse and resistance, gender identity and community. Her two current research projects focus on supporting people who have been labelled with an intellectual disability to tell their stories and same sex attracted young people, dominant homophobic discourses and resistance. Her research has been used to inform educational and health policy at state and national levels. In 1999 Lynne was awarded a National Health and Medical Research Council post-doctoral fellowship to investigate aspects of community and youth homelessness. Lyn Harrison and Lynne Hillier have worked together on many projects and as a result have co-authored a number of articles on their work. They have presented their research at national and international conferences and published in both Australian and international journals.

Ann Kesting is currently employed as a Community Mental Health nurse at the Murray Mallee Community Health Centre, where she has worked for five years, following eleven years in district nursing in both rural and metropolitan areas, and ten years in hospitals. She is proud to be part of the collaborative work of Women's Health services, as without such a framework, the daily problems of dealing with poverty and social issues can be overwhelming.

Helen La Nauze strived to achieve social justice and structural change. She was a champion of women's rights, particularly in rural areas. Sadly, Helen died on 25 February 1998, at the age of 49, after battling cancer. Since graduating with Honours in Social Work, Helen's career path spanned a number of areas including community work in the Albury-Wodonga area, and as an academic with the social work program at the Wodonga Campus of La Trobe University. In the first edition of *Women in Welfare Education*, Helen's paper entitled 'Rural Welfare Practice and Rural Women: A Review of the Australian Literature' was published. In this paper, she called for the need for research and theory-building around women-centred rural practice. She heeded this call in her own MSW thesis, completed in 1996 under the supervision of Wendy Weeks, which conceptualised feminist community practice in the Albury-Wodonga region.

Margaret Lynn has lived in Gippsland in rural Victoria for 26 years, and practised as a social worker for ten of those years, until she moved into higher education, teaching Social Welfare. She is currently head of the School of Humanities, Communications and Social Sciences at Monash University and co-chair of the Centre for Rural Communities Inc.

Peter Munn is principal lecturer in Social Work at the Whyalla Campus of the University of South Australia. He is particularly interested in human service delivery in rural and remote South Australia. He is currently undertaking PhD studies focused on service co-ordination of human services in rural South Australia. He teaches Rural Social Work to students at several Campuses of the University of South Australia as well as to students in other Universities based in rural locations. Peter is the leader of the Centre for Rural and Remote Area Studies, a small research group at the Whyalla Campus. He enjoys living and working in Whyalla and sees himself as fortunate in his position which enables him to teach and undertake research in other rural communities.

Kevin O'Toole is a senior lecturer in the School of Australian and International Studies at the Warrnambool campus of Deakin University. He has spent many years working and researching the impact of change in rural areas and has published a range of research papers. Following the work of his PhD, Kevin has focused on local government, especially in rural areas. Most recently he completed a research report entitled 'The Competitive Edge: Competition Policy and Local Government in Rural Victoria', which studied some of the issues associated with competitive tendering in rural Australia. He is also responsible for the development of the National Local Government research data base and web site that will include an electronic journal on local government in the near future. His work in rural Australia has been recognised by the journal *Rural Society* which has Kevin on the editorial panel.

Eversley Ruth spent 1994–96 in the north-west of Western Australia, as the regional community services manager of a multi-service non-government organisation. She has thirty years experience working with communities, and in non-government and government agencies in a variety of roles, and has published many reflections on her work.

Shirley Rutherford identified violence against women and children as a major local issue in Albury-Wodonga. She was a key worker in developing regional strategic responses for women's health. She is currently employed as director of Primary Care by Colac Community Health Services, an integrated agency which includes acute care, aged care and a wide range of primary and community support services.

Helen Sheil is a Community Development educator and researcher with particular interest in the future of rural communities. Her learning from practice and involvement in rural women's programs has provided her with a basis from which to develop a theoretical framework and methodology to achieve transformative change. She is a founding member of the Centre for Rural Communities Inc., an alliance of tertiary education institutions and rural communities, working to provide a clearing house, networking and research in a responsive and supportive capacity to individuals and communities on issues of rurality.

Len Smith is an epidemiologist at the National Centre for Epidemiology and Population Health at the Australian National University. His PhD dissertation was the first definitive account of the demography of the Aboriginal population of Australia, later published by the Academy of the Social Sciences. He was involved in the establishment of the first Aboriginal Medical Service in Sydney, and has published on Aboriginal health and health services, and on related information issues. He is a former director of the Australian Institute of Health and Welfare, and has worked as an advisor to the Fred Hollows Foundation.

Alan Thorpe completed his Master of Arts in Community Education at the University of Canberra, with a thesis titled 'Sexuality and Straitjackets: Issues affecting gay men in rural communities'. His interest and experience in the area has developed through employment as an HIV project officer for a rural health service and as the education manager of an AIDS Council. He has presented on numerous occasions at conferences covering gay and lesbian issues, particularly in relation to rural health services. He is currently with the Commonwealth Department of Health managing the national HIV/AIDS education program.

Wendy Weeks is associate professor in Social Work at the University of Melbourne. She has a long-standing interest in feminist policy and practice, and has written on part-time work, feminist community work and women's services. She is co-editor of *Issues Facing Australian Families: Human Services Respond*, published by Addison Wesley Longman (1991 & 1995), and *Women Working Together: Lessons from Feminist Women's Services* (Longman 1994). Wendy was Helen La Nauze's research thesis supervisor. As colleague and friend in the Women's Studies Research Unit in Social Work at the University of Melbourne, she enjoyed working with Helen enormously, including all the lively debates about research methods and practice.

Chris Williams is senior lecturer in Social Work and Community Welfare at James Cook University where he teaches social policy. He has a particular interest in social policies that affect older people. He is currently researching the impacts of National Competition Policy and related reforms upon human services, in particular those relating to home and community care services for the elderly. Chris has previously taught at the University of New South Wales and at Charles Sturt University.

John Wilson has been Health Services co-ordinator at the Nganampa Health Council for the past four years. Prior to that he has taught social work and community welfare at James Cook University and the Royal Melbourne Institute of Technology. He is the author of a biographical novel called *Lori* published by Magabala Books, Australia's first Indigenous publishing company. John is also the author of several social welfare text books, and a book about single fathers.

Introducing
rural practice

1

Setting the scene
Unravelling rural practice

Linda Briskman

Introduction

It has never been quite fashionable to advocate on behalf of rural communities. City dwellers frequently perceive rural settings as being inherently conservative, increasingly racist and resistant to what is 'talked up' as necessary change in the global economy. Yet such views ignore the diversity and creativity that are part and parcel of rural life, and in particular the survival against the odds at a time when rural communities are confronting agricultural decline, service withdrawal and funding cuts.

The forgotten achievers of rural areas are those human services workers who have little opportunity to speak of their creative responses to the context in which they work. Whether the setting is a large bureaucracy in a regional centre, a small hospital in a medium-sized town or a one-person service in a remote community, these practitioners have had to learn and apply remarkable skills of adaptation. At a time when rural communities have been struggling to keep up with the pressure of imposed change, rural workers are refocusing their practice to incorporate changing philosophies and perspectives, while remaining responsive to the communities in which they live and work.

This collection of Australian writing provides an opportunity to promote rural practice, to acknowledge the contribution made by a variety of professional groups and to present strategies which students and professional workers may find helpful in their own learning and practice.

Murky waters

The term 'rural' refers to an elusive concept, and in this book we draw on notions of plurality and diversity to avoid being trapped in the contested ground of what is, or is not, rural. In so doing, we draw together a range of perspectives which, although standing on their own, hopefully will give some direction and heart to other professional workers grappling with the complexities of rural practice. Although each element of practice is unique, there are, we believe, some lessons that are transferable and adaptable to a variety of settings.

La Nauze (1994, p. 62) refers to the 'murky waters' of the definition and usage of the term 'rural', characterised by ambiguity and lack of consensus. Contest over definition and scope has in fact occurred since serious research and writing about rural issues began. In analysing the array of literature that has emerged, it is evident that, in conceptualising rural, some refer to size, yet others to the nature of the economic activities undertaken, others to values and characteristics. All have difficulties. There has been a trend at times to refer to the concept of non-metropolitan, but this lapses into presenting a false dichotomy, 'othering' rural and obscuring differences in terms of gender, race and social class (La Nauze 1994, p. 63).

Our thrust is encapsulated by the definition by Cox and Vetiri (1992, p.13) who state:

> *The word* rural *is a descriptive term which can be used to describe a location, a person or a perspective. The terms:* the country, rural and regional, rural and remote, rural communities and non-metropolitan *are often used interchangeably. Some people find these terms are used too loosely and would prefer clearer boundaries and more absolute definitions. There is however, no one all encompassing definition which will capture the whole meaning of 'rural' for all people. Any attempt to come to a singular, all encompassing definition only serves to restrict rather than to encourage an understanding of the great wealth of diversity that is rural.*

Rurality implies geographic location beyond the city, characterised at the very least by sparser population distribution, paucity of service infrastructure and a relationship with primary industry. Remoteness is typified by greater distance from major cities, a narrower economic base such as pastoral or mining industries, and isolated communities. What is significant is a recognition that rural areas are no more homogeneous than urban, incorporating a range of aspirations, values, beliefs, affiliations and needs (Frances & Henderson 1992, p. 21). Although common threads and themes will emerge throughout this book, the recognition of diversity is a key concept. Yet, despite difficulties of definition, the term 'rural' certainly conjures up different images for different people. 'Rural' can be perceived as denoting care and social harmony or, by way of contrast, social control and perpetuation of patterns of inequality (Frances & Henderson 1992, p. 19). When a remote dimension is added, the picture may change from a romanticised ideal of sunsets over miles of river or mountain views to one of hardship, lack of access and distances beyond the comprehension of most urban dwellers (Briskman 1997, p. 65).

Whatever interpretation is applied, there is little doubt that rural issues remain marginal to mainstream policy agendas, and rural communities often feel excluded from the policy development and implementation process. A recurring theme in the literature is that of a metropolitan perspective dominating professional practice, models of service delivery and the allocation of resources (La Nauze 1994, p. 63). Whiting and Martyn (1992, p. 26) assert that national policies do not take into account rural realities, and Cox and Veteri (1992, pp. 105–106) have identified the frustrations rural workers and groups experience in attempting to participate in state-level planning for the delivery of community services to rural communities. An assumption exists that urban models and programs can be readily transferred to rural areas (La Nauze 1994, p. 63). Furthermore, when reference is made to rural policy issues, this is often taken to mean social policies that impact on the 'man on the land'. Within this framework rural is synonymous with agriculture, and is conceptualised in terms of economic activity as it effects the total nation. Hence definitions of farmers as 'the backbone of the nation' or 'the salt of the earth' abound (Briskman 1997, p. 65).

Ideologies of particular governments have a significant impact on rural residents. When conservative governments are in power, the farming sector is often given increased recognition and increased resources. For social democratic governments greater priority may be given to justice for a range of groups, particularly the most significantly disadvantaged. Within this ideology, there are a number of groups in rural settings which are seen to experience such disadvantage, including women, Aborigines and people with disabilities (Briskman 1997, pp. 65–6).

Identifying rural culture

The question that springs to mind is whether it is possible to identify components of a rural culture, and the rural literature provides some leads. Rural areas are frequently labelled as being politically conservative. Interestingly, however, according to Campbell and Moore (1991, p. 15), while support of conservative political parties characterises Australia and New Zealand, this is not a global phenomenon, with rural constituents in some countries having been involved in radical reform. Yet, in the Australian context, rural residents, particularly community leaders, are said to be the upholders of traditional values and beliefs.

This is manifest in a number of ways, with critiques of rural areas focusing on characteristics that may be labelled 'racist' or even 'redneck', 'sexist' and 'anti-diversity'. These attitudes are seen to have a significant impact on policy development and implementation in rural areas.

Particularly pervasive to rural areas is the phenomenon identified by Schaffer (1990, p. 12), which denotes the categories of 'real' Australian as including all Australian-born men (as long as they are heterosexual); Anglo-Irish Australian-born men and women; Australian bush dwellers (but never the Chinese); 'mates' involved together at important moments of national life, including diggers, Anzacs and union comrades; naturalised English-speaking migrants (without 'foreign' accents); other naturalised citizens (as long as they are white); rarely, naturalised citizens from Southern European or South-East Asian backgrounds, and Aborigines. Such categorising demonstrates long-established ideological underpinnings, which have a particular impact on migrants and Indigenous peoples.

The lack of acceptance of difference transcends other areas of rural life. Rural residents are perceived as being more homogeneous than urban communities, with less exposure to different life styles. They are seen as less tolerant of diversity and more concerned with maintaining the status quo (Roberts 1992, p. 13). Those considered to be outside the dominant norm include gay men, ethnic groups, and young people who challenge conventional lifestyles. These areas will be covered in subsequent chapters.

Resistance to change is often presented as an entrenched characteristic of rural areas, yet change generates mixed responses. For example farmer ideology can result in farmers maintaining a belief in a traditional view of farming, despite their actual practices, which may engage with the increasing corporatisation of agriculture (Halpin & Martin 1996). Local government may resist encroachment on its autonomy, but embrace new government directions of competitive tendering. The non-government sector may cling to a focus on needs-based services, while co-operating with requirements to rationalise programs and produce quantifiable outputs.

Is rural practice different?

One purpose for producing this collection is to demonstrate, within the professional discourse, the distinctiveness of rural practice, and each of the contributors has drawn this out in their work. These distinctive elements are not static, but responsive to the changing nature of the rural environment. Such adaptations by rural human services workers create context-dependent frameworks that govern practice, consistent with 'bottom-up constructions of wisdom' (Ife 1995, p. 249) central to the reflective examples in this book.

Human services workers, in our framework, are those practitioners involved in service provision in rural areas. They include nurses, medical practitioners, social workers and educators, as well as those who conduct research in rural communities. In the examples presented in subsequent chapters, it is evident that professional practitioners not only *do* their practice, but by necessity adopt a reflexive approach to their work, combined with a critical understanding of the context in which they work. The practitioners who are writing about their experiences have a variety of experience in rural areas. Some 'pass through' in the delivery of programs, others are long-term residents, and the most adventurous have relocated themselves to a rural setting for employment purposes. Others, located outside the rural areas, demonstrate a commitment to rural communities by striving to address policy issues and to enhance rural practice. Each of the researchers who have contributed chapters have applied their findings to practice perspectives, and provide leads for improved policy formulation and service delivery.

Most human services workers in rural areas perform their roles in a co-operative manner, within a multi-disciplinary framework, with people who are differently trained or perhaps without a formal qualification, but with an abundance of practice wisdom. The rural tradition of people working together, particularly in hard times, is an indication of community strength (Ife 1995, p. 117) and partnerships between human services workers and community organisations are common. Human services workers in rural and remote areas, as in urban, operate in a variety of settings and come from a range of disciplines. In this book we try to span a range of disciplines, settings and fields of practice.

Gender, race/ethnicity and class

An analysis of the functioning of rural areas would be incomplete without attention to the dimensions of gender, race and class.

In bringing these constructs to the forefront of our book, we are adopting a structural approach which critiques social structures as being oppressive and inequitable or, as labelled by Ife (1995, p. 53), as 'blaming the system'. This perspective analyses social problems in terms of power issues, which in rural areas are linked to elites dominated by white, middle class men. Within this paradigm, social institutions are viewed as functioning in such a way that they discriminate against people along such lines as class, gender, race, sexual orientation and disability (Mullaly 1993, p. 122). A number of the programs described in subsequent chapters are an attempt to introduce new models that challenge the inherent limitations involved in bringing about structural change in rural areas. Underpinning our approach is a commitment to social justice principles and a human rights perspective: the necessity for all rural residents to share a sense of connection and to have access to an equitable share of resources and services. Traditional attitudes to gender and race are common in many rural communities, and these can serve as barriers to working within a social justice framework (Ife 1995, p. 118).

Although Australian rural sociologists have written extensively on the application of class concepts, class politics have had a minimal analysis in terms of rural human services *practice*. The existing analysis tends to focus on the notions of 'deserving' and 'undeserving' poor. Such a conceptualisation does little to acknowledge the differential access that people have to economic rewards as well as to sources of power. Thus, for those who take a structural or radical perspective, implicit in their analysis is an ongoing critique of existing social, political and economic arrangement, a commitment to protecting individuals against oppression by more powerful individuals, groups or structures and goals of personal liberation and social change (Fook 1993, p. 7).

The gendered nature of rural life is being increasingly researched and reported in the Australian literature (Alston 1990, Poiner 1990, Dempsey 1992, La Nauze 1996). Yet despite the changing nature of women's participation in rural areas, and despite the exposure of rural women to feminist aspirations, overt and covert pressures ensure that sexism and discrimination on the grounds of sex are more difficult barriers for rural women to confront than they are for their urban counterparts. Moreover, as women become more active in advocating change at a variety of levels, they have been confronted with what Alston (1996, p. 82) describes as a 'gender backlash'.

Much of the gender stereotyping emerges from the national mythologies that have been perpetuated in Australia, with the celebration of a particular style of white masculinity embodied in the Australian bushman (Grimshaw, Lake, McGrath, & Quartly 1994, p. 2). Poetry, art and literature that romanticises the patriarchal construction of rurality reinforces such mythologies and renders women invisible in depicting the rural identity. Dixson (1994, p. 58) posits that 'the most striking feature of our national identity is a womanlessness that amounts in some sense to her obliteration'.

British writer, Ruth Lister, argues that women have alway been involved in struggles for formal admission to citizenship, which has been on different terms to those enjoyed by men, with the question of women's inclusion in the public realm as involving complex issues concerning their status as 'other' (1997, p. 71). Australian rural writing has documented this exclusion in relation to civic and sporting events (Dempsey 1992), relegation of duties to a limited sphere such as the 'Ladies a Plate Please' syndrome (Freedman 1989) and to an invisibility in rural literature (La Nauze 1994). In a content analysis of rural social work writing, La Nauze (1994, p. 85) observed that a picture was presented of rural life in which women were characterised as powerless in the public domain, while making considerable but largely unacknowledged contributions to rural economic and community life.

Based on his study of a Victorian country town, Dempsey (1992) stresses the interconnections between dominance and oppression in one sphere, including domestic labour, and exclusion or subordination in others, such as the paid labour force or recreation. He argues that men's superior economic power produces dependency of rural women on male partners. This view is supported in the Canadian context by Collier (1993, pp. xiv–xv), who postulates that both the concept of private property and of the patriarchal farm emerged during the transition from subsistence to market agriculture, where men owned the property, monopolised most of the important agricultural skills and demanded obedience from women and children.

There is considerable evidence that the women's movement has had little effect on farm women (Alston 1990, p. 23). Poiner (1990), in a study in a New South Wales rural community, found that farm women, who were making an enormous contribution to their enterprises, were not developing a feminist consciousness.

Constructs of race and ethnicity are differentially applied in rural areas. False fears of an 'Aboriginal land grab', combined with the ethnic homogeneity of many rural areas, results in less acceptance of diversity. Many rural communities have a relatively high number of Indigenous residents who are shunned by the dominant community and subject to stereotyping, racism and exclusion. In rural areas, Indigenous people are often underemployed, less likely to complete secondary schooling than their non-Indigenous counterparts and over-represented in arrest and imprisonment statistics (Briskman 1998, p. 70).

An urban/rural analysis of voting patterns in the much vaunted Federal referendum of 1967, which restored constitutional right to Aboriginal people, provides some telling results. Of the ten electorates with the highest 'no' vote, nine were in rural areas (Attwood & Markus 1997, p. 56). In 1970, only three years after the passing of the referendum, Lippman published a study of race relations in Victorian country towns which revealed both a lack of understanding of Aboriginal people and prejudiced attitudes. This is despite the fact that Indigenous Australians were instrumental in developing the pastoral industry in Australia, often providing to leaseholders access to traditional lands (Whyman 1997, p. 15). To many commentators it appears that little has changed in the 1990s, with the rise of the One Nation Party, and the 'backlash' against native title provision. Despite the backlash, there are numerous examples of effective work being undertaken with Aboriginal communities, and examples are included in subsequent chapters.

People from non-English speaking backgrounds experience marginalisation, exclusion and lack of acceptance. Some of the older established migrant groups from Europe have, within an integration model, been accepted into rural communities. This acceptance, however, frequently applies to the employed male partner of a migrant family, with women experiencing greater discrimination in terms of access to services and involvement with community organisations. Although there has not been a spate of Asian relocation to rural Australia, much of the anti-Asian migration thrust in recent years has emerged from country areas. Concerns about the migration settlement experience will be reflected in the book.

The wider challenges

All these factors combine to create barriers to the role of human services practitioners trying to work in a manner sensitive to their communities, transcending traditional attitudes which act against the interests of rural constituents. Such challenges have led to a variety of service responses, which have required recognition by rural workers of the vulnerability of many of the communities in which they lived, based on both attitudinal and demographic characteristics.

The decline in small towns, the relatively low income levels, the loss of young people to the cities and the ageing populations all result in the need for a vigilant response. The vulnerability frequently extends to the practitioners themselves who are not sure, in uncertain times, whether they will continue to be employed. Such uncertainty is pitted against rural mythology in popular culture, which presents rural living as being healthy and stress free. The mythology flies in the face of research and documentation which emphasises, for example, the poor health status of rural dwellers (Humphreys 1993), poverty and deprivation as the norm in many parts of rural Australia (Rolley & Humphreys 1993, p. 248) and lack of access to services (La Nauze 1994). In recent times, publicity has been given to the high suicide rate of young men in rural areas (an issue explored in this book), as well as to the fact that country people 'die younger, receive less medical attention, less education and often inadequate telecommunications services' (Wahlquist 1998, p. 23).

From a global perspective, the International Federation of Social Workers (1990, p. 44) notes that rural communities throughout the world have been caught up in a process of socio-economic and political change over which they have had little or no control. Hill and Phillips (1991, p. 4) point out that rural 'crises' have always been a significant feature of our physical and social history, in part precipitated by a harsh and vulnerable landscape. In the Australian context a restructuring of rural Australia has occurred in which the historical dependence on agriculture and mining has declined (Share & Lawrence 1993, p. 15). Such structural change or rural adjustment in Australian agriculture has eroded the economic base of rural communities (Rolley & Humphreys 1993, p. 246).

The impact of such changes is not only profound for farming communities, but groups such as the young, the elderly, women and Aborigines have been adversely affected by structural readjustment in the rural economy (Rolley & Humphreys 1993, p. 250). For people who do not have 'life's fundamentals', including a job, a house and good health, living in rural and remote areas can be seen as a risk factor in itself (Gregory 1998, p. 155). Alston (1998, p. 20) points out that the farm crisis, combined with economic rationalist agendas, has resulted in widespread repercussions in rural communities, including closures of banks, hospitals and a range of government services, with a large number of businesses also going 'to the wall'.

From policy to practice

The diverse nature of rural areas has constrained those policy-makers who, in their attraction to a monocultural, measurable and output-based approach, adopt 'one approach fits all' policies. The rural amnesia of urban-based politicians and policy-makers has resulted in criticism levelled at the city. Those professing to speak on behalf of rural constituents, such as the National Party and farmer organisations, are often perceived as representing a limited constituency, primarily serving the needs of agricultural communities, rather than the full range of rural residents. Constraints from within also exist, with dominant power elites, often enshrined in local government structures, viewed as non-inclusive of the full gamut of constituents. It is not the norm, for example, for rural local government to advocate in support of Indigenous groups, single mothers and people with HIV/AIDS.

Collingridge (1991, pp. 3–4) sees the major problems in the provision of rural community services as being connected to issues of resource distribution, planning and co-ordination, and management and delivery. In terms of resources, he identifies both funding shortfalls and the lack of human resources to deliver services.

As we approach the new millennium we observe how rural areas are confronted with issues connected with 'new managerialist' approaches, driven by economic rationalist agendas. These themes emerge in the next chapter and in some of the later contributions to this book. Such approaches result in top-down decision making, and stringent accountability to irrelevant government benchmarks. Rural areas are increasingly exposed to rationalisation and privatisation, with more responsibility being passed on to the voluntary sector (Dunn & Williams 1992, p. 10). Other consequences include less flexibility and responsiveness to need, with rigid programmatic categories dictated by economies of scale, and a belief in standardisation of services.

Giving voice to rural practitioners

Rural practitioners from a range of disciplines have been working for a long time with little recognition. Their experiences have created considerable practice wisdom, but this wisdom is not often documented and disseminated. In recent years, however, there has been a burgeoning of conferences in which practitioners tell their stories, creating greater awareness and understanding and helping them to move forward as the context changes.

From 1977 until 1991 I lived in a rural area of Victoria. Coming from urban Melbourne, there were many challenges for me, both personally and professionally. From an early stage in my employment as a social worker, I attempted to conceptualise my practice by drawing on the work of overseas theorists and practitioners, and rural sociologists. But it was hearing the voices of the practitioners that worked best for me. It was at those Friday night gatherings in the 'local' where the highlights and lowlights from the week were relived and recounted, that change possibilities were explored and working partnerships nurtured.

In trying to find a pathway through the difficulties confronting rural practice, the development of 'global' strategies, which have an appeal to policy-makers, has proved to be a formidable task. For the past two decades, we have seen the release of government reports which recommend new strategic developments for rural locations. A number of these reports appear to be ungrounded, with the 'how to do it' principles not seen as relevant to the day-to-day practice realities. It is for these reasons that human service workers reject 'top-down' imposition on rural communities of 'urbo-centric' policy proposals. The challenges facing many of the contributors to this book relate to the future of rural communities, in terms of their ability to retain local ownership of their programs while adapting to new conditions that can be community-enhancing rather than community-destroying.

By giving voice to individual practitioners, practice wisdom becomes more visible and accessible. The contributors to this book, in documenting their own practice and presenting their research, are also giving voice to previously ignored constituents including gay men, young women and migrants. Through innovation, celebration of diversity and a responsiveness to rural and remote communities in turbulent times we believe the examples provided have the potential to challenge and influence rural policy and practice.

References

Alston, M. 1990, 'Feminism and farm women', in *Australian Social Work*, vol. 43, no. 1, pp. 23–7.

Alston, M. 1996, 'Rural women make formidable activists', in *Social Change in Rural Australia*, Lawrence, G., Lyons, K. & Momtaz, S. (eds), Rural Social and Economic Research Centre, Central Queensland University, Rockhampton.

Alston, M. 1998, 'Social work and the decline of the bush', *National Bulletin*, Australian Association of Social Workers, vol. 8, issue 2, p. 20.

Attwood, B. & Markus, A. 1997, *The 1967 Referendum, or when Aborigines didn't get the vote*, Australian Institute of Aboriginal and Torres Strait Islander Studies, Canberra.

Briskman, L. 1997, 'Rural issues', in Briskman, L. & O'Toole, K., *Critical Social Policy*, Study Guide, Deakin University, Geelong.

Campbell, H. & Moore, D. 1991, 'Crisis time for rural crisis meetings: Ruralia contra mundum, in *Rural Society*, vol. 1, no. 2, pp. 15–16.

Collier, K. 1993, *Social Work with Rural Peoples*, New Star Books, Vancouver.

Collingridge, M. 1991, 'What is wrong with rural and community services', in *Rural Society*, vol. 1, no. 2, pp. 2–6.

Cox, D. & Veteri, D. 1992, 'Influencing social policy from a distance', in *Community work: Solution or illusion*, ed. M. Coppin, papers from the second Australasian Conference on Rural Social Welfare Practice, Kookynie Press, Perth.

Dempsey, K. 1993, *A Man's Town: Inequality between women and men in rural Australia*, Oxford University Press, Melbourne.

Dixson, M. 1994, *The Real Matilda*, 3rd edition, Penguin Books, Melbourne.

Dunn, P. & Williams, C. 1992, 'Human service delivery to the elderly', in *Rural Society*, vol. 2, no. 3, pp. 17–20.

Fook, J. 1993, *Radical Casework: A theory of practice*, Allen & Unwin, Sydney.

Frances & Henderson 1992, *Working with Rural Communities*, Macmillan Press, London.

Freedman, L. 1989 'Ladies a Plate Please', in *Network*, Rural Women's Network Newsletter, Victoria, Spring, pp. 3–4.

Gregory, G. 1998, 'Few positives for rural communities', in *Rural Society*, vol. 8, no. 2, pp. 155–6.

Grimshaw, P., Lake, M., McGrath, A. & Quartly, M. 1994, *Creating a Nation*, McPhee Gribble, Melbourne.

Halpin, D. & Martin, P. 1996, 'Agrarianism and farmer representation: Ideology in Australian agriculture, in *Social Change in Rural Australia*, Lawrence, G., Lyons, K. & Momtaz, S. (eds), Rural Social and Economic Research Centre, Central Queensland University, Rockhampton.

Hill, J. & Phillips, C. 1991, 'Rural people in times of recession', in *Children Australia*, vol. 16, no. 4, pp. 4–10.

Humphreys, J. 1993, 'Planning for services in rural Australia', in *Regional Journal of Social Issues*, no. 27.

Ife, J. 1995, *Community Development: Creating community alternatives—vision, analysis, practice*, Longman, Melbourne.

International Federation of Social Workers 1990, 'International policy on conditions in rural communities', in *Australian Social Work*, vol. 43, no. 1, pp. 44–5.

La Nauze, H. 1994, 'Rural Welfare Practice and Rural Women: A review of the Australian literature, in *Women in Welfare Education*, no. 1, 1994.

La Nauze, H. 1996, *Conceptualising feminist community practice in a major rural centre*, unpublished MSW thesis, University of Melbourne, Melbourne.

Lawrence, G. 1996, 'Rural Australia: Insights and issues from contemporary political economy', in *Social Change in Rural Australia*, Lawrence, G., Lyons, K. & Momtaz, S. (eds), Rural Social and Economic Research Centre, Central Queensland University, Rockhampton.

Lippman, L. 1970, *A Survey of Race Relations in Selected Country Towns*, Centre for Research into Aboriginal Affairs, Monash University, Melbourne.

Lister, R. 1997, *Citizenship: Feminist Perspectives*, Macmillan Press, Hampshire.

Mullaly, R. 1993, *Structural Social Work: Ideology, theory and practice*, McClelland & Stewart, Toronto.

Poiner, G. 1990, *The Good Old Rule: Gender and other relationships in a rural community*, Sydney University Press, Melbourne.

Roberts, R. 1992, 'Men who have sex with men in the bush', in *Rural Society*, vol. 2, no. 3, pp. 13–14.

Rolley, F. & Humphreys, J. 1993, 'Rural Welfare: The human face of Australia's countryside', in *Prospects and policies for rural Australia*, Sorenson, I. & Epps, R. (eds), Longman Cheshire, Melbourne, pp. 241–57.

Schaffer, K. 1990, *Women and the Bush: Forces of desire in the Australian cultural tradition*, Cambridge University Press, Cambridge.

Share, P. & Lawrence, G. 1993, 'Structural change for rural communities', in *Impact*, vol. 24, no. 4, pp. 15–17.

Wahlquist, A. 1998, 'Great Dividing Range', in *The Weekend Australian*, 26–27 September, pp. 23, 26.

Whiting, L. & Martyn, R. 1992, 'Mental health social work practice in a rural and urban setting: A comparative study', unpublished BSW Honours thesis, Department of Social Work, Monash University, Melbourne.

Whyman, H. 1997, Address to Rural Australia: Toward 2000 Conference, Centre for Rural Research, Charles Sturt University, Wagga Wagga.

2

Setting the scene
Exploring the context

Margaret Lynn

Introduction

A focus on rural human services brings into sharp relief the issues and processes that are often invisible in the dominant rural discourse, which focuses largely on agriculture and climate, commodity prices and interest rates, capital and land, technology and transport, innovation and tradition. This chapter will examine that broader rural context and some of the points of contact and influence between the dominant view of rural issues, and the perspective that human services occupies, identifying a vacuum in rural development policy that needs to be addressed (Sher & Sher 1994). Rural Australia is experiencing change at an unprecedented rate, and the political and economic infrastructure that supports it is arguably out of date and out of touch with the new realities, while the social infrastructure has become an ideological casualty of change.

Rural organisations and politics

Despite the increasingly urban nature of the Australian population, rural organisations have played a dominant role in mainstream conservative politics in all states, and nationally since federation. The National Party (by various names) has had a close alliance with the National Farmers Federation (NFF) formed in 1979, and its antecedent organisations, which pursue the interests of the farming community. This is done not only through direct representation of commodity market and land issues, but by representing the interests of capital versus labour in its enduring opposition to unionism. The NFF was closely involved in the conservative government's attempt in 1998 to break the Maritime Union's influence over the waterside workers' conditions, in the alleged interests of improving the efficiency of the waterfront, a site which has a determining role in the cost of exporting primary products.

Within the rural sector, the NFF and its state counterparts and a range of industry-focused groups have operated to serve the market interests of primary producers, and have frequently taken up broader political issues on behalf of their constituency. A range of geographically located commissions, for example The Murray-Darling Basin Commission established in 1987, mediate solutions to problems caused by combinations of environment, climate and misuse of the land. Additionally, Landcare, founded in the mid-1980s, is a politically bipartisan organisation which is committed to environmental sustainability and operates through several thousand groups around Australia. Other rural issues become politicised from time to time when they gather sufficient strength to arouse an organisational response (for example the gun lobby, made up of groups and sub-groups arguing against government restrictions on gun ownership).

Women's organisations have existed as a forum for women's issues in country areas. In its early years the Country Women's Association (CWA), founded in the 1920s, while not challenging the male orthodoxies surrounding power relationships and resource distribution in country towns, was responsible for the widespread development of a number of key services now accepted as universal in the country, such as infant welfare centres and hospitals. The CWA is now seen as a conservative and consensual organisation, and has difficulty in attracting new, younger members (Teather 1994).

Successors to the CWA in carrying the mantle for country women could be said to be Women in Agriculture, the Rural Women's Networks in several states, and the Foundation for Australian Agricultural Women. These groups are still evolving and taking up new challenges and new directions. It was the Australian Women in Agriculture that organised the first International Farm Women's Conference in Melbourne in 1994, and the same key women have had significant and continued success in organising women nationally and internationally, including the staging of a further world conference in the United States in 1998. The new rural women's movement is inspired by feminist principles and seeks a more equitable share of power at all levels, from the farm, family and community to national and international levels (Teather 1995).

Many organisations take a conscious and deliberate approach to achieving aspects of social, political and economic change in the rural environment, but few organisations synthesise these perspectives to take as their central tenet the sustainable development and support of rural communities and their populations. Indeed, policies of either political party implicitly or explicitly adopt the social darwinist view that many rural communities are not sustainable. This applies even when the same governments operate Departments of Primary Industries, Agriculture or Natural Resources, with programs aimed at assisting rural communities or businesses. Some programs are designed to assist farmers to 'adjust out' of farming, on the premise that they will not be able to achieve or return to viability. This view is perhaps unfairly applied to some communities that have been allowed to decline through official neglect.

The Australian political agenda, concentrated in but by no means confined to rural Australia, has become skewed away from the 'social' and in the direction of the 'economic'. The ascendancy of economic rationalist policy has seen a greater split than ever between the thinking and aspirations of ordinary men and women in the way they expect their nation to be run, and the actual performance and outcomes of political and economic policy. Such outcomes have been a drastic reduction in the visible community infrastructure: the closure of schools and health services; the regionalisation, and hence distancing from most people, of large numbers of direct services—postal, banking, support services, employment, communications and transport. Other professional services that depend on the existence of these operations are undermined, and add further to the decline of community infrastructure. A number of factors have created barriers to the community identifying with existing services, and engaging in finding solutions to their own problems. These include:

- the creation of a new language to define and measure the inputs and outputs (not outcomes) of the social sector;
- the introduction of competitive tendering, frequently leading to the employment of people and organisations not previously involved in or aware of the needs of the local area; and
- the ensuing commercial-in-confidence nature of the development of human services.

Kevin O'Toole's chapter discusses some of the dilemmas for human services which are created by economic rationalism, and presents one community's response. As other chapters demonstrate, the human services field is currently in the process of determining the extent to which it will adapt to the new demands, and can in turn influence the policy that sets such requirements.

There has been a dramatic shift in the popular rural discourse in very recent times. Commentators have all identified a growing sense of disempowerment and disillusionment with the political process as a vital ingredient in the rise of deeply conservative or reactionary views being espoused. These views were previously mumbled by a disaffected minority of disadvantaged individuals who believed that forces conspired to give some community sectors more than they deserve. These same views have always formed the platforms of tiny but extreme right wing groups, such as the League of Rights, based on supremacist or oppressive philosophies. It is new in Australian politics that such views have been given a mainstream audience, and espoused by those who claim to be tolerant but fed up with their own marginalised positions. This new political presence has become the voice for many groups who wish to oppose what they see as unacceptable erosion of their rights as Australians:

- recently introduced gun control measures;
- the perceived threat to land tenure of recent land rights and native title legislation;
- immigration levels seen as adding to current levels of unemployment;
- perceived inequities in providing any services designed specifically for Aborigines;
- multiculturalism replacing assimilation;
- support for single parents (read mothers) to remain out of the workforce to raise their families.

The platform appears to be based on a fear that diversity and cultural pluralism is harmful to national unity, and that there are only limited ways for Australia to progress which essentially preclude further diversification. Many of these issues do not apply specifically to rural Australia, nor did they translate into electoral success at the 1998 federal election as many predicted. However, they are being popularly identified with a rural backlash, whose aftermath will predictably have a long-term impact on Australian politics, and will serve to raise the political necessity of attending to rural infrastructure issues that have been increasingly neglected.

The rural agenda in the late 1990s has thus been changed in reactive ways, and a new progressive agenda has not yet sufficiently emerged to offer hope for communities that have experienced considerable losses. Simplistic responses appear to provide approaches to the disillusioned. Rural communities are caught in the emotional crossfire between pride and despair, and need the sort of policies that offer support and resources for establishing autonomous and locally relevant structures and viable lifestyles, as well as ways of being fully integrated into the social and economic environment of Australia and the world. A progressive policy for rural Australia will be complex and contested, and will need to be negotiated through many organisational and political lenses to deliver the sort of outcomes that can appeal to a disparate constituency and multiple sectional interests. Some chapters in this book, for example Helen Sheil's, offer some hope that such a policy may be advanced.

Government impacts on the rural setting

Local government has always been seen as the level of government closest to the people, and hence more knowable, more able to be influenced, and more involved in matters of community relevance. With the move in some states during the 1990s towards the amalgamation of local government areas, the sense of local ownership and participation in this form of government is faltering. Australia is moving further away from localism to regionalism and to larger and more impersonal government. The dominance of state and national interests means that local government is acting increasingly as an agent of higher levels of government. Larger groupings of councils on behalf of regional economic interests further erode local control. The capacity of local government to create local employment is disappearing with the imperatives of competitive tendering, and the consequent changes to job definitions through unit costing and notions of core business. Privatisation means that all services aim to make a profit. The purchasing of services by government has been separated from the provision of service by government or private providers, an 'efficiency' aimed at avoiding conflicts of interest and undue influence, but which adds to the complexity of service delivery for consumers at a local level.

Many decisions about local community activity are the result of programmatic decisions taken centrally at state or federal level. Programs in health, education and community services, employment, policing and public safety are frequently established according to metropolitan models and priorities, and it is the extent to which local professionals and service users can exert influence over their implementation and allow a degree of local ownership that determines their success or failure at the local level. The dominance of urban-based policies that masquerade as universal policies adds further to the rural policy vacuum alluded to, by which many of the needs of rural people and communities go unrecognised and unmet. Eversley Ruth's chapter highlights the impacts on communities of the loss of human services networking and collaborative needs identification, grounded in local knowledge.

Most government-funded programs currently operate under the policy rubric of economic rationalism. This partly explains the policy vacuum for rural communities, because the critical social issues are not economic or market-driven, but it is also true to say that rural policy has always been dominated by agricultural and hence market sector interests, and not the broad needs of people. The 'social' has traditionally been left to the informal sector.

In the late 1990s, communications policy has emerged as a key policy concentration with major rural implications as government moves to divest itself of responsibility for managing telecommunications, and is faced with the need to ensure that rural and remote Australia is adequately served by the new private corporations who will own the infrastructure and deliver the services in the industry of the future. The Networking the Nation Project, while ironically funded from the partial sale of Telstra in 1997, offers some hope for adequate rural telecommunications service provision, but receiving submissions from regional and community organisations as a means for meeting policy objectives ensures that progress will be patchy for some time. David Barlow's chapter analyses some of the opportunities but also the dangers for rural and remote communities in an expansion of electronic service delivery that may be used either to provide new and valued services or to dehumanise or to replace those that already exist.

A national health strategy acknowledges that health outcomes for rural residents are worse on all indicators than for urban residents. It includes incentives to encourage doctors to the country, and supports research on rural health. It is difficult to get accurate figures on rural health expenditure, but equitable distribution is unlikely when the most expensive specialist procedures are only conducted in cities, consuming disproportionate amounts of the federal health budget. Aboriginal health, particularly in rural and remote areas, is a matter of national shame, and official responses move between expressions of scapegoating, paternalism, helplessness and concern. Garry Brian and Len Smith's, and John Wilson's chapters demonstrate the complexity of the task if Australia is to have policies and practice models that serve the health needs of all people and communities. However, they both argue for a change in the centralist perspective that creates policies inadequately grounded in the context in which they will apply.

Policy that sees rural human concerns as central, and hence requires an integrated approach to social, economic and environmental issues, is the challenge for government and rural organisations. However, at the end of the twentieth century, it appears that Australian governments are retreating from all but economic considerations.

Rural social and economic change

While rural communities are being exposed to global change at an accelerated pace, it would appear that the healthiest and most lively communities are those that actively engage with shaping their response to these impacts. Smaller communities that organise to plan alternative economic options, that rally to discuss bank closures or march in large numbers to celebrate cultural diversity, are better placed to deal with change than those places and people who have been so demoralised by the speed of change that it has left them without the resources to respond, or too divided to find a voice. The greater the population, by and large, the greater the dependency on formal organisations to catalyse a change process, and therein lies the dilemma for many communities where large organisations see their future viability requiring them to identify with the external sources of change, usually government or large corporations. The Latrobe Valley in Victoria thus lost ten thousand jobs and gained no government financial compensation in return, because unions, local government and the power generators, then in public hands, were unable to separate themselves from the political and economic forces and make compelling demands for the community.

In smaller geographically focused communities, informal networks have the potential to operate powerfully to shape information, provide support and material assistance, and act as agents of social control. In my own community of Gippsland I have observed that networks that accept the inevitability of change are exercising significant influence over community affairs, particularly when more traditional organisations have lost their capacity to lead. While in 'the good times' power elites can apply economic influence fairly invisibly to control much at a local level, in times of change the old structures are under pressure to respond differently. Participatory and democratic processes may actually prevail at a local level and produce responsive structures, as discussed in some chapters of this book. The towns of Maleny in Queensland and, on a smaller scale, Mirboo North in Victoria both provide excellent examples of communities that believe in their own capacity to create positive change, and as a result continue to generate significant co-operative solutions to community need.

The rapidity of social change in the last few decades has impacted no less on rural communities than elsewhere. Life and work have become profoundly more complex, as almost constant change adds layers of process and choices to be made for every action. Values have become less an arena for certainty than for contest, as more and more decisions are required to be made in areas where competing values are inevitably confronted. The rise in the 1990s of independent candidates for political office, for example in West Gippsland and Mildura in Victoria, demonstrates that more diverse value positions are publicly emerging, and a less consensual form of politics is being adopted, at least in the short term.

Divergent value positions have always been expressed in rural communities in the tension between the valued tradition of self-help and the lesser value ascribed to those seen as needing assistance. Rural subsidies for diesel or other tax concessions, or drought relief, are never seen as compromising the self-help ethic, and are not put in the same category as welfare. However, attitudes towards welfare have been challenged, even in the most conservative sectors of communities, by the dramatic increase in the number of rural people needing unemployment benefits. Since the rural downturn of the 1980s, unemployed people have been seen much more as receiving necessary help rather than a heavily stigmatised service, and unemployment is now more recognised as a structural matter rather than an indication of personal failure. There is evidence that certain value positions are being renegotiated in rural communities through force of circumstance. Current community agendas are being shaped by a number of factors. These include women's awareness of the impact on families of economically driven policies, as well as the forces of globalisation, which are changing the nature of farming and the economic base.

Recognition of gender issues is, for some women at least, becoming unavoidable as employment practices are less regulated and the nakedness of gender discrimination becomes apparent. Conservative rural values still frequently privilege male breadwinners over female for employment, while some farm management practices still marginalise the role and contributions of women. Privatisation, corporatisation, deregulation are all forces that have changed the nature of relationships in the workplace. The closure of businesses and the relocation of services have reduced diversity in employment, and in many cases, diminished the proportion of jobs available to women. The rationalisation of banks and the demise of rural schools, both traditional employers of women, illustrate this trend.

Unemployment and industrial restructure have major impacts on rural towns. Forced mobility and out-migration leaves infrastructure under-utilised, leading to further retractions; house prices drop, and the capacity to attract other industry and new residents is diminished, as the town is seen as less attractive. The cause may be identical in the city for a company to be taken over and downsized, but the impact on a smaller community with a narrower industrial base will be frequently experienced as a crisis for the whole community, not just the individuals directly involved. Rural community relationships and processes are more visibly dynamic and personalised.

Many parts of rural Australia have a significant unemployment crisis, especially among youth, and will require a change in policy direction to enable real change to occur. There is a greater acceptance of the need to provide new markets and new employment opportunities in rural areas. Although this will be facilitated by government support, it is increasingly recognised that positive change requires new ways of thinking that are less dependent on major capital injection than on good ideas and people working together.

Most parts of the rural farm-based economy have always been heavily dependent on export markets, and subject to the vagaries of commodity price shifts and international politics. The challenge for the rural economy would appear to be further market diversification and the development of value-adding processes, though Lawrence (1994, p. 14) argues that farmer preference for the traditional bulk commodities suggests that niche markets are unlikely to grow very rapidly. He argues that farming practices involve social and personal processes, and are not simply the result of impersonal economic forces. Governments traditionally and inevitably find it difficult to develop policies that will produce fundamental and positive shifts in the management of whole industrial and community sectors, and find it easier to talk down as being time-limited or anachronistic those sectors seen as unproductive or dependent. The days of massive rural subsidies are over, and restructuring now demands greater competitiveness. Much government rhetoric suggests a belief, or a wish, that small rural communities will die away when economic change further undermines their viability. History has produced many ghost towns, but it also demonstrates that creativity and diversification can revive seemingly moribund areas, or prevent such decline occurring at all.

Perhaps as an antidote to rationalisation and corporatisation, co-operative developments are slowly occupying a greater share of production and marketing strategies in Australia, though we are well behind other Organisation for Economic Co-operation and Development (OECD) countries in most areas of co-operative development in primary industry. Co-operatives have the capacity to transform not only local economies but local communities, as they involve a fundamentally different approach to work and to notions of competition, to capitalisation of enterprises, and to management. Co-operation in rural communities can provide a powerful answer to the problems posed by economic restructuring. Australia has produced some very exciting recent examples of co-operative development in the primary, secondary and service industries that provide models that could be adopted anywhere. Co-operatives can bridge the gap between the local and the global by taking a holistic, not a partial, view of the enterprise and its place globally. People involved in true co-operatives are encouraged, trained and even obliged to understand the total process from initial source to final delivery. They share the benefits and the problems, the profits and the losses. Co-operative service delivery can provide services for a community where the economic multiplier effect of the investment can be far greater than an external employer could achieve, and the social multiplier effect creates a vibrant and empowered community. Yeoval Health Services in New South Wales demonstrate such effectiveness, where a community of 450 has taken co-operative ownership of its hospital which was threatened with closure, has created 40 jobs and turns over millions of dollars per year (see Helen Sheil's chapter). Yeoval was assisted by the positive co-operative legislation of the New South Wales government, while similar attempts in Victoria are made much more difficult by poor legislative and organisational support. Co-operatives have a history going back to Rochdale in 1844, when co-operative principles were first enunciated and the first worker co-operative was established. While they may be seen by some as anachronistic structures in the face of globalisation, the evidence would suggest that they have great capacity to meet economic and social needs of their members, as well as offering the flexibility of operation that can cope with a context of any size, locally or globally.

And yet globalisation will change rural communities for ever. Businesses will be as likely to communicate across the world as across the river. Inexpensive electronic access will mean that information is available from anywhere in the world, though the telecommunications revolution has not yet provided such access to all parts of Australia. Education is developing in less formal ways, and more people are taking up adult education options, while at the same time more emphasis than ever is being put on formal qualifications, as international study opportunities expand and preparation for global employment becomes more real. The rural sector, which has traditionally placed less store by formal education, is facing the need to catch up and improve its school retention rates, and the role of regional universities could change as a result, providing an environment that is more comfortable than city campuses for many rural residents, as well as being key institutions for flexible modes of learning off-campus, and major resources for regional economic and social development. While these dramatic changes will produce some seamless transitions from rural to urban, and local to global, rural Australia is challenged as never before to shape an agenda that is inclusive, so that the divide between rich and poor in resource and information terms does not polarise the nation.

Social justice and injustice

Considerations of social justice in the country require an examination of the meaning of access, equity, human rights and distributive justice. How do such notions apply in some of the most remote parts of Australia? Even applied relatively, is it possible to argue that all Australians have rights to services that will be made accessible to them, rights to be treated equitably, and to have legal protection from any type of exploitation, abuse or exclusion. Can the existing factors of distance and lack of choice in services, compounded by the recent closures of so many services and programs, provide at all adequately for the health, education and support needs of all Australians? The answer, of course, is that Australia has never had the sort of commitment to social justice and an equitable allocation of resources that could ensure universal provision of adequate, culturally appropriate programs and services, the laws and regulations to back them up, and the funding to maintain them. This applies even if it may be argued that we have done as well or better than comparable countries in this regard.

Recent changes to industrial legislation have alerted Australians to the fragile nature of human rights that were once assumed to have been won for ever. The erosion of award conditions and the limiting of factors that can be covered by awards make it clear that social justice is ephemeral and needs to be constantly guarded and recontested. The performance of global capital enterprises in developing countries that do not have environmental and industrial protection laws of any kind demonstrate how necessary legal regulation is to ensure conscionable corporate behaviour.

Questions of social justice bring us back to the roles and responsibilities of human services. These are defined very broadly to include not only professional services and programs, but the activities of communities, through organisations and individuals, who are engaged in meeting their needs for sustainability, justice and mutual care. Human services operate at the interface between individual and community interest, minority and majority perspectives, autonomy and advocacy, care and control. The tension between these potentially polarised positions must be recognised and worked with. In rural communities the human services task is very often to argue for resources in a climate that does not give priority to the social, to promote meaning when young people see no hope, to assert rights when others would deny them, to help people use their abilities rather than be defined by their disabilities. In rural Australia, as elsewhere, the dominant discourse is not about integrated development and social justice, and so it is necessary for human service workers to set their sights on shifting the balance, and remaining optimistic.

This chapter has attempted to explore the context in which rural practice operates. I have defined this context in terms that are essentially political, and as shaped by policies and lack of policies addressing rural needs, on the one hand; and rural people's and organisations' direct or indirect actions to influence the development of more responsive policies on the other. While there is no final consensus on what these needs and appropriate policy responses are, Sher and Sher (1994, pp. 27–8) discuss the need for a comprehensive rural development policy. They identify goals in expanding the rural population, growing and diversifying the rural economy and employment base, providing to rural people and communities an equitable sharing of the rewards derived from rural resources, and creating an improved quality of life and stronger, more cohesive rural communities.

The chapters that follow develop a number of the themes addressed in this introduction, and provide a range of socially just, strategic approaches that argue for equitable resourcing and recognition of the strengths of rural communities, while acknowledging their shortcomings and challenging their limitations. They also argue for a sense of ownership rather than alienation, a sense of community rather than atomisation, and human development rather than economic measures alone.

References

Lawrence, G. 1994, 'Rural Adjustment Revisited: in Defence of a Sociological Approach', in *Rural Society*, vol. 4, no. 3.

Sher, K. & Sher, J. 1994, 'Beyond the Conventional Wisdom: Rural Development as if Australia's Rural People and Communities Really Mattered', in *Journal of Research in Rural Education*, vol. 10, no. 1.

Teather, E. 1994, 'CWA at the Crossroads', in Franklin, M.A., Short, L.M., & Teather, E., *Country Women at the Crossroads*, UNE Press.

Teather, E. 1995, 'Origins of the New Farm Women's Movement in Canada, New Zealand and Australia', in *Rural Society*, vol. 5, no. 4.

Section 1

Changing communities

Introduction

The causes and effects of change are complex, and this section represents both the range of individual and community responses to change and a diversity in the writers' approaches to conceptualising, analysing and negotiating change in a rural context. The kinds of changes experienced in rural communities in the 1990s evoke responses typical of grief reactions: denial, anger, depression, reconciliation, reintegration. Reintegration for some communities involves creating new opportunities; others are left in a more precarious position, with access to resources seemingly out of their control. In exploring change, and responses to change, some of these chapters reflect felt experience, others provide an analytical framework, but all examine practice tools for facilitating constructive change. Themes of collaboration and community building, and creating inclusive practice through recognising and working to reconcile tensions and difference, pervade this section.

We start with Helen Sheil's appraisal of a rural Victorian community, which, in the late 1990s, is reeling from the political, economic and ecological blows it has been dealt, but is learning to respond in highly constructive ways. Helen's visioning of confident and revitalised communities achievable through transformatory education for co-operation, is optimistic and challenging.

David Barlow's sharp analysis of the promises offered by the communications revolution raises the spectre of communities further impoverished through lack of access to information if the revolution remains incomplete, and also the risk of depersonalisation when information and support are provided electronically without human contact.

Eversley Ruth reflects on the question: how do communities sustain themselves in the face of such a paradigm shift as economic rationalism? She takes us on a personal journey through years of practice in Western Australia, towards the end of which the rules changed. The new approach to human services has resulted in the undermining of the human values of co-operation and local ownership, and has replaced them with competition and imposed models of service, increasing vulnerability rather than enhancing communities.

Expanding on these conceptual and political shifts, Kevin O'Toole analyses the transition from a service focus to a market-driven focus. He describes one Victorian shire's response which acknowledged the nature of imposed change, and developed new coalitions with tasks consistent with the new technological and economic challenges. Both Kevin's and Eversley's chapters affirm the value of processes that have always been important in building community and encouraging local ownership and control.

Helen La Nauze's chapter introduces gender as an organising theme and as a means of identifying a different, highly process-oriented and personally invested form of practice. Although gender analysis is not explicit in earlier chapters in this section, the same emphasis on process and reflection is evident in some. Helen also develops the theme of tensions between opposing forces such as mainstreaming and marginalisation, which can be addressed by inclusive and reconciling stances.

Brian Cheers draws together a form of practice that is effective because it authentically reflects compatibilities with rural and community interaction in its emphasis on connectedness, visibility and a holistic view of community. Social care creates social integration, and balances individuality with belonging.

3

Building rural futures through co-operation

The need, the dream, the reality

Helen Sheil

Introduction

This chapter discusses a project from rural Victoria, Building Rural Futures through Co-operation. The project incorporates core principles of collaborative education guided by the goals of community development theory: ecological sustainability and social justice. Two major themes are significant. First: how we work will determine the culture and capacity of the outcomes. Second: guided by the goals of community development, collaborative educational strategies will provide a means to facilitate balanced development of rural communities. The aim is to create an 'ethic of hope' that can heal the divisions caused by policies that have been too narrowly focused to allow a uniquely Australian rural story of integrated development to emerge. The chapter seeks to model the methodology and utilises narrative as a tool for transformation.

A response from rural Victoria challenging the vision of success

The vision of success is frequently determined by the dominant thinking of the time. Yet what is success in one era can be viewed differently in the next.

My community, Mirboo North, is situated between the coalfields of the Latrobe Valley and farming country along the Strzlecki ranges in South Gippsland, a place of wonderfully rich soils and normally high rainfall. Known for its prolific growth, visitors learn of this region producing the tallest trees in the world. The Tarra Bulga National Park is a wonderful example of how the red soils were enriched by the massive forests that developed over thousands of years. Nearby on a ridge in a now barren paddock is a metal sign: 'The world's tallest tree grew here'; A massive Mountain Ash (*Eucalyptus regnans*) of over 400 feet. The tree was cut down in the 1890s. There is still no replanting on this hill. The steep country lends itself to landslips and washes away. Those who felled the tree were concerned with the present and not the future.

How far have we come? The twentieth century view of success is tied up with continued growth of market commodities. Economic rationalism, with goals of increased gross domestic product, dictates policy and action in every area of life: health, education, natural resource management, finance, religion and arts, all now operate as businesses with a primary concern for profit. Our thinking is permeated by the language of globalisation, centralisation, restructure, down-sizing, amalgamation, out-sourcing, take-over, speculation, efficiency, productivity and competition: words from a very recent concept of economics (Max Neef 1991, Waring 1988).

The predicted terminal decline based on the sustained and continuing population losses of more than half of Australia's rural communities (Sorensen & Epps 1993, p. 2) is a similar indicator of thinking which takes no account of the future.

The need for change can be found in the words of David Suzuki (1997):

> Just as the key to species survival in the natural world is its ability to adapt to local habitats, so the key to human survival will probably be the local community.

Jim Ife's model of balanced development (1995, p. 132) provides a framework I have adapted to look more closely at the state of my community under economic rationalist policies of centralisation and globalisation. Was decline inevitable?

The local situation

Politically Rural people feel themselves to be outside a responsive political system and unrepresented by the major political parties who concentrate on their large urban majorities. The amalgamation of local government areas, appointment of urban-based managers and policies of tendering out 50% of services has radically altered the concept of local government.

Economically The impact of policies of privatisation, centralisation and out-sourcing has drastically reduced employment, stability and populations. Local bank closures and no evidence of support for drought affected farmers see little money circulating locally, and businesses close.

Socially Longer hours of working, less security in employment, and fewer people result in less capacity to engage in community projects vital to the functioning of the town. Diminished resources in schools and out-sourced health services struggle to take on the demands created by extra stress in the community.

Personally and spiritually There is less space 'to have a life' that had personal expressions of creativity and spirituality. Churches have less money and smaller congregations and have also been closing.

Cultural development Generally a welcoming community, tolerant of difference, where young people are valued but there is little future for them in remaining in the district.

Environmentally A major dilemma exists while concerns about basic resources of water and land use increases, resources to implement good policy and practice decline and become increasingly remote.

A new vision for Australia's rural and regional communities is needed, one which recognises and values the contribution of rural communities to the national well-being: economically, socially, culturally and ecologically. The measure of success for the twenty-first century must embody qualities that plan for the long term. How could our work in education and community development contribute towards this change? These issues framed the current work of the Centre for Rural Communities and led to the project, BuildingRural Futures through Co-operation. (Sheil 1998)

The project challenges the 'conventional wisdom' of placing economic interests above those of every other aspect of life. The world as we knew it has changed; our once plentiful resource base in this country is diminished as it is globally. Within all nations there reaches a point where increased rates of extraction and production begin to impoverish the land and the people who depend upon it (Sher & Sher 1994, Max Neef 1982, Henderson 1991). It is a concept of development that has passed its use-by date.

Each age has expanded into new areas of learning in response to challenges of the time. This age demands the development of skills, attitudes and knowledge, which recognise the interdependency of life. The need is for collaborative learning to reconnect knowledge that has become specialist and isolated to the point of destructiveness. Learning that is collaborative and supportive of finding new futures for rural people and communities has a key role. Learning that can include and value rural perspectives, that can develop skills for working together, can forge partnerships and heal past divisions and wounds. Such work is not new. Theoretical perspectives exist which strive to tap the potential of people and place to support quality of life into the future, offering sound strategies (Freire 1973, Postman 1996, Vella 1994, McTaggart & Kemmis 1996).

What is new is the application of this work to safeguard the future of rural communities. It can be used to educate ourselves and those in key positions about new ways of working with the diversity of communities named 'rural'.

The dream that inspires me is to plan for the future by ensuring collaborative learning strategies guided by the community development goals of social justice and ecological sustainability, which are accessible as planning tools within rural communities, and have been used to initiate action in Gippsland. Such a strategy can provide a process to reframe the understanding of the status of rural communities in the national well-being, and facilitate the establishment of partnerships capable of learning with rural communities how best to ensure a vibrant future for rural Australia.

> *For Australia to be a clever nation as well as a lucky one, we stress the need for everyone to move beyond the conventional wisdom and to embrace a vision of rural development in which the well being of rural people and communities really do matter.*
>
> (Sher & Sher 1994)

In 1995 a new partnership focusing on issues of rurality formed the Centre for Rural Communities Inc. linking the knowledge and resources of Monash University, the Technical and Further Education sector and Gippsland Regional Council of Adult Community and Further Education, with concern to ensure access to information and resources for struggling rural communities.

The project model was inspired by Landcare, operating on a philosophy of management by local people who knew best the existing barriers and opportunities, and where people could be resourced on matters that required further skills, knowledge and research (Chamala & Mortiss 1990, Hogan & Cumming 1997). Two years of preparing submissions to every level of government and institutions with responsibility for rural affairs saw the Centre still unfunded. Responses from government consistently suggested referring to other levels of government, usually ending up with local government, who at this time were facing significant fiscal problems. Regional initiatives were the responsibility of economic groups whose targets were set within the short-term market-driven agenda. Centralisation was the current thinking and the benefit of local people working in partnership was not understood. Rural communities' potential to survive further deteriorated.

But inspiration came from resourceful rural communities, which had begun co-operative ventures. Yeoval in New South Wales, a town of 450 people, had established a Community Hospital Co-operative in 1988 in response to the closing of the local hospital. It now provides the local community's health care needs and a major source of employment in the community. Yinnar in South

Gippsland formed a Co-operative Hotel 25 years ago when the local owner died and the town wanted to maintain its meeting place. The profits from the hotel fund the football club, bowls club and school. In Queensland, Maleny's development from a declining beef and dairy area 15 years ago to the present thriving community started with the opening of a fruit and vegetable co-operative. From this a Community Managed Credit Union began in 1984 to provide affordable finance and circulate money locally. The co-operative way of working is infectious and Maleny now has a co-operative club, enterprise centre and school, waste management business and more. Inspiration from the knowledge that decline could be turned around urged us on.

Building Rural Futures through Co-operation as a proposal began to take shape within the Centre with the aims to enable rural communities of up to 10 000 population in Victoria to co-operatively develop projects that would have long-term benefit, and to assist rural communities reclaim some control over their future through establishing locally owned ventures. Common areas of concern included: local finance, as withdrawal of banks provided opportunities for local involvement in financial ventures; health services that had become centralised and unsatisfactory; agriculture, where the family farm needed to work differently; agro-forestry which was becoming a growth area needing assistance; and power (gas, electricity and water) where privatisation had altered issues of access and payment. Discussions with funding bodies and local communities now had a focus. The next challenge was how to provide access to educational strategies that would strengthen the development of a co-operative culture within rural communities. Philanthropy provided the opportunity. Funding for the first stage of the Building Rural Futures through Co-operation project came from Philanthropic Trusts in 1997. The Co-operative Federation of Victoria has also been involved.

Study circles were chosen as an accessible format, encouraging involvement that could include diverse interests. Solutions to issues are not the domain of any one group and require involvement by all to bring about changed attitudes and practice (Study Circles Resource Centre 1997).

The theoretical work in developing material within the study circle kit is guided by Jim Ife's model of balanced development, recognising that

> *we require thinking which takes account of our social development, our spiritual development, our political development, our economic development, our personal development, our cultural development, and for all these we are dependent upon our environmental development (1995).*

The practical focus is the exploration of the potential of co-operative ventures as a creative response to change, guided by transformative learning.

The methodology is developed from the analysis of key strategies utilised within rural women's projects resulting in personal and community development (Sheil 1996, 1998, 1999).

Nine steps of collaborative learning for transformation

- **Dialogue** provides a forum to develop language and legitimacy for the range of concerns close to the heart of rural people. Encouraging participation and respecting views that come from different life experiences begins the process of learning as individuals and as a community. Sharing of stories is a major strategy: stories offering hope, stories voicing concern for what is valued, stories offering solutions, support and development (Freire 1972, Field-Belenky et al. 1986).

- **Networking** provides the opportunity to extend understanding of potential solutions and is facilitated through regional and state gatherings, and locally initiated trips and invitations (Mitchell 1994).

- **Co-operative culture** requires skills of good communication, clear processes and abilities to resolve conflict. The transition from individual hopes to shared dreams requires group participation in exploring the potential of working together on projects of common interest (Peavey 1986, Sheilds 1991).

- **Visioning** is the opportunity to be invited to speak of dreams, to describe the desirable community, to set the goals.

- **Local ownership** is vital because local people know best what they are experiencing. Skill development, resources and research to complement local solutions can support this knowledge. The potential for local groups to combine resources on particular projects facilitates the beneficial interchange of knowledge and skills (Max Neef 1991).

- **Time** to develop trust and acceptance of difference and to learn skills of working together is essential, and a four- to six-month period has been found to be a minimum time.

- **Reflection** ensures regular evaluating and ability to constructively identify situations needing attention. Individuals and community grow stronger together if this method of lifelong learning underpins the way of working (Wadsworth 1984).

- **Action** is fundamental as every act of working to care for people within our community or care for the environment educates others. Such action reaffirms the importance of belonging to a healthy community, increases understanding of responsibility, interconnectedness and mutual development of all life.

- **Transformation** comes through celebrating and educating the capacity of rural communities to lead the way in balanced development, transforming the isolated individuals who began the journey. Each cycle of learning adds new partnerships and potential that were once only dreams (Sher & Sher 1993).

Development of the project

The steps identified above were built into the production of the study circle kit. Response from across rural Victoria has been constant, keen and interested, from groups diverse in focus and geography. A structure offering support not direction appealed, as did the knowledge that the initiative came from within rural communities, itself a partnership between previously separate groups. Communities welcomed a process with the flexibility to respond to local issues, acknowledging the uniqueness of each locality.

Local people involved in co-operative ventures spoke at project launches in rural Victoria. Ventures as diverse as Sweet Corn Co-operatives, a Co-operative Hotel, Pine or Beef Co-operatives, Community Newspapers, and Credit Unions evoked equal passion and enthusiasm, providing inspiration in the current climate. Invitations to participate in statewide and regional forums regarding the project came from groups responding to constant change: from Adult Education, the Association of Neighbourhood Houses and Learning Centres, Rural Leadership programs, participation in the Women on Farms gathering, Rural and Regional Strategy Forum, and the Uniting Church Rural Synod, local government, co-operatives, businesses, environmental planning and community welfare organisations.

Responses to forums have been enthusiastic. The interactive group process provides a way for local people to explore solutions to issues they deal with daily. The process invites people to look first at the current situation, then to share their dreams of how life could be, followed by discussion of how to achieve this. Answers are spontaneous, sometimes it is so simple laughter erupts in recognition of the possibilities.

New stories of resourcefulness are shared. In Ouyen the desire to provide local quality care for older people within the community resulted in the purchase of a motel which was for sale. Accommodation is not clinical, couples are not separated and family can visit. Residents are proud of their ability to ensure good quality care. A new motel was built as the need arose (Torpey 1998).

Interest in the project has exceeded our expectation. Requests for information have come from several states and from government departments of primary industry, human services, recreation, economic development, natural resource management and infrastructure; from all levels of adult learning, across disciplines of business, social sciences, education, agribusiness, and finance. People rang to discuss adapting the material. Consultants and industry groups recognised the interconnectedness of rural life, and the importance of skill development required to strengthen communities.

The expectation that study groups would be established without support has proved unrealistic in the current climate. Despite interest and enthusiasm, the study circle kit has not been used as designed, except where a person is in a funded position. There is an urgent need to resource key people within communities to take on the role of facilitation in a recognised and supported capacity. Those groups that began are groups with some level of funding and structure: Landcare, church groups, neighbourhood centres, natural resource management, TAFE outreach centres. Community groups motivated by loss of banks and services are applying for grants through the federal funding program Advance Agriculture Australia to enable them to use the kit more adequately. Interest in the use of the kit as a local planning tool is significant.

Outcomes so far (September 1998)

A weekend workshop (in May 1998) drew together rural policy makers and one hundred people from across rural Victoria facilitating connections and further understandings of co-operation. It led to a number of productive outcomes for the project: state government departments offered to facilitate briefing sessions with regional managers, and charitable trusts indicated their willingness to be involved in next stage discussions.

Ventures with similar interests made links and connections across the state: in health, in media and communications, in agriculture, in art and local finance. Local government has became actively involved by participating in discussions on the potential of co-operative ventures between local governments in the area of local financial institutions to maintain services in rural communities.

The challenge is to build on the enthusiasm and potential generated by the Building Rural Futures through Co-operation project by ensuring that collaborative learning strategies continue to be accessible in rural communities, in partnerships with relevant expertise, research and training. Two essential steps in building on the development and potential of the study circle kit are the creation of a clearinghouse and networking role, and extending the use of the methodology.

The project has resulted in the central accumulation of contacts and knowledge of resources across community, government, philanthropy, industry, religious and human rights organisations, the co-operative movement and rural development. The funding of a networking and clearinghouse role for the Centre would build on this work. The current material is designed for use at a local level with the involvement of policy and planners. Material, design and content can be adapted in consultation with public and private sector groups interested in utilising the effective strategies trialed in this methodology.

Research and consultancy is a further strategy to make accessible the expertise and knowledge of those involved with the project. Contact with agribusiness and with infrastructure has already begun as they have learnt of the current work being undertaken. New links with universities involved in rural research will extend the capacity of the Centre for Rural Communities to ensure access to relevant information, for example work carried out in relation to quality assurance in cattle care training, undertaken by University of Tasmania legitimated the Beef Co-operatives' approaches to Wodonga TAFE College for local training (Falk, Kilpatrick & Morgan 1997).

Conclusion

The material produced through the project is designed for use at a local level with involvement of policy makers and planners. Material, design and content can be adapted in consultation with public and private sector groups interested in utilising the effective strategies trialed in this methodology. The steps of transformative learning are transferable, and relevant to move from this age of economics and technology to 'the healing century' (Theobold 1998).

> *We begin planning when we sit together 'in vulnerability' to learn from each other andwe are required … to ensure that the outcomes of our exchange are not known in advance. We begin one of the tasks of repair when we refuse to determine milestones, and thus make ourselves available to be surprised by what our fellow human beings, and the world, may want of us.*
>
> (Bird 1997)

Learning that is not limited by the current paradigm has a key role in such a process for it provides a mechanism to work towards a vibrant future in our rural communities. The use of collaborative learning strategies guided by community development goals can produce positive outcomes for the future of rural Australia, locally, regionally and nationally. The project described is still in progress and has not yet reached its potential, but those of us involved are very optimistic about its capacity to create change for the long term, its relevance in the current climate and its growing positive reception with government and planning bodies.

References

Chamala, S. & Mortiss, P.D. 1990, *Working together for Landcare*, Australian Academic Press, Brisbane.

Falk, I., Kilpatrick, S. & Morgan, H. 1997, *Quality Assurance in Agriculture: Promoting access for beef producers*, Launceston: Centre For Research and Learning in Regional Australia, University of Tasmania.

Field-Belenky, M., McVicker Clinchy, B., Rule Goldberger, N., Mattuck Tarule, J. 1986, *Women's Ways of Knowing: The Development of Self Voice and Mind*, Basic Books Inc. New York.

Freire, P., 1972, *Pedagogy of the Oppressed*, Penguin, Hammondsworth.

Henderson, H. 1991, *Paradigms in Progress: Life beyond Economics*, Knowledge Systems Inc. Indianapolis.

Henshall Hansen Associates 1988, *Study of Small Towns in Victoria*, (revised edition) Department of Agriculture and Rural Affairs, Victoria.

Hogan, E. & Cumming, B. 1997, *More than a Question of Numbers*, Commonwealth of Australia.

Ife, J. 1995, *Community Development. Creating community alternatives—vision, analysis and practice*, Longman Australia.

Kenny, S. 1994, *Developing Communities for the future. Community Development in Australia*, Nelson Australia.

Kenny, S. 1996, *Community Development Journal*, vol. 31, Oxford University Press.

Max Neef, M. 1991, *Human Scale Development*, Apex Press, New York.

McTaggert, R. & Kemmis, S. 1996, *The Action Research Reader*, Deakin University, Geelong.

Peavey, F. 1986, *Heart Politics*, New Society Publishers, Philadelphia.

Postman, N. 1996, *The End of Education: Redefining the Value of School*, First Vintage Books Edition, New York.

Rose Bird, D. 1997, 'Indigenous ecology and an ethic of hope', Conference paper *Global Ethics for the 21st Century Conference*, University of Melbourne.

Sheil, H. 1996, 'People, Places and Learning', in *Education in Rural Australia*, vol. 6, 21–29, Society for the Provision of Education in Rural Australia, Charles Sturt University, Wagga Wagga.

Sheil, H. 1997, 'Rural is not the enemy: strategies for rural sustainability', Conference paper Rural Australia: Toward 2000, Charles Sturt University, Wagga Wagga.

Sheil, H. 1998, 'Building Rural Futures through Co-operation', Study Circle Kit, Centre for Rural Communities, Monash University, Gippsland Campus, Churchill.

Sheil, H. 1999, 'The Gippsland experience of establishing partnerships with rural women. Extending the methodology to technology', Conference paper, Technology and Community Leadership Project, Uniting our Rural Communities Conference, April, Churchill, Victoria.

Sheilds, K. 1991, *In the Tiger's Mouth*, Millennium Books, Newtown, NSW.

Sher, K. & Sher, J. 1994, 'Beyond the Conventional Wisdom: Rural Development as if Australia's Rural People and Communities Really Mattered', in *Journal of Research in Rural Education*, vol 10 no 1, 2–43.

Sorensen, T. & Epps, R. (eds) 1993, *Prospects and policies for rural Australia*, Longman Cheshire, Melbourne.

Study Circles Resource Centre: Pomfret, USA.

Suzuki, D., with McConnell, A. 1997, *The Sacred Balance*, Allen and Unwin, St. Leonards, NSW.

Theobold, R. 1998, *The Healing Century. A message of hope for the new millennium*, Radio National Transcripts.

Vella, J. 1994, *Learning to listen, learning to teach: the power of dialogue in educating adults*, Jossey Bass, San Francisco.

Wadsworth, Y. 1984, *Do it yourself social research*, Victorian Council of Social Services and Melbourne Family Care Organisation.

4

W(h)ither rural human services in an 'online' information age?

David Barlow

Introduction

> *Australians have progressively abandoned their open spaces and magical landscapes*
> *because most of us have had no choice. There are not enough jobs, there are too few*
> *prospects for a full lifestyle, there are not enough opportunities for learning and there is*
> *no access to the levels of community service that we regard as acceptable in today's world*
> *... Professionals, investors, and families confront the tyrannies of distance, isolation,*
> *high costs, second rate services—and see no future ... The communications revolution*
> *can change all of this.*

(Information Policy Advisory Council 1997, p. iii)

Today's era has been variously described as an 'information', 'communications' or 'knowledge' society and more recently as the 'information age' (see for example: Telecom Australia 1994, p. 4; Broadband Services Expert Group 1995, p. 2; Australian Science and Technology Council 1994, p. 1; Information Policy Advisory Council 1997, p. iii). Whatever the preferred nomenclature, it is an era characterised by a 'knowledge explosion, increased use of communications technologies, technological convergence between computers and telecommunications, and associated social changes' (Barr 1994, p. 93). Garnham (1986, p. 28) suggests these developments have occurred as a result of concurrent initiatives by predominantly Western governments pursuing new growth opportunities and multi-national corporations seeking fresh global markets.

A prerequisite for a nation's participation in the information age is advanced telecommunications infrastructure and the concomitant information and communications services (Cavill 1994, p. 1). Aiming to increase Australia's economic growth prospects and international competitiveness, the Keating ALP government signalled Australia's entry into the information age with plans to extend and upgrade the nation's information and communications infrastructure. 'Visions' for Australia's future were provided in reports such as *The Networked Nation* (Australian Science and Technology Council 1994), *Networking Australia's Future* (Broadband Services Expert Group 1995) and *Matching Science and Technology to Future Needs* (Australian Science and Technology Council 1995). The latter report argues that Australia's future economic prosperity and general well-being will be dependent on its use of new information and communications technologies, which, it is suggested, could help 'revitalise rural and remote communities across Australia' (Australian Science and Technology Council 1996, p. 29).

For rural communities, many of which already lack the services, amenities and choices available in metropolitan areas (see for example, Cheers 1992; Collingridge & Dunn 1993; Crellin 1994; Lawrence & Killion 1994; MacDonald 1994), there are obvious attractions in acquiring advanced information and communications technologies to help overcome problems of distance and isolation. However, in the context of a globalising economy where the power of the nation-state is in decline (Lewis & Slade 1995, p. 275), and where commercial imperatives undermine notions of public service, private interests supersede public interest, and 'smaller government' leads to the contracting-out and/or privatisation of human services (see, for example, Hoatson, Dixon & Sloman 1996; Lawrence and Killion 1994, pp. 15–16), the availability of advanced information and communications technologies should not be considered a panacea.

It is against such a backdrop that this chapter considers the provision of rural human services in an 'online' information age. It does this in three parts, drawing on recent policy initiatives, theoretical ideas and practical examples for its substance. First, the communications divide between metropolitan and rural Australia is considered in the context of moves to introduce advanced information and communications networks nationwide. Second, with electronic service delivery high on the agenda of all governments, consideration is given to how the introduction of online services will impact on the users and providers of rural human services. Finally, assumptions that advanced information and communications networks will empower rural communities are challenged, with a reminder that the same technologies have the potential to undermine community infrastructure and further disenfranchise some rural dwellers.

For the purposes of this chapter, rural communities are considered to include all settlements outside the major metropolitan centres, but the author is particularly interested in the myriad smaller communities beyond the provincial regional centres and larger country towns. While recognising the value of distinguishing between rural and remote (Cheers 1992, p. 11; MacDonald 1994, p. 82), in this instance, remote will be considered a subset of rural (Lawrence & Killion 1994, p. 3).

Bridging the city/country communications divide?

Whether all rural Australians will be able to fully participate in the information age through the use of advanced information and communications technologies remains to be seen. Amongst others, Telecom Australia (now Telstra) have questioned the 'spin' and optimistic projections associated with the provision of such services to rural communities (Cavill 1993). In a submission to a Commonwealth Government Regional Development Task Force, Telecom Australia suggested the following factors were likely to mitigate against the provision of advanced information and communications services in rural communities: the provision of infrastructure driven by market forces leading to investment in capital cities, major regional centres and the business corridors between them; the Universal Services Obligation only applying to basic (voice telephony) rather than advanced (data transfer) telecommunications services; and the unequal distribution of information and infrastructure leading to spatial inequalities between regions and inevitable differences in the cost and availability of telecommunications services (Cavill 1993, p. 2). A cursory overview of the current 'state of play' in rural Australia suggests these concerns were valid.

A recent audit of communications services and needs in regional Western Australia concludes that there are 'significant gaps in the provision of communications services between metropolitan and regional areas' (The Boshe Group 1997, p. 13). On the basis of anecdotal evidence, it is highly likely that similar audits conducted in other parts of Australia would reach the same conclusion. But aside from the generally reduced choice of television and radio services, newspapers, and the limited variety, availability and inflated cost of transport in rural Australia, it is the limitations of the standard telephone service and the Analogue and Digital Radio Concentrator Systems that have attracted recent attention. This is because each of these telephone systems lacks the speed and capacity (bandwidth) to meet the increasing need for data transfer facilities required for facsimile (fax) and Internet services.

There is also dissatisfaction with mobile telephony services beyond the capital cities and larger regional centres where demand is high but coverage limited (Austin 1997, p. 11). For example, in Western Australia mobile telephones operate in and around the major centres of population which constitute only 5% of Western Australia's landmass (The Boshe Group 1997, p. 2). With the government planning to withdraw the analogue mobile telephone network by the year 2000, there are concerns that some rural areas will be left without a mobile telephone service. Pricing mechanisms have also penalised rural telephone users (Buckeridge 1996, pp. 30–31; The Boshe Group 1997, p. 6), and the limited (but growing) availability of Internet Service Providers has resulted in Internet access varying in price from $1.60 to $30 per hour in rural Australia (Cavill 1996, p. 12). Variation in the national communications infrastructure is also sharply illuminated when reminded of those rural dwellers without a reliable twenty-four-hour power supply who face the inconvenience and additional costs of providing their own power to access communications services (The Boshe Group 1997, p. 7). While some of the above problems are likely to be resolved as a result of Telstra's roll-out of an Integrated Services Digital Network (ISDN) and upgrading of the Analogue and Digital Radio Concentrator Systems (Buckeridge 1996, p. 32; Information Policy Advisory Council 1997, p. 37), the implementation process has attracted some criticism:

> *The pace of the roll-out can be glacial and may never progress to the furthest points,*
> *especially as it is not seen to be commercially viable to do so.*
>
> (The Boshe Group 1997, p. 3)

Despite these concerns, Telstra's initiatives are expected to provide 96% of Australians with access to high speed digital quality telecommunications by the year 2000, enabling voice, data, fax and video conference transmission (Austin 1997, p. 12). But due to ISDN technology only having an effective range of five kilometres, the remaining 4% (estimated at 40 000 customers who are mostly rural producers) will be without a digital capacity for the foreseeable future because they reside more than five kilometres from a telephone exchange (Austin 1997, p. 12). Whether access to digital telecommunications will ever become universally available is uncertain. Presently, the Universal Services Obligation (USO) ensures all Australians have access to a standard (voice grade) telephone service on an equitable basis (Given 1997, pp. 12–13). This is achieved through a process of cross-subsidisation, whereby profitable services (in metropolitan centres) are used to finance infrastructure in unprofitable (rural) areas (Broadband Services Expert Group 1995, p. 53). Although one of the goals of the recent *Telecommunications Act* 1997 is 'the universal availability of a "digital data capacity" ... by the year 2000' (Given 1997, p. 8), it is not yet clear whether this enhanced level of provision will be designated as a new minimum standard of service and incorporated into a future USO.

However, it is important to note that having access to digital telecommunications or having them *available*—the terminology used by the legislators and policy makers—does not automatically mean having such a facility at home or work. In other words, the service will be 'universally accessible but not universally provided' (Austin 1997, p. 14). Whether due to a lack of infrastructure, the costs involved, or other factors, the Broadband Services Expert Group (1995, p. 51) has acknowledged that all Australians are unlikely to have access to such services at home. To ameliorate this situation they have recommended the use of 'access points' in schools, libraries, community centres or information kiosks as a way of providing the 'unconnected' with access to the Internet and government services (Broadband Services Expert Group 1995, pp. 56–8). It is, therefore, not surprising that the delay in providing rural communities with information and communications technologies that 'metropolitan markets take for granted' (Ferguson 1997, p. 12) has prompted some to question whether the introduction of digital technologies will actually widen the communications gap between urban and rural Australia (Buckeridge 1996, p. 36).

Online services—supplement or substitute?

One of the most recent and influential reports examining the information and communications needs of rural Australia has been generated by the Information Policy Advisory Council (IPAC), a body appointed by the Howard Liberal– National Party Coalition government to advise on how the provision of online services and technologies can contribute to Australia's prosperity. Pivotal to IPAC's thinking is that all Australians need to become 'location independent' through access to advanced information and communications networks, thereby overcoming the tyranny of distance both within the nation and between Australia and the rest of the world (Information Policy Advisory Council 1997, p. 11).

The IPAC report, imaginatively entitled *rural&regional.au/for all* (Information Policy Advisory Council 1997), argues for rigorous, immediate and stimulative efforts by government—in partnership with industry and community—to develop and introduce telecommunications infrastructure to enable the introduction of online services (Information Policy Advisory Council 1997, p. 4). While IPAC is primarily concerned with facilitating opportunities for electronic commerce, great emphasis is also placed on government usage, with particular encouragement for the delivery of online health, education and social services (Information Policy Advisory Council 1997, p. 11). IPAC's reference to how 'the Internet and the technological platforms of the 'information age' [can] transform the possibilities for rural Australia' (Information Policy Advisory Council 1997, p. iii) also reflects the thinking at all levels of government. The key question for rural communities is whether online services will supplement or replace current human services provision.

With advanced information and communications infrastructure in place, IPAC envisages an era in which rural communities will have access to services never before imaginable (Information Policy Advisory Council 1997, p. 29). Even a cursory examination of some recent developments indicates how new technologies have changed the nature of service delivery. Under the banner of 'telehealth', clinical consultation, clinical diagnosis, remote counselling, public health information, and administrative and professional development services are now being made available to rural communities by way of advanced information and communications systems (Information Policy Advisory Council 1997, p. 52). Examples include: the South Australian Renal Dialysis Telemedicine Project, which allows doctors and allied health professionals to communicate through video conferencing facilities with patients and staff at four regional locations up to 300 kilometres from Adelaide; the Metropolitan and Country Healthcare Network in Victoria, which provides tele-radiology, tele-pathology and tele-immunology services to a regional hospital and enables doctors to perform pre- and post-admission examinations using video conferencing facilities; and, tele-psychiatry programs in South Australia and Western Australia, which enable city-based counsellors, psychologists and psychiatrists to provide assessment and consultation services through video conferencing facilities to service users in rural locations (Information Policy Advisory Council 1997, pp. 53–4).

The same developments are also evident in the education and justice systems. For some time, telematics, television, video conferencing and satellites have been used to provide education and training to primary, secondary and tertiary students in rural Australia (Broadband Services Expert Group 1995, p. 79). Using the Internet's World Wide Web (WWW) information retrieval system, students can now access course material and other information at a time and place of their own choosing. This has prompted some universities to reduce lectures and other traditional face-to-face delivery and make no distinction between on-campus and off-campus students (Information Policy Advisory Council 1997, p. 63). Advanced information and communications technologies have also been incorporated into the justice area, with police using video conferencing to interview witnesses in rural areas and the courts in Victoria and Queensland adopting similar means to conduct some stages of court proceedings (Deliotte Touche Tohmatsu 1995, p. 453; Information Policy Advisory Council 1997, pp. 65–6). In addition to the 'real time' services provided through video conferencing links, the WWW sites—which are growing exponentially—allow workers access to information on a vast array of topics and services on a twenty-four-hour basis, and the availability of chat lines, bulletin boards and electronic mail (e-mail) provides the opportunity for advice and support from colleagues in Australia and overseas.

While governments are enthusiastic about using advanced information and communications technologies to deliver services, progress is variable. This has prompted criticism of patchy and unco-ordinated developments which further exacerbate the current service disparities between regions (Information Policy Advisory Council 1997, p. 29). Leading the innovators is Victoria, which is committed to the provision of all government services through information kiosks, interactive telephone centres and the Internet by the year 2000 (Connolly 1997, pp. 8–9). Victoria expects to make its advanced communications network available to the wider community and federal government with the aim of aggregating services and making it financially viable to extend the roll-out into remote areas (Cavill 1996, p. 6). Moira, a local government municipality in regional Victoria, is establishing community based information kiosks as one-stop shops for government information and intends to provide all ratepayers with local call access to the Internet (Information Policy Advisory Council 1997, p. 81). Developments such as these will be assisted by the Coalition's Regional Telecommunications Infrastructure Fund (RTIF), launched under the banner of 'Networking the Nation', and its Online Public Access Initiative (OPAI). Administered by the Department of Communications, Information Economy and the Arts, both programs aim to enhance and extend communications infrastructure in rural Australia to help catalyse the development of online services.

However, recent research into the delivery of human services by electronic means draws attention to a number of concerns (Australian Council of Social Service 1996). Three areas are of particular interest: one, that in their haste to provide online services, governments appear to be more interested in the delivery technologies rather than the content and quality of the services being provided; two, that online services do not necessarily provide the user with the opportunity for advice, support and/or advocacy that is normally available from a trained worker in a traditional interview situation; and, three, that the introduction of advanced information and communications technologies may be seen primarily by governments as a cost cutting opportunity (Australian Council of Social Service 1996, pp. 121–2). There is also some disquiet about how service users will react to the increasing use of electronic service delivery. Those most likely to be concerned about the introduction of online services are thought to be the aged, people with disabilities, people on low incomes, people concerned about privacy, people with literacy problems, people from non-English speaking backgrounds and members of rural communities (Connolly 1997, p. 9).

Revitalised communities or electronic ghettos?

The more optimistic predictions suggest that advanced information and communications technologies will not only end the current trend towards centralisation, but facilitate a process of decentralisation. It is argued that once the necessary infrastructure is in place, there will be a population drift back to rural areas which will facilitate economic growth, create jobs and require the provision of services comparable in quality and range to those available in metropolitan centres (Information Policy Advisory Council 1997, p. 24; The Boshe Group 1997, p. 4). Conversely, the introduction of advanced information and communications technologies has the potential to impact negatively on rural community infrastructure, perhaps even accelerating population drift and leading to further decline.

Community infrastructure is generally thought to include the physical structures, financial institutions, social and other services that enable a community to function. Civille (1995, p. 1) also adds another component, that of 'community information infrastructure', interpreted as 'the sources and conduits of information for a community' and considered essential for socio-economic development (George 1995, p. 2). Two trends that are particularly apparent in the transition towards an information age are changes in the type of ownership—public to private—and changes in the structure of ownership—local to global (George 1995, p. 2). The consequences of both these trends will be evident to all who live or work in rural communities.

The privatisation and corporatisation of previously public enterprises is already challenging traditionally free and relatively easy access to public information in a number of ways. For example, moves by governments to contract out services have been a boon for the 'secrecy movement' as access to information can be denied on the grounds of 'commercial-in-confidence' (Administrative Review Council 1997, p. 21). The use of electronic information technologies in public libraries will increasingly involve charges for users (Griff 1994, p. 22), which will become more prevalent as physical library holdings are reduced in favour of accessing new material by electronic means (Melody 1990, p. 11). Access to information under Freedom of Information legislation will also be curtailed due to escalating costs for searches and government restrictions on the availability of certain types of information (Fagan 1996, p. 5). Also, the current trend towards deregulation either eradicates regulating bodies or reduces their power to acquire information and make it public (*Communications Update* 1994, p. 16).

These developments are seen as inevitable in the transition towards an information age in which 'public information will shift from a public good to that of a privately appropriable commodity' (Garnham 1986, p. 29). This is clearly evident in the now dominant 'user pays' regime. With some local governments entering into commercial partnerships to provide community information, Kelly (1994, p. 57) suggests that published information may be targeted towards particular interest groups, reduced in size and/or quality, and only made available for a fee. With funding cuts being experienced by a wide range of community organisations, charging for access to information may be seen as a legitimate means of maintaining service levels. Developments such as these prompt questions about who owns 'community information' and whether some people will be denied access because of their inability or unwillingness to pay (Ethell 1995, p. 31).

With the emergence of electronic service delivery, the implications for agencies providing community information services are ominous. Under the guise of eradicating allegedly duplicate services, local information providers may be rationalised and the information provided through the Internet or a 'touch screen' at community access points (Ethell 1995, p. 31). These developments have the potential to undermine the physical and human resources that constitute community information infrastructure and exacerbate the gap between the 'haves' and 'have nots'.

Changes in the structure of ownership from the local to the global are epitomised by the 'bigger is better' syndrome—even though it may mean further away! In the private sector, the search for more powerful alliances has led to corporate mergers and take-overs which result in local ownership transferring to larger corporations whose 'economic interests transcend the specific needs of a community' (George 1995, p. 2). In the public sector, the local to global transition is evident in the continuing drift of services from rural communities to metropolitan or regional centres. With loss of local ownership reducing corporate accountability, civic participation and access to key decision makers, the 'disintegrative tendencies' inherent in this form of vertical integration can impact deleteriously on personal, professional and civic networks (Warren 1966, pp. 194–5).

Just a few examples illustrate the extent of the changes occurring at the local level. Utilities that were previously publicly owned are shifting from the lower-left cell to the upper-right as they are privatised and subject to distant (and increasingly overseas) ownership. Likewise, private enterprises that were previously locally owned are moving from the lower-right cell to the upper-right. These changes are made easier with the introduction of new information and communications technologies, since there is little need for a physical presence if a service can be provided adequately (or profitably) by electronic means. This factor helps accelerate movement from the lower to upper cells irrespective of whether services are in the private or public domain. Taken to an extreme, these developments conjure the idea of electronic ghettos, as community infrastructure—in the form of jobs, services and local networks—evaporates in the face of 'virtual service' provision from metropolitan and regional centres through advanced information and communications networks (Barlow 1997, p. 7). While this scenario might appear somewhat pessimistic and far-fetched, it is acknowledged as a probability for some rural communities:

> At the margin, there will be some branch rationalisation and closures, as electronic information and service delivery systems demonstrate their efficiency, so some rural villages may lose physical infrastructure. Certainly, there will be rationalisation of government service delivery points within an individual town, to achieve large savings in public funds.
>
> (Buckeridge 1996, p. 46)

Such developments are expected to help consolidate the larger provincial centres at the expense of smaller peripheral communities. The trade-off, according to Buckeridge (1996, p. 46), will be a much improved range and quality of services that residents of rural communities will be able to access through electronic means at a time and place of their own choosing. But with the transition to electronic service delivery and online services already occurring, it is somewhat concerning to find IPAC acknowledging that research findings are yet to confirm

> *the kinds of content and applications rural communities want from online services; [the]*
> *services and information currently being provided; [the] key impediments to the*
> *development of services and infrastructure; the real potential of new technologies and*
> *services; and, [the] likely economic benefits to flow from adoption of online services in*
> *regional and rural Australia.*

(Information Policy Advisory Council 1997, p. 31)

Conclusions

The extension of advanced information and communications technologies into rural Australia presents both threats and opportunities. While moves to electronic service delivery are likely to assist in overcoming problems of distance and isolation, and to help repopulate and revitalise some rural communities, the same developments may assist in the decline or demise of others if locally based services and traditional forms of service delivery are simply displaced by electronic infrastructure and services in online form. Electronic service delivery may also help perpetuate (and entrench?) the traditional city-centric control over and approach to the delivery of human services in rural communities (Collingridge & Dunn 1993, p. 89; Lawrence & Killion 1994, p. 8; Cheers 1992, p. 13).

The speed at which electronic service delivery is being introduced is also cause for concern, as are questions of ownership and control. To what extent, if any, will human service workers and service users in rural communities be involved in the design, operation and control of online services and the systems delivering them? Even IPAC acknowledge the risk of 'big companies and big governments' foisting online services on rural communities as a 'means of cutting costs and further withdrawing face-to-face services' (Information Policy Advisory Council 1997, p. 12). The developments in Victoria underline some of these concerns. After reviewing Victoria's moves to deliver services by electronic means, Connolly (1997, p. 9) queries whether there has been adequate community consultation and notes that while the government is indicating electronic delivery will supplement existing services, there are no guarantees into the future. Suffice to say there appears little doubt that the information age will pose yet more personal, professional and political dilemmas for rural human service workers.

References

Administrative Review Council 1997, *The Contracting Out of Government Services*, Issues Paper, Australian Government Publishing Service, Canberra.

Austin, J. 1997, 'Deregulation of the telecommunications industry: What it means for rural Australia', in *Reform* (a quarterly publication of the National Farmers Federation), issue 1, Autumn, pp. 11–14.

Australian Council of Social Service 1996, *Electronic Communication and the Community Sector*, ACOSS Paper No. 81, September.

Australian Science and Technology Council 1994, *The Networked Nation*, Australian Science and Technology Council, Canberra.

Australian Science and Technology Council 1995, *Matching Science and Technology to Future Needs: Key Issues for Australia to 2010*, Australian Science and Technology Council, Canberra.

Barlow, D. M. 1996, 'Non-profit community media as community information infrastructure in the information society', in Aoun, S. & Sherwood, P. (eds), *Regionalisation, Successes, Myths and Realities*, proceedings of the 2nd National Regional Australia Conference, 23–26 September, WA Centre for Rural Health and Community Development, Edith Cowan University, Bunbury.

Barlow, D. M. 1997, 'Electronic community networks in rural Australia: A model for social development in the information society', in *Australian Social Work*, vol. 50, no. 1, pp. 3–8.

Barr, T. 1994, 'Australia's information society: clever enough?' in Green, L. & Guinery, R. (eds), *Framing Technology: Society, Choice and Change*, Allen and Unwin, St. Leonards, NSW, pp. 91–104.

Broadband Services Expert Group 1995, *Networking Australia's Future*, Australian Government Publishing Service, Canberra.

Buckeridge, R. 1996, *Rural Australia Online*, Rural Industries Research and Development Corporation, Barton, ACT 2600.

Cavill, M. 1993, Telecom Australia's Submission to the Task Force on Regional Development, Telecom Australia, Melbourne.

Cavill, M. 1996, *A Discourse on Regional Community Networking*, Centre for International Research on Communication and Information Technologies (CIRCIT), Melbourne.

Cheers, B. 1992, 'Rural Social Work and Social Welfare in the Australian Context', in *Australian Social Work*, vol. 45, no. 2, pp. 11–21.

Civille, R. 1995, *Building community information infrastructure: Universal service for the information age* [online], Center for Civic Networking, Washington DC 20035, gopher gopher.civic.net 2400.

Collingridge, M. & Dunn, P. 1993, 'Rural Australia: people, policies and services', in Inglis, J. and Rogan, L. (eds), *Beyond Swings and Roundabouts: Shaping the Future of Community Services in Australia*, Pluto Press, Sydney, pp. 81–96.

Communications Update 1994, 'Consumers and the 1997 Review', in *Communications Update*, issue 102, August, pp. 15–16.

Connolly, C. 1997, 'Virtual Government leaves little room for citizens', in *Communications Update*, issue 138, November, pp. 8–9.

Crellin, I. R. 1994, 'The Australian Telecentre Program: A New Approach to Technology Transfer and Rural Community Development', paper presented to the XX11 International Conference of Agricultural Economists, Harare, 22–29 August 1994.

Deloitte Touche Tohmatsu 1994, 'Broadband Services in the Government and Public Information Sectors', in *Demand for Broadband Services: Consultancy Reports Prepared For The Broadband Services Expert Group*, Australian Government Publishing Service, Canberra.

Ethell, L. 1995, 'Taking a CAB into the 21st Century', in *Community*, no. 37, pp. 29–33.

Fagan, D. 1996, 'Secret is out, but don't tell anyone', in *Australian*, 22 January, p. 3.

Ferguson, S. 1997, 'rural & regional.au/for all?', in *Communications Update*, Issue 134, July, pp. 12–13.

Garnham, N. 1986, 'The Media and the Public Sphere', in *Intermedia*, vol. 14, no. 1, pp. 28–33.

George, K. 1995, *Review of Community Networks* [online], e-mail: cybergeorge@igc.apc.org.

Given, J. 1997, 'OFTEL revises Universal Service for the UK', in *Communications Update*, issue 136, September, pp. 8–9.

Griff, C. 1994, 'Low Income People', in *Planning for an Information Society Project: Population Group Discussion Papers & Policy Issue Discussion Papers*, Telecom Australia, Melbourne, pp. 17–28.

Hoatson, L., Dixon, J., & Sloman, D. 1996, 'Community development, citizenship and the contract state', in *Community Development Journal*, vol. 31, no. 2, pp. 126–36.

Information Policy Advisory Council 1997, 'rural & regional.au / for all: Report of the Working Party investigating the development of online infrastructure and service development in regional and rural Australia', Department of Communications and the Arts, Canberra.

Kelly, C. 1994, 'New Developments in Community Information and their Implications in the Provision of Quality Service', in *Community Information: The Super*

Highway to Social Justice, selected proceedings of the Sixth National Community Information Conference, Community Information and Referral Service of the ACT Inc., Canberra, pp. 57–60.

Lawrence, G. F. & Killion, F. 1994, 'Challenging the Equity Divide in the Age of Efficiency', proceedings of the ACOSS National Congress 1994, 26–28 October, Brisbane, Australian Council of Social Service (ACOSS), Sydney.

Lewis, G. & Slade, C. 1994, *Critical Communication*, Prentice Hall, Sydney.

MacDonald, L. 1994, 'The Rural and Remote Sector', in *Planning for an Information Society Project: Population Group Discussion Papers & Policy Issue Discussion Papers*, Telecom Australia, Melbourne, pp. 81–101.

Melody, W. H. 1990, 'The Information in I.T.—"Where Lies the Public Interest?"', in *Intermedia*, vol. 18, no. 3, pp. 10–18.

Telecom Australia 1994, *Planning for an Information Society Project: Population Group Discussion Papers & Policy Issue Discussion Papers*, Telecom Australia, Melbourne.

The Boshe Group 1997, *Communications Audit: The Needs of Regional Western Australians*, The Boshe Group, West Perth.

Warren, R. 1966, 'Vertical and Horizontal Patterns', in Warren R. (ed.), *Perspectives on the American Community: A Book of Readings*, Rand McNally & Company, Chicago, pp. 194–200.

5

Beyond economic rationalisation— towards community building
A critique of new approaches to funding community services in remote areas[*]

Eversley Ruth

Introduction

I drove down in August on my last trip through to Perth. Around 1400 kilometres of near desert between Karratha and Wubin—beautiful in spring and desolate in the height of the summer. Driving into Wubin everything changes—green pastures, fences, water. Rural not remote. Just a hop and a step here to the big smoke (less than 300 kilometres)—not days of driving to find minimal services like in the remote north. If you travel from the Kimberley, just add three extra days of driving with towns scattered about the places you need a petrol break.

It would take several volumes to adequately discuss what is happening out bush today. And when you are on the ground there is not much time there for

*Adaptation of a paper first delivered at the 40th Anniversary Conference of WACOSS, in November 1996

pure research. So I am selective in what I have to say—selective and probably subjective, philosophical rather than empirical, intuitive rather than factual. And that feels okay, as an older woman looking to move beyond economic rationalisation—beyond the rational if you like.

My intention is to look at how to sustain community in remote areas, and move beyond an economic rationalist approach to community services which can profoundly negate community building. I realise in writing this chapter that, far from experiencing economic decline, many of the remote towns in which I have worked still experience a boom. So this discussion tries to incorporate the wide range of decline and boom experiences of the remote towns of north-western Western Australia.

Some background. I am concentrating on the remote north—north of the 23rd parallel has been my patch for three years—through the Gascoyne, Murchison, East and West Pilbara and East and West Kimberley, or if you like from Meekatharra (actually just south of the 23rd) to Port Hedland and from Carnarvon to Kununurra. I managed forty staff thinly spread across aged care, financial counselling, day care, migrant community work and general pastoral care to station people. We also carried some flamboyantly creative work over the last 25 years, including early intervention programs in the Aboriginal towns of Halls Creek, Fitzroy and Roebourne, and a Social Justice Project, also in Roebourne. It was all tough work—tough and challenging like most remote area work.

No two remote communities are the same and most are not in decline. Like suburbs in Perth, there are pecking orders. I lived in the dress circle town, Karratha, where you can be forgiven for forgetting you live on the edge of the desert. Travel the ring road, get lost in the cul de sacs and shopping centre and you could be anywhere in suburbia, in any city of Australia. A rich, mainly 'white Anglo Saxon' town full of dollars dragged from the bowels of the earth or piped from under the ocean. The airport is said to be the busiest outside a capital city, full of fly-in fly-outs changing shift.

At the other end of the territory, there is the one example of the many poor relations—Wyndham—stripped of services to make way for the new town of Kununurra, it has become a Cinderella town. An endearing Cinderella with more characters per square inch than any other town I have grown to love. And fiercely defended by its mainly Aboriginal population. Cinderella before the ball nevertheless, battling to provide services that many Australians take for granted.

Across the Pilbara and Kimberley there are fundamental survival issues involving degradation of land, falling prices for sheep and cattle, and contested land title. The dilemma for those in community services in the North arises from remoteness, diversity and the (mostly) tiny populations. How do you spread thin the resources across wealthy clean mining towns, dusty,poor, poor mining towns and camps, Aboriginal towns and remote Aboriginal communities, grand scale pastoral leases, river agricultural communities and wealthy tourist towns? There is a special concern about working in the Pilbara, which has the greatest number of non-English speaking background people outside Perth. The North West is not one but many diverse communities.

People of the north are fiercely independent and proud of their hard-won self-determination in near impossible environments. They win community the hard way, forging it in countless daily interactions for survival. They hate to be patronised; they do not need to be told how to do things. They hate most people from the city visiting for two days in the middle of the magnificent winter to tell them what to do, or hoping to resource them. The Kimberley even resents the Pilbara trying to help, and the Pilbara certainly does not think it has much to gain from the Kimberley.

So this is the backdrop to the community services work in these settings. I would now like to shift gears and talk about the programs, the people and relationships worth sustaining in this rich territory, which breathes like the soul of our country.

Enter new funding relationships

Into this environment enters a new way of contracting community services. In Perth in 1991–92, a Community Services Industry Review (1993) was undertaken by the (then) Western Australian Department for Community Services. This completed an audit of all government funding to non- government community service organisations. Every program was visited and structured interviews checked the numbers of clients seen, the numbers of dollars used, the numbers of services given. Funding was frozen and the new economic rationalist approach began to develop. How to market services to people, like marketing sheep or oranges overseas. It was intriguing and exasperating to watch it working out its life far away from the city where it was designed. And I have to say several years later, there is no evidence that communities have benefited from the change.

For example, a major family support project in the regional centre of Karratha was closed. This project had been initiated in the 1970s when the town was just beginning to take shape, and had been instrumental in being the catalyst for a number of different programs: the occasional day care centre, the migrant program, financial relief, a toy library, caravan park outreach. Right through its life it was the central focus for many visiting services from government departments, training workshops for both the staff and the community, and it maintained a large community centre in the centre of town which was used by a range of different groups. By the 1990s the town of Karratha had a range of other community services as well, and many of the independent programs spawned by the family support program were semi-independent. The funding body, as part of the Community Services Industry Review, decided that the figures no longer added up. The community development role of the project was not easy to measure under the guidelines of the Review, which found difficulty in counting heads of welfare clients in services developed by the family support program.

The closure of the program, however, had dramatic effects on all the other programs which had developed from its enthusiasm. It took several years of hard, unfunded work by the regional office of this peak agency to ensure that each of the satellite programs became sustainable. At the end of three years they remained fragile, without the umbrella program to advocate on their behalf. The community continued to ask for support, but there was no longer a staff person on the ground to resource their various needs.

Another progressive family program in neighbouring Roebourne targeted young Aboriginal children and their mothers. Perhaps before its time, it sought to provide a base for language and early childhood development prior to formal pre-school, through a range of activities such as sewing, play group, men's carpentry. The original funding initiative for a one-year program had come from the Western Australian Department for Community Services, but with changing personnel and changing times, it was no longer seen as a priority and funding was stopped. Federal funding was gained and supported for two more years to keep the program alive. Then, similar review processes in the Department of Commonwealth Human Services and Health funding ended the project.

The Aboriginal families involved had been some of the more marginal in the community and were devastated by the closure. Their building was well equipped from donated resources from all over Australia, but, with no funding for staff, it hiccupped along with volunteers for several years, never really giving up hope that something would change and their Centre would reopen.

As I left the Pilbara, a new early intervention program was beginning in the same small town, managed directly by the original funding body which, since the Industry Review, had become the Western Australian Department of Family and Children's Services. As might be expected, it was having great trouble gaining any commitment from the now totally disillusioned families who had once been so anxious to attend their centre every day.

Roebourne, in the Pilbara of Western Australia, is littered with such stories of services begun with all good intentions and later defunded for newer and brighter models, contributing to major distrust and factionalism within the Aboriginal community. The Northern Australian Social Justice Project based in Roebourne traced many of these trends over a two-year pilot during 1994–95. In its Final Report it suggested that 'future government funded projects must be planned on the basis of rigorous and all-inclusive community consultation, and an intention to facilitate community control of such projects' (Northern Australian Social Justice Project: Roebourne 1996, p. 41).

Many services had probably outrun their use-by date—if you could measure human behaviour as easily as seems to be thought. (As an aside, this measuring job is probably the work of a research psychologist, not a local community services worker or a voluntary management committee, as is often expected by government funding bodies!) But had these services run out of time if you measured something more intangible—the role these services provided in community building? Many other community services programs have been sustained this is true, but with no CPI increase and funding levels based on city formulas, the services are providing less and less to fewer and fewer.

We lost other things, like relationships with those who thought they could measure us and then found us wanting. The tendering process was very disempowering. The partnership between government and non-government, which thrived in the decade prior to tendering, deteriorated. We no longer planned together what services we might provide collaboratively because that would contaminate the tendering process. This is a process that tries to depersonalise work so people can be seen as things to be measured.

The Northern Australia Social Justice Project in Roebourne found the lack of a co-ordinating culture within government departments as key to problems experienced in promoting better planning and co-ordination in Roebourne's human service provision (Northern Australian Social Justice Project: Roebourne 1996, p. 46). Some of this related to enormous workloads that meant department planning officers drew strict role-defining boundaries which excluded a co-ordinating function. High turnover in remote areas only exacerbated the difficulties.

And we lost community relationships. It is hard to sustain community in a small town when everybody is double-guessing who is competing for the fragile resources and when the process starting from identification of a need to implementing funding can take more than three years. On average, mining towns have turned over half their population in that time.

The worst example of this process occurred in the small town of Exmouth, where a twenty-year-old family support program was suffering from lack of resourcing. An internal non-government organisation review undertook community consultations, found out what funding was needed, and tried to negotiate with government for its provision. Because the previous submission funding process was now dead, the community waited many years for the development of tendering, while entrenched camps emerged in the community around different possible programs and sponsors. Finally an agency which had never worked in Exmouth received funding by the Western Australian Family and Children's Services, no doubt because it was perceived as neutral. It had not participated in the earlier community consultations, nor been involved in any way with community service provision in the town before this. The local groups were ignored, the original funded non-government organisation was discounted and so were its attempts to ensure a community building approach. The community by this time was polarised, and many years' work would follow before their commitment was regained. New services funded in this manner do not resource a community building component. Services are given to the community rather than the community participating in resourcing itself, with the whole concept of community empowerment being ignored in the new funding guidelines.

I am painting a dismal picture. But I am committed to being part of a solution. So let me now turn to how we could build on the tough independence and the vision of remote communities in the north.

Valuing community above economics

Let us begin a new way of doing things (or is this a return to a well-worn path?).

First, we need to connect with the local community. We need to build on existing strengths and relationships, knowing this is the beginning of our community service work. This differs from a staff selection process (on which it seems tendering is often modelled). The way any of us enters a community (non-government organisation or government) will reflect the way our work is achieved in the future. If we fail in this beginning process, we will live to work through broken relationships at a later date.

It follows, secondly, that we need to value the work of local communities. This means seeing the successful community building process as a major criteria of any selection process. Any tendering process involves wide communities of interest, beyond the tendering organisations. For example, in a country town, the need for a service usually arises from that community in some form and is then communicated to government. Long before any 'Expression of Interest' is advertised, years of work may have been given to research and involvement by the community.

Thirdly, small, local community groups have enormous ability to command the confidence of remote communities. The latter criteria can get lost in the accountability process. While large well-resourced city-based organisations may be able to meet criteria relating to how they met outcomes in previous work, they may eventually prove unable to 'make the work happen' in a remote location. The current level of literacy needed to even read a tendering document means local community groups may never write such a document for a local community service, let alone successfully receive funding.

Fourthly, we need to almost double the amount of funding necessary for a functional service in a remote community. Unlike the city, there are recruitment and removal costs, long distances to travel, major housing issues, district allowances, remote area equipment breakdowns and expensive repairs, and extra supervision expenses. These all need to be included if we are serious about skilling staff who often have limited qualifications, while attempting to produce outcomes. Government commonly provides incentives for their own staff, and these need to be translated into the non-government sector in remote areas.

Similarly, if an agency is to seriously tender for a service it needs to set a realistic dollar budget, rather than be expected to cut the cloth to meet metropolitan expectations. It is not adequate for funding bodies to expect remote communities to fund-raise to meet the gap, as is commonly assumed for city programs. Even in wealthy towns, commitment from a transitory population is difficult to command. In declining towns, their survival is often dependent on a transfer of resources from the more wealthy areas of Australia.

Finally, any funding process needs to find a way around the possible competitive cycle. I have already mentioned that sensitivities in remote communities run deep. There may be integrity in confidentiality, but not when speculation fuels community conflict. Better is a process that allows for regular, open and honest communication: between community members, between community members and potential non-government organisation sponsors; and between either of these and the government funding body.

This may require rethinking a strict economic approach, and acknowledging that community services are not merely producers of services. Early collaboration by funding bodies in wide community consultations will help identify the way to proceed. Local steering committees for new programs have worked effectively for many decades. It may require an adaptation of the submission method of funding, rather than the pursuit of hard-nosed competitive tendering. In remote areas there is often only one logical service provider, or services can be spread too thinly between different sponsors. Where possible, services need to remain grounded in the community, not continually absorbed by a large national service provider which becomes increasingly remote from the community's needs.

Identifying community needs has to be a collaborative process, and because the needs analysis itself influences the community it can never be pure, unadulterated research. At best, it is picture building and relationship building. Ultimately the hallmark of a good contracting process is one that leads to community building in the long term.

In today's funding environment workers will need to be skilled in learning both the language of economic rationalism and the language of community development. It is possible for them to co-exist where there is the will and the resources. New programs and old can keep alive the networking and community building processes that involve the community, while ensuring there are measurement mechanisms put in place to provide the numbers for the funding bodies. Mechanisms that are simple and automatic need to be negotiated with management. Time-consuming documentation will only frustrate workers committed to community building. Figures are important, but funding bodies have a responsibility to assist in designing these together with sectors of the human services industry to ensure they are both adequate and simple. Home and Community Care programs in the Kimberley had the benefit of an excellent relationship with the regional funding office, which worked with co-ordinators to design simple statistical collection check sheets.

Involving the community in a reference group attached to each program became the best way we could find in remote areas, where the local expertise was limited. Each worker was expected to call regular meetings to discuss their work, and to receive input about future planning. For example, each migrant program in the Pilbara involved a range of ethnic community members who came together every couple of months. Members also participated in designing and implementing the program wherever possible.

When a local community has adequate resources to maintain its own programs, larger national organisations have a role in assisting them to form their own incorporated organisations during the development stage of programs. Rather than claiming long-term ownership of what could rightfully be run by the local community, they can include skill development through participation on committees, which ultimately leads to an 'out of town' sponsor being able to leave, and the sponsorship being handed back to the community. This is challenging in towns where there is constant population change, but very important in towns where local community interests are more constant and the town can develop its own expertise.

Conclusion

To sum up, we desperately need to work together: non-government organisations, government and community. The resources are too thin on the ground in remote areas to do anything else.

It is more important to build community than it is to market services. We are involved in a service industry. We do not produce tangible resources like barges of iron ore or tanks of gas which we can sell overseas. We need to develop processes not products.

A market driven approach accentuates the hard data issues—cost measures, outcomes, accountability measures, skills in reading and writing business contracts. Strong communities are more likely to be brought about by less tangible qualities—networking, participation, inclusion, empowerment, communication, negotiation, evolution, affirmation and valuing skills.

We are part of building rich, sensitive, immensely precious and yet often immeasurable relationships which build strong families and strong communities.

Our knowledge of human endeavour is at best limited. We cannot yet know that a service that meets hard data outcomes is better for the community because those very outcomes are elusive and time consuming to measure. What we can know intuitively is that communities that work together, grow together. Whether our remote communities face economic decline or renewed development, the need for people on the ground to work together to decide their own destinies is fundamental to their personal futures. We discount mechanisms of local community building at our peril, for we will be left with communities no longer motivated to resource themselves, but which expect others far away to determine their lives.

So we end by finding there is a higher concern than economic rationalism—one found in the quality of community relationships. Just in case any of us thinks any of this is new, I'd like to quote just one line I came across in Jostein Gaarder's wonderful philosophical treatise, *Sophie's World*. It is a quote from David Hume who lived over two hundred years ago:

> *Acting responsibly is not a matter of strengthening our reason,*
> *but of deepening our feelings for the welfare of other.*
>
> David Hume 1711–76

References

Department for Community Services 1993, *Community Services Industry Review*, Perth.

Gaarder, J. 1996, *Sophie's World: A novel about the history of philosophy*, Phoenix, London.

Uniting Church Frontier Services 1996, *Northern Australian Social Justice Project: Roebourne Planning, Coordinating and Related Issues Affecting Human Service Delivery in Roebourne*, Final Report vol. 1, Karratha, 1996.

6

Competition and marketisation
A small town responds

Kevin O'Toole

Introduction

To lead locally and compete globally may be the catch cry of central governments who seek to marketise the role and functions of governance in Australia. But the use of universal criteria for public sector management practices has left many regions lagging in their attempts to compete globally. This chapter looks at the outcomes of marketisation of public policy upon one regional local government area in South West Victoria. First, the chapter locates the marketisation of public policy in its global context. Secondly, there is an analysis of the initial impact upon the shire of Moyne. Thirdly and more importantly, the chapter discusses some of the ways in which local initiatives have attempted to counter the negative effects of marketisation policies upon their local area. The chapter concludes by arguing that while the effects of marketisation upon many rural shires has been catastrophic, there are some lessons to be drawn from the Moyne initiatives.

I use a case study approach in this chapter as it has a number of advantages for small area research. First, small area data is often difficult to extrapolate from large-scale statistical collections, and there is often a need to collect more in-depth information at the local level. In this instance data gathered from local documentary evidence, the Australian Bureau of Statistics (ABS), and education and health sources, was supplemented by interviews with ten leading people in the shire of Moyne. Notes from these unstructured interviews were used to construct a paper that was then verified by the interviewees. In this sense the participants were treated as experts and not just sources of data.

The public sector and marketisation

The marketisation of the state sector has been driven by three significant strands: globalisation, economic rationalism and new managerialism. The term globalisation is used in a number of contexts to indicate the greater interconnectedness of the international world (Fagan & Webber 1997).

This has arisen in a number of areas: the growth of technologies that link people more directly to other people in other parts of the world through computer, communication or transport facilities; the expansion of service industries such as accounting, law, finance, insurance and consulting across the international arena; the development of international industries such as fast foods that are not tied to any one national economy; the integration of different industries such as the car industry across national borders.

All of these practices have heightened the use of the term globalisation. But it is not the existence of technologies that is central to globalisation, but rather the way that public policies throughout the world have allowed a more liberal approach to the exchange of material and intellectual resources. Sassen (1991) argues that globalisation is not particularly novel especially with regard to places like Australia. However, the pressure to conform to the rules of the new international economy has had a significant impact upon the public policies of many countries (Stilwell 1997). Much of this pressure comes in the form of economic rationalism that supplies the basic value framework for a good deal of public policy making.

Economic rationalism has been defined by a number of writers in recent times (Horne 1992, Carroll 1992, Pusey 1991). What is important here is to identify the common elements amongst those who call themselves economic rationalists. In this chapter, economic rationalism is defined as a belief in the efficacy of free market forces as a mechanism to determine the allocation of scarce resources among alternative uses. This belief leads to the political discourse of 'let the market decide' and 'the market knows best'. Economic rationalists advocate a minimalist role for government in the operations of the economy. They argue for the dominance of what is termed 'market forces' which means that the role of government should be limited. Consequently the discourse of economic rationalism involves a belief in what is termed the 'free' market or a general move to the marketisation of all goods and services.

New managerialism applies to the internal structures of government administration. According to Hughes (1994) much of the change in the management structures of the state is driven by the attack on the public sector in terms of its scale, scope and methods. Scale refers to the sheer size of the state which is accused of absorbing too much of the scarce resources available. Scope refers to a wide range of state activities that could easily be done in the private sector. Methods refer to the bureaucratic organisation of the state that is seen as cumbersome and inefficient in the delivery of its services. The assumption is that the actions of public servants are all aimed at maximising their own position in the state. This results in continuing state programs justified by the self-interest of public servants and without a market mechanism to test the efficiency of the program, there is no proper accountability to the public. Accordingly, Osborne and Gaebler (1993) argue that for governments to perform properly there is a need for the separation between policy and management or what they call steering and rowing. That is the state is meant to steer by setting the policy framework within which the rowers, the service providers, carry out the activities on behalf of the state. The result for Australia is a significant downsizing of the operations of the state (Codd 1991).

In applying the market test the commonwealth, state and territory governments agreed to examine a national approach to competition policy in 1991, engaging Professor Fred Hilmer to head up a National Competition Policy Review (National Competition Policy Review 1993). When his report was released in August 1993, the commonwealth, state and territory governments began extensive negotiations on implementation of its recommendations. The outcome was the *Competition Policy Reform Act* 1995 that changed the environment of public sector activity by marketising the activities of government. The 'Shield of the Crown' immunity for state and territory government businesses was removed and the reach of the *Prices Surveillance Act* was extended to the business enterprises of state and territory governments (ACCC 1996). The extension of competition to the public sector means that there has been increased privatisation and contracting out of services to private agencies to carry out the work of the state. The managers in the state move from being managers of services to managers of contracts on behalf of the government and the people. In the parlance of competitive tendering there is a purchaser/provider split.

However, it should be remembered that competition policy is essentially about competitive neutrality and the applications of competition policy are separate political decisions. As the National Competition Council has argued:

> *While the CPA does not require competitive tendering and contracting per se, competitive tendering and subsequent contracting out is nevertheless one means by which governments might meet their competitive neutrality obligations. And examining the cost (on a competitively neutral basis) of providing a service in-house will help determine whether providing a service in this way is a sensible approach. However, in considering the relative merits of in-house and external provision, it is appropriate to*

examine factors in addition to the relative cost of in-house and external provision. One consideration is the value of keeping workers employed in a local region. Another is the convenience of having people readily available to provide a service.

(National Competition Council 1996)

Nevertheless, governments have embraced contracting and privatisation as a major tool of administration in the past few years.

Victoria: marketisation and competition

In Victoria, the marketisation of government took on a greater urgency with the election of the Kennett government in 1992 (Alford & O'Neill 1994). The policies pursued by the Kennett government were informed by reformist zeal to reduce the size of government and apply market principles to public sector management. The outcomes were: the privatisation of as many government business enterprises as the government could manage at one time; the downsizing of the public sector with changes to the internal structures of accountability based on a new set of performance indicators; a concomitant reduction in services based on efficiency principles or the 'bottom line'; the reorganisation of local government to assist the introduction of Compulsory Competitive Tendering (CCT) and the application of measurement processes built on financial criteria, often without due regard to other criteria such as location.

Together with the downsizing in federal government and private sector firms, the reforms in Victoria resulted in an accelerated downturn in regional workforce and its services. Three of the most significant local public institutions in regional Victoria were schools, hospitals and local government. All three not only supplied work in the local community, they also supplied a local community focus. Any dislocation to these services would often mean that many local communities would become unsustainable. Despite all this, the Kennett government, driven by its zeal to reinvent the total processes of governance in Victoria, proceeded with their reforms.

Local government was totally overhauled in the state. In a phased program all local government bodies were sacked and replaced with commissioners in the new amalgamated units. The number of local government authorities was reduced from 210 to 78 between 1993 and 1996. The amalgamations caused a good deal of community reaction across both urban and regional Victoria and took the focus off the major changes planned by the government; compulsory competitive tendering, rate capping and the purchaser/provider split. However, in regional areas many smaller communities suddenly discovered the loss of local resources in the form of buildings, workers and equipment.

The cuts to health care funding in Victoria also had major repercussions for the regions. But the cuts were not as damaging as the introduction of casemix funding, the health equivalent of the purchaser/provider split. Casemix is an output-based funding approach that allocates resources to hospitals on the basis of the number and type of patients treated. By focusing on specific specialty activities, hospitals could attain sufficient throughput to attract large blocks of funding to afford the medical technology and staff required. Under such a system, smaller hospitals in the regions were unable to attract the numbers of cases required with the resultant loss of many small rural hospitals. The old model of the local hospital run by community fund raising and subsidised by state government funds was destroyed by casemix.

The third major government service affected by the Kennett government was education which also suffered major funding cuts in the 1990s. By setting universal benchmarks for student/staff ratios, regional differences were not taken into account and the result was the closure of many small rural schools and the amalgamation of others. Further, the government also moved to introduce competition between schools by devolving more responsibly in the 'Schools of the Future' program. McGuire (1994) argues that both casemix funding and Schools of the Future did introduce competition, but it was more competition for scarce budget resources than paying consumers.

Corporatisation and privatisation of utilities at both state and federal level also affected regional Victoria, especially in electricity, water and telecommunications. Further, government reforms to the public sector have meant the reduction of government agricultural services to regional Victoria, a function that affects major areas of production. The downsizing in private sector provision of such activities as banking has also reduced services in regional Australia (Beal & Ralston 1998). All in all many communities in regional Victoria were severely affected by the global forces of rationalisation.

Shire of Moyne and the impact of marketisation

The impact of marketisation and competition upon Moyne shire was no less than that experienced by other parts of regional Victoria. The shire of Moyne was created from the former shires of Belfast and Minhamite, the borough of Port Fairy, and parts of the shires of Mortlake, Warrnambool, Dundas, Mount Rouse and Hampden on Friday, 23 September, 1994. The shire is mainly characterised by agricultural production with dairying, sheep and beef grazing, cereal crop growing, potatoes and onions as the main pursuits. It also has significant export industries that include bluestone products, baked products, pharmaceuticals, seafoods and a large multinational presence in processed dairy foods. The five main population centres are Port Fairy (pop. 2625), Mortlake (pop. 989), Koroit (pop. 998), Macarthur (pop. 238) and Peterborough (pop. 150).

Over the last decade the area that now constitutes the shire of Moyne has suffered significant changes to its services. The Shire itself is subject to the strictures of the CCT regime, but has managed to reach 72% of its cash

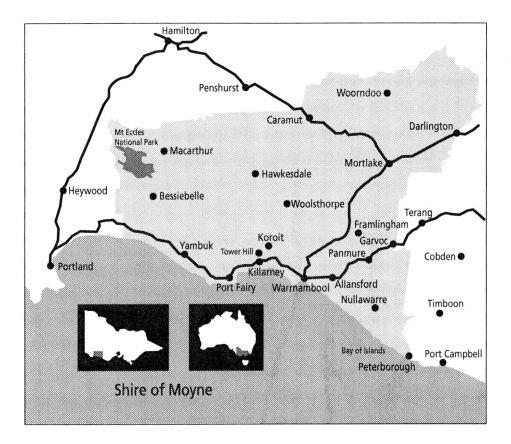

Shire of Moyne

expenditure on contract tendering with 80% of contracts for the 1998/99 budget still in-house (Shire of Moyne 1998). The focus of this chapter, however, is not CCT but rather service provision in the shire.

Major local government services have been withdrawn from three of the main population centres. The Koroit merger with the old Warrnambool shire in 1985 was a voluntary process that was welcomed by most of its residents. However, the mergers of Mortlake shire and the Minhamite shire into the new Moyne shire under the Kennett government were forced mergers. Both raised the ire of Mortlake and Macarthur residents who lost most of their local government facilities, staff and equipment. The Minhamite municipality shared its local government facilities between Macarthur and a nearby township of Hawkesdale, a town of around 150 people, which felt the effects of the merger very heavily.

The area serviced by the shire also had four major hospitals which have all undergone significant change over the past decade (Mahnken, Nesbitt & Keyzer 1997): the Koroit hospital has been reduced to a nursing home facility; the Macarthur hospital lost its acute care and GP at the same time and has been reduced to an outreach centre; and Mortlake has had its hospital amalgamated into the Terang-Mortlake Health Service. Only Port Fairy has maintained its hospital, but it has been reconstituted as the Moyne Health Services and has incorporated acute care, nursing hostel and day care facilities under its auspices. In an attempt to avoid incorporation into the nearby Warrnambool base hospital, the management and board of the Port Fairy hospital have negotiated a deal with the government to be part of a 'Health Streams' pilot project (Victorian Department of Human Service 1998). Certainly, the local community is very supportive of its local hospital, raising $2.2m out of a $4m building fund.

The shire has also lost a number of schools and had others amalgamated. Nine small rural schools closed between 1993 and 1998 and two other primary schools have been amalgamated with local secondary schools in Mortlake and Hawkesdale to form what are known as P12 schools (Victorian Education Department 1992, 1998). The loss of schools, hospital functions, local government facilities and other government services is demonstrated in the drop in government employees in the shire from 289 in 1986 to 169 in 1996 (CData 1996).

The effects of private sector downsizing have also been felt in the shire. Banking facilities in the smaller towns have generally been wound down: Macarthur lost its last major bank; the Port Fairy bank had its status reduced and the management services transferred to Warrnambool; and Koroit had its bank reduced to two days trading. Added to the decline in service delivery, there has been a 5% reduction in the labour force in the shire over the decade from 1986 to 1996 (CData 1996). This is despite the expansion of dairy processing with its multiplier effects, especially in areas like transport (CData 1996).

Community reaction to marketisation

The reaction of communities to loss of services in the shire has been universal anger. However, that anger has been changed by the growth of a number of development groups in the shire. There are three significant groups that have arisen over the past two years: Macarthur Advancement Development committee or MAD; Koroit Development Association; and the Mortlake Community Development Committee (MCDC). Each of these groups has developed a broad definition of development to include everything from the street-scaping to new business enterprises.

The Koroit committee has been successful in developing a number of local events, especially the annual Irish Festival which fits in with long family connections to Ireland. The festival is now into its third year and continues to attract larger numbers of people from outside the region. While it is not on the scale of the annual Port Fairy Folk Festival, which is now an event of international standing, the Irish Festival is rooted in its local history. The KDC has also been instrumental in developing discussions between the local nursing home and other such facilities in the nearby City of Warrnambool.

As an organisation MAD attracts a good deal of local support. One of the most significant events for MAD was the closure of the local bank. With the assistance of the Moyne shire council, especially the mayor, Macarthur was able to replace its bank within twelve months with an 'agency' from the Bank of South Australia. By using a local business that opens seven days a week from early morning to late evening, the people of Macarthur were able to achieve a seven day a week banking operation.

However, perhaps the most outstanding response to marketisation in the public sector has been the Mortlake Community Development Committee (MCDC). The MCDC grew out of community reaction to three significant events in the town: the closure of the hospital; the relocation of the shire office to Port Fairy; and the relocation of the primary school to the secondary school site, establishing what is called a P12 school. Following two mass meetings of around one hundred concerned citizens in November 1996, the MCDC was established with a working group of fourteen people who were 'charged with being the watch dog and a point of voicing community concern' (MCDC, 1997). From the outset the MCDC was a committee that included a wide range of people who had a broad ranging view of local economic development.

The MCDC soon went beyond a watch dog role to a proactive role in local development of the town. To maintain momentum the MCDC invited speakers to the town, especially from the executive level of the shire and the health services. These speakers were deemed to be an important strategy in turning the anger of the community into constructive ways of re-establishing the town. At the same time contacts were established with local and regional organisations that showed some promise of offering assistance to the town. This assistance was not purely financial but rather in terms of supportive ideas, contacts and networks that would allow different sections of the community to engage with the town. These groups included tourist associations, adult education groups, land protection authorities, health services, local water authorities, arts councils, rural counselling services, the local university campus, local governments, and government departments at state and federal level such as Natural Resources and Energy and the Primary Industries and Environment.

Together with two other community groups, the Buskers Festival Inc and the Central Hopkins Land Protection Group, the MCDC established the Mortlake and District Visitor and Business Information Centre. The aims of the centre are: to promote Mortlake and District; to promote the shire of Moyne and the region; to provide a focal point for the community, promote participation and ownership and provide community outlet; to increase job prospects and re-entry to the workforce for volunteers, by providing training in tourism, tour guiding, desk top publishing and computer skills, customer service, and to promote local industry, businesses and events.

The MCDC is a grass roots organisation that has sought to bring all aspects of the development of Mortlake under one banner. This does not mean controlling all activities but rather linking the different development processes. The MCDC as a development agency has produced some results for the town. For example they have developed a telecentre with a full-time manager. The telecentre is a co-operative enterprise between three rural counselling services and another telecentre in a town north of Hamilton, Cavendish. The idea of the centre is to supply a number of interests: an 1800 number and a meeting place for rural counselling services; an adult education centre for computing and telecommunication; a local centre for townspeople to use email, computing and secretarial services; an instrumentality for developing information banks for agencies such as tourist associations; an instrumentality for the training of e-commerce for local businesses.

The MCDC seeks to link Mortlake to as many external agencies as possible. For example the MCDC has sought linkages with Deakin University in Warrnambool with which it is developing research and development programs. The outcomes of the liaison with the university have led to a number of projects, including a national soldier settlement and war memorabilia museum. The MCDC also believes in creating projects in the town that develop internal linkages. Co-locating an art gallery with the existing swimming pool would help to construct an indoor pool that could also be used for hydrotherapy.

As a group the MCDC is proactive, studying the experiences of successful development in other localities. For example they have studied the experience in other towns of introducing new banks or creating community banks after bank closures. At the same time the MCDC has been successful in helping to attract fourteen new businesses into Mortlake (Annual Report 1997).

The MCDC has been able to gain support from the shire and other levels of government. The shire is not only supportive with its resources, it also uses the MCDC as a major consultative committee for the Mortlake region. The MCDC has been able to attract $90 000 from the Rural Communities Program and has had members chosen for community development training with the Victorian Department of Natural Resources and Energy. It has also been successful in attracting money from other sources for local projects. Local businesses are also supportive, especially the pastry factory, which holds an export licence for its products.

Lessons from community action

There are a number of lessons to be drawn from the community activity described in the reactions of the community to marketisation and competition. These can be summarised under four major headings; 'bottom up' approach; leadership; training and research; and shock treatment.

'Bottom up' approach

Beer and Alaric (1996) argue that 'organisations need empowerment ... and for an organisation to survive it must be empowered by "bottom up" support from community, "top down" support from the State or Commonwealth Government, or both'. Since the local development groups described above have been developed from the grass roots, they are locally empowered. It is not the existence of the development groups that is important, but rather the wide ranging community representation and support. By establishing formal links with different groups in the town through the use of sub-committees, the MCDC has been able to co-ordinate and assist development across a number of different activities. Through this mechanism the leaders in the town are brought together to co-operate in developing the town as a whole.

At the same time the MCDC is fully aware that unless it becomes financially secure it will flounder (Annual Report, MCDC). Accordingly the second aspect of its strategy is to seek 'top down' support from local, state and federal governments. In 1997 the MCDC applied for funding across a number of different organisations: Heritage Victoria for the purchase and restoration of the mill; Street Life for the commencement of a town plan; the Premier's office to fund a tourism co-ordinator; Veterans Affairs for War Memorial funding; the Shire of Moyne Community Support fund; and Pride of Place. Most of these applications have been successful.

Leadership

McKinsey argues that leadership is an essential part of regional development but leadership comes in many forms (McKinsey & Co 1994). A significant feature of the Mortlake, Macarthur and Koroit experiences is the discovery of local 'talent'. Where before people in the community were content to allow the local municipal authority to take the initiative, now there is a vacuum that is being filled by retired and semi-retired people filled with enthusiasm to try out their own ideas. Since their commitment is to the maintenance of their own local infrastructure, and there is not the formality associated with bureaucratic structures, most of the new leadership is prepared to give their time in trying out their own ideas.

Training and research

A specific strategy adopted by the MCDC is training and research. Members of the committee have been chosen to attend special training courses in community development. Further, the MCDC has adopted strategies to gather information on successful practices adopted by other regional communities. By sifting the available literature the committee is able to plan for possible changes in their local economic and social environment. The linkages with other local and regional agencies have also provided a good source of information and research.

The search for information by MCDC is a process carried out by many communities around Australia. If the networks are easily accessed or the community has people with research training then the process achieves good results. However, there is probably a need to create a central clearinghouse for information to rural communities. This could involve a web site and database as a first stage in the distribution of information.

Shock treatment and community development

The emergence of local groups like those described above was dependent upon the local impact of central government policies. Where once many rural communities were dependent upon the allocation of resources by central governments to their locality on an on-going basis, they now depend upon competition with other communities for resources. In the past, the response by local communities to loss of government services has led to delegations of local luminaries trekking off to Melbourne or to the local member's office, where they could usually negotiate some resurrection of the lost service. But all this has changed. The once 'taken-for-granted' services of education, health and local government provision have either been removed or transformed to meet the criteria of economic indicators established by the central policy makers.

Those places that have seen services removed or renovated have reacted angrily at first and in some instances, like those described above, there has been the emergence of local survival committees. Where there has been little or no change, it is often hard to galvanise local support. Or, in some instances there has been positive resistance to any amendments to local life styles. A township like Peterborough in the Moyne shire is one such example, where 'development' is treated with great resistance. This township has not had any of the three major services of education, health or local government and accordingly has not had to suffer any losses to the social fabric of the town.

Conclusion: the bigger picture

While supporting the growth of local 'bottom up' agencies, Beer and Alaric (1996) argue that there is another level of development that needs to be considered. They argue:

> Communities, usually with local government involvement, will continue to create 'bottom up' agencies as they struggle to deal with local problems. However, they are generally unable to create the upper level, regional, organisations that are needed to deal with issues such as industry rather than firm development, major infrastructure, and the pressure and opportunities of the global economy.

Groups like the MCDC recognise that they will survive in the new global economy only if they spread their connections upward and outward. Accordingly the group is involved in collaborating with other regional players to co-ordinate developments in infrastructure and planning. The Moyne shire is also aware of the issues and seeks to incorporate the directions of the MCDC into its strategic planning, especially in tourism and multi-media development. The MCDC is also collaborating with other municipalities in the region. Similarly the Greater Green Triangle Incorporated, the local regional organisation in South West Victoria, is involved in the processes of up-grading infrastructure, especially in telecommunications (O'Toole 1998).

However, in my opinion, governments at state and federal level should review their approach to marketisation and competition. Competition for funding between different regions is not the way to develop a prosperous economy in regional Australia. 'Shock treatment' may have developed some renovation of local communities, but it is a shortsighted approach to public policy. Communities like Mortlake may have been jolted into action by the marketisation policies of the Victorian state government. However, if the general policy of the application of universal criteria to resource allocation in government service delivery continues, towns like Mortlake will continue to suffer losses, despite the magnificent efforts of the MCDC. The argument is not about handouts to regional Australia but rather having the insight to see that a significant aspect of market failure in national terms is the monopoly over decision making by one theory of development. Marketisation of government policy making does not lead necessarily to better outcomes for all Australians.

References

ACCC 1996, *Summaries of the Trade Practices Act*, http://www.accc.gov.au/docs/summary/sumnov98.htm

Alford, J. & O'Neill, D. 1994, *The Contract State: Public Management and the Kennett Government*, Centre for Applied Social Research, Deakin University.

Australian Bureau of Statistics 1996, *Cdata*

Beal, D. & Ralston, D. 1998, 'Economic and Social Impacts of the Closure of the Only Bank in Australian Rural Communities', in Staples, M. & Millmow, A., *Studies in Australian Economic Development*, Centre for Rural Social Research, Charles Sturt University, Wagga Wagga.

Beer, A. & Alaric, M. 1996, *Effectiveness of State Frameworks for Local Economic Development*, Geography Department, Flinders University.

Carroll, J. 1992, Economic Rationalism and its Consequences, in Carroll, J. & Manne, R., *Shutdown: The Failure of Economic Rationalism*, Text Publishing, Melbourne.

Clark, G. 1992, 'The Auction Proposal', in Carroll, J. & Manne, R. *Shutdown: The Failure of Economic Rationalism*, Text Publishing, Melbourne.

Codd, M. 1991, *Federal Public Sector Management Reform: Recent History and Current Priorities*, Public Service Commission, AGPS, Canberra.

Fagan, R. & Webber, M. 1997, *Global Restructuring: The Australian Experience*, Oxford University Press, Melbourne.

Horne, D. 1992, *The Trouble with Economic Rationalism*, Scribe, Newham, Victoria.

Hughes, O. 1994, *Public Management and Administration: An Introduction*, Macmillan, New York

Mahnken, J., Nesbitt, P. & Keyzer, D. 1997, *The Rural Nurse Practitioner: A Pilot Project to Develop an Alternative Model of Practice*, Deakin University: Faculty of Health and Behavioural Sciences: Warrnambool.

McGuire, L. 1994, 'Service Delivery Agreements: Experimenting with Casemix Funding and "Schools of the Future"', in Alford, J. & O'Neill, D., *The Contract State: Public Management and the Kennett Government*, Centre for Applied Social Research, Deakin University.

McKinsey & Company 1994, *Lead Local Compete Global: Unlocking the Growth Potential of Australia's Regions*, McKinsey & Company, Sydney.

Mortlake Community Development Committee 1997, *Annual Report*.

National Competition Council 1996, *Considering the Public Interest under the National Competition Policy*, Melbourne.

National Competition Policy Review 1993, *National Competition Policy (Hilmer Inquiry)*, AGPS, Canberra.

Osborne, D. & Gaebler, T. 1993, *Reinventing Government: How the Entrepreneurial Spirit is Transforming Government*, Plume, New York.

O'Toole, K. 1998, 'Economic Development in the Green Triangle: A Need for Reassessment in the New International Environment', in Staples M. & Millmow, A., *Studies in Australian Rural Economic Development*, Centre for Rural Social Research, Wagga Wagga.

Pusey, M. 1991, *Economic Rationalism in Canberra*, Cambridge University Press, Melbourne.

Pusey, M. 1992, 'Canberra Changes Its Mind', in Carroll, J. & Manne, R., *Shutdown: The Failure of Economic Rationalism*, Text Publishing, Melbourne.

Sassen, S. 1991, *The Global City*, Princeton University Press, New Jersey.

Shire of Moyne 1998, *Annual Budget*.

Stilwell, F. 1997, *Globalisation and Cities: An Australian Political-Economic Perspective*, Urban Research Program, Australian National University, Canberra.

Victorian Department of Human Service Rural Health Services Unit 1998, *Programs*, http://www.dhs.vic.gov.au/rural/rurprogr.htm

Victorian Education Department 1992, *Barwon-South Western Region Government and Non Government Schools: Alphabetical Listing*.

Victorian Education Department 1998, *Barwon-South Western Region Government and Non Government Schools: Alphabetical Listing*.

7

Conceptualising feminist community practice in a regional area*

Helen La Nauze with Wendy Weeks

Introduction

Women's community practice in Albury-Wodonga in the 1980s can be understood in the context of 'an active women's movement and a reforming labor government' (Curthoys 1992, p. 436) and the specific national action which resulted in the 1973 declaration of Albury-Wodonga as the National Growth Centre. This chapter reports on Helen La Nauze's research, completed in 1996, which addressed two questions: 'What has been the nature of feminist community practice in Albury-Wodonga?' and 'How can this be understood in relation to women's local experiences, as well as in relation to the broader Australian women's movement?'

---

* This chapter is an edited version of parts of Helen La Nauze's Master of Social Work thesis at University of Melbourne, which was awarded first class honours in 1996. Wherever possible Helen's own words have been retained.

In researching feminist community practice La Nauze (1996, p. 5) acknowledged that 'feminism', 'community practice' and 'rural' are all contested terms. Her approach, as she interviewed local women community workers, was to start out using the terms loosely, seeking not to prejudice what she heard, but allowing the women to define how they thought and spoke about it. Operationally she defined 'feminist community workers' as women who were identified by the researcher or others as having been active participants in organisations, events and/or networks that were working for change for women. From the in-depth interviews La Nauze drew themes which conceptualise the nature of women's community practice.

The sample of participants

The participants in the study had lived in Albury-Wodonga or district from 8 to over 30 years. Four had lived in the area since childhood, 3 had moved there prior to the development of the area as a growth centre, 2 arrived in the 1970s and 4 in the 1980s. Twelve of the 13 participants were still resident in the area at the time of the research. As described above, participants were women who had extensive involvement in community work in the 1980s. Twelve had worked in paid positions in community services, including full-time, part-time, short-term contract and casual employment. Twelve had been involved with neighbourhood houses in one or more roles. For example, 5 had been in paid employment as community workers; 7 had been members of committees of management; and 3 had done sessional work at one or more houses. Twelve of the women had been involved with the Women's Collective (which began in 1980 at the Social Planning Unit and later met at the Women's Centre). Seven women had been involved with the YWCA in paid or unpaid committee membership positions, and 6 with the Women's Centre. Three women were involved in the committee which developed Mobile Child Care, which began in 1984 as a Community Employment Program, and several had been employed or on committees with the Social Planning Unit of Albury-Wodonga Corporation. Other organisations in which more than one participant was involved included the Upper Murray Consultative Council, the Women's Refuge, the Albury-Wodonga Children's Resource Group, and the local TAFE (Technical and Further Education) Board.

The theoretical and practical context of the research

Feminist activity is conceptualised and named differently within the different discourses and historical and national traditions. The accounts of women's community action found in Bookman and Morgen (1988) are viewed as political practice, while Adamson, Brisken and McPhail (1989) write about feminist organising for change. Within the professional discourse, feminist community work and feminist community action are terms used by Dominelli and MacLeod (1989) and Dominelli (1990) writing in the British tradition, while Weil (1986) and Brandwein (1987) in the American context write of feminist principles for community organisation. Hyde (1989) adopts the concept of 'macro-practice'. Australian debate has taken place using the term 'feminist community work' (Dixon 1993; Weeks, 1994b). La Nauze adopted the term 'feminist community practice' as an umbrella term which subsumes community organising, community action and community development.

La Nauze used the term 'women's movement' to encompass the broad-based but often loosely structured inter-weaving complex of groups, organisations, networks and campaigns that has evolved since the early 1970s in Australia to work for the political and social equality of women. She noted that there was no intent to suggest uniformity, but to assume a diversity of currents of thought and ways of organising which have evolved since the resurgence of activity since the 1970s. Defining the nature and form of the local women's movement was a task of the research.

The meaning of the term 'rural' is also contested. Australian and international rural practice literature recognises the ambiguity and lack of consensus around definitions of rural, which may be characterised by demographic, occupational and/or socio-cultural characteristics. La Nauze accepted the broad, pragmatic definition of rural as 'non-metropolitan' (following Dunn 1989, p. 13; Lynn, 1990, p. 6). The literature that reports experiences of rural women reflects the ambiguity of definition that characterises other rural literature. Women who live outside metropolitan Australia have been variously defined as 'country women', 'rural women' or 'women in rural Australia' (James 1982; Alston 1990; Dallow 1992; Franklin, Short & Teather 1994). The experiences of women in larger regional centres are not clearly articulated in the rural literature, and La Nauze's work sought to fill this gap.

The site of La Nauze's research was Albury-Wodonga. Situated on the Murray River, the border between Victoria and New South Wales, Albury is in New South Wales, 600 kilometres south-west of Sydney, and Wodonga is on the Victorian side some 300 kilometres from Melbourne. The 'twin cities' have rail, road and air links to the respective capital cities, and are separated by the river and flood plains over three kilometres. The state border means that a variety of policy and service provision differences intervene in the way people and organisations conduct their activities. The 1973 Albury-Wodonga Development Agreement established a statutory authority, the Albury-Wodonga Development Corporation (AWDC) with a charter to build a vigorous new city with attention to physical and social planning. The national strategy was abandoned in 1976, with plans for development being modified, and the centre supported as a pilot in decentralisation. Nonetheless there has been considerable population growth, particularly in Wodonga. The population of Wodonga, which was 13 150 in 1971, doubled in the following 20 years. In the same period Albury grew from 29 150 to

40 560 (AWDC 1994, p. 1). Taken together this is the largest population growth of all regional centres in Victoria and New South Wales for the period. In these years of growth, 35% of the population arriving were between 25 and 34 years with many young families. The local women's movement activity documented in La Nauze's research was set in this rapidly growing regional centre, described by one of the participants as 'shaking the foundations of the community', not just about 'new houses on the edge of town'.

Feminist practice in a major regional centre

The participants' stories showed that women related to notions of feminism and the women's movement in different ways. They varied in the extent to which they spontaneously embraced the term 'feminist' as defining their participation or saw their involvement as part of the women's movement. Some women unhesitatingly identified themselves and their involvement as feminist, but this was not always the case. Is it, then, appropriate to continue with the inclusive approach of using the term 'feminist community practice' to cover the involvement of participants, whether or not they self-identified as feminist? La Nauze decided it was. Similarly, Graveline et al. (1991, pp. 134–5) writing about feminist community organising in northern Canada acknowledged that not all of the network were self-named feminists, but the work was 'woman-oriented' and the goals were about equality for women and the network she described appealed to 'feminist-thinking women'. Alternatively, however, La Nauze was mindful of Rowbotham's (1992, p. 234) warning of caution in ascribing people with a consciousness they do not claim.

In drawing themes from the stories of the Albury-Wodonga women community workers, La Nauze rejected developing a typology in favour of a more dynamic approach. She found parallels with Laura Balbo's metaphor of patchwork quilting: the language of

> piece-bags, sorting out, piecing, patching and quilting ... the servicing, the pooling, the packaging of resources, the self-help activities, emotional work and survival networks; how women keep at their endless tasks, how they put their vision into planning and design of their own and others' lives whose responsibility they carry.
>
> (Balbo 1987, p. 46)

It is a metaphor that captures both the whole and the parts, the integrating threads and the many designs that women produce. La Nauze found parallels, too, in the way Gilkes (1988, pp. 54–5) describes Black women community workers 'building in many places'. Her study within an urban locality tells of how women built 'Black-oriented' institutions in the places they worked, used friendship networks, membership in various organisations and diverse 'pragmatic affiliations' to produce 'a connectedness and cohesion within a pluralistic Black community'. The third influence was the approach of Canadian writers Adamson, Brisken and McPhail (1989) who emphasise feminist practice as within the tension of mainstreaming and disengagement. The themes that La Nauze drew from the stories of the Albury-Wodonga community work are creating a women-centred focus around different sites and issues; networking, connection and connectedness; providing service to women as well as working for change; and linking local activity to the broader movement.

(1) Creating a women-centred focus around different sites and issues

Women's community practice in Albury-Wodonga in the 1980s can be described in Gilkes' (1988) phrase 'building in many places'. Women worked in and from a variety of organisational locations, in a mix of paid and unpaid capacities, building on and around the social development they initiated in response to external forces and opportunities. They were active in both generalist and women-specific organisations, traditional and new women's organisations, and statutory and non-government community-based organisations. There was no one pattern of activity, development or location, as the following examples show.

The planned development of Albury-Wodonga as a National Growth Centre was important because it precipitated an influx of newcomers and stimulated the provision of infrastructure, such as the Development Corporation (started in 1974) and neighbourhood houses. The ways in which women built their practice approaches around these initiatives, and the catalytic effect of the women in the Social Planning Unit of the Development Corporation clearly emerges from the women's stories. Women described how they incorporated a women-focused analysis of issues into generalist planning roles. They built and maintained strong grass-roots connections with women and with the community in general, and supported the work of women in other organisations by providing information and resources, and by being involved in committees and working groups. Women's development of the organisational mandate and related opportunities provided important leadership for local women.

A second example is the development of the Community Educational Centre (CEC). Increased access to funding for community-based adult education occurred across Victoria and in this context local women built a team of workers who developed a women-specific program, as well as a more women-focused general service. The program model developed included co-operative planning, building women-friendly space and consciousness-raising approaches to teaching. Women at the Centre were also active in stimulating connections between women in the different education sectors, formal and informal, and in working for increased access for women to education at all levels.

Mobile Child Care was the outcome of workers from both these organisations seizing the opportunity of Commonwealth Community Employment funding to develop an innovative service which took child care activities to women and children in a variety of locations in the area. The model developed was collaborative and involved women from a number of organisations and groups in shared decision-making and shared resources.

At the YWCA, which had originally begun in the 1940s, women undertook the difficult task of bringing together a traditional women's organisation with the more feminist-oriented ideas and energies of younger women from the Wodonga branch. A viable local organisation, with a focus on young women, and with strong state and national ties, resulted from the union. Specific women's services such as the Women's Centre and the Refuge were developed 'from scratch', and women with different perspectives grappled with working together in a hostile environment. In sum, the varied settings and patterns of development of women's practice highlight the importance of a feminist practice which is contextually sensitive, and therefore responsive to the particular opportunities for change in time and place.

Despite very different structures and organisational bases, two practices were common. Firstly, women frequently worked together to develop 'women-friendly' spaces and places. Some spaces were women-only, while others were not exclusively so, but encouraged an environment that was safe, both physically and emotionally, friendly and open to women. This is consistent with 'creating women's safe space' which was argued by Weeks (1994b) to be a separate practice principle in light of the amount of energy and time the women's movement has spent creating spaces and service organisations for women. Hyde(1989), Guitierrez and Lewis (1994) and Dominelli (1990) all refer to the importance of safe and supportive environments for women. A study (1992) of the Country Women's Association suggests that the provision of space for women is not just a characteristic of urban-based movements but also has a history in rural women's organising.

Second, co-operative ways of working were common among women, either within organisations or between them. Co-operative and participatory ways of working are frequently claimed as a hallmark of feminist organising (Weil 1986; Hyde 1989; Brown 1992; Guitierrez and Lewis 1994; Weeks 1994a). Focus in the literature is often on collectivity as total organisational form. In this study, co-operative and democratic approaches were most evident in the day-to-day processes and the informal structures, rather than in the structural 'collective' form.

(2) Networking, connection and connectedness

The many facets of connection and inter-connection emerge strongly from the picture of women's community practice in the 1980s in Albury-Wodonga. The women were multiply connected—through workplaces, friendship networks, involvement in community organisations and historically. Their connections were actively pursued, not just incidental happenings. This study highlights the importance women placed on building strong, local, inter-personal ties with other women. Through their strong connections women shared information and resources, built their understanding and/or consciousness, developed a sense of shared purpose and identity as women, provided support to each other in an environment that was perceived and often experienced as hostile to women's liberation. They learned from each other and derived enjoyment, friendship and companionship. They used their connections to enhance work practices, lobby, increase women's participation on boards and committees and to develop new ventures.

The practices of creating women-friendly places and working in co-operative and participatory ways enhance an involvement which is a full personal engagement, not reducible to professional or organisational roles, nor indicative of homosexual preference. They are practices that minimise social distance and facilitate trust and connection. Connectedness, too, is enhanced by the interweaving of different spheres of women's lives in their work and community (such as around child care or children's sports), referred to by one participant as 'the meshing that women can do so well'.

Connection, relationship, 'relatedness', networks and networking are concepts that resonate with aspects of the rural and feminist community practice literature. According to Dominelli and MacLeod (1989) networking forms the basis of feminist community work and yet is fluid and diverse in form. Weeks (1994a, 1994b) asserts that networking, a non-hierarchical linking strategy, is a practice principle in reaction to women's fragmented everyday lives, and a development of the role of women 'gossiping' which historically meant passing on important information.

Networking emerged as a central feature of the Albury-Wodonga study (see also, Hyde 1989; Lynn 1990b; Metzendorf 1990). The importance of reviewing the various associated meanings of these concepts is highlighted by Dixon's ambivalence about aspects of feminist community practice. She argues that some feminist practice writing risks reducing the political to the personal and introducing an 'essentialist feminist logic', implying that some processes are uniquely female (Dixon 1993, p. 25). She claims that the focus should be on concepts based in the power discourse, on the 'dynamics for change they unleash, rather than on the assumed masculinist or feminist properties' (Dixon 1993, p. 26). In contrast, Canadian scholar Angela Miles' (1991) central concept of 'integrative feminism' affirms women's specificity as well as their equality. She asserts that building on women's specific experiences and their concomitant concerns and values is a political, not a biological, claim which seeks to transform humanity.

The pertinent question for practice is not whether the experience can be understood as 'essentially female', but whether there can be a claim to an effective practice which is built around women's networks, relationships and connections. The present study supports the line of interpretation developed by Acklesberg (1988) who places importance on 'relatedness' which she sees as characteristic of the lives of many women and their engagement in organising. In reference to working class women's activism, she states:

for many of the women discussed in these studies, the process of coming to political consciousness seems to be the process of making connections—between their lives and the lives of others, between issues that affect them and their families in the neighbourhood or community and those that affect them in the workplace, between the so-called differing spheres of their lives.

(Acklesberg 1988, p. 305)

In her view, giving central place to a human connectedness is not about asserting 'women's values', but an expression of how people live and engage in political activity. Mitchell (1994, p. 141), reflecting on her six years with the Victorian Rural Women's Network, claims that the network grew in strength through the personal connections women made, but which she pointedly distinguishes from 'private' connections. Women participants in this study emphasised the fluidity of networking, with women grouping, regrouping and establishing themselves in multiple settings, addressing a host of different issues.

Brown (1992, pp. 70–71) argues, in her study of women's organising, that networking is a core skill of organising. She describes it as about 'forming peer relationships with interdependent others [and] is enacted through transactions and exchanges'. It serves the purpose of gaining information about the environment in which one is working, and assists in understanding and analysing it. Arguably it is a crucial skill for feminist practice in a conservative rural context.

A further claim is that personal connection can form the deeper bonds of support and friendship which provide the motive energy and vision for change, as well as buffering painful periods. In this study, these bonds are conveyed in the language used by the women, such as a sense of 'constructing what we were on about', a 'sense of common purpose', 'developing intimate knowledge and trust in each other'. The need for and provision of mutual support was also reported. The reports are consistent with the reviewed feminist practice literature, including those writers such as Hawkeshurst and Morrow and Weeks who write of building feminist community as a practice principle.

Raymond's (1986) visionary analysis of female friendship conceptualises the potential of female friendship as political. She does not portray it as romanticised bonds, reducible to emotions, but as relationships which are fully human in their intellectual, spiritual and affective ties and expressed in actions with common purpose. The significance of female friendship is in its potential to create the vision and means for a reality that is constructed by women acting as 'self' rather than 'other'. (Raymond 1986, p. 20) She argues that the personal becomes the ground for the political.

The paradoxical effects of women's closeness and interconnection that were reported in this study concur with other accounts of feminist practice, which report experiences of personal conflict and hurt, along with the empowering

(Raymond 1986, p. 7; Hyde 1989; Weeks 1994a). Women's close working relationships can also create boundaries and exclusion. Feminism as ideology can operate as a unifying force, but may concurrently deny diversity and power differences, as Ristock reported in Canadian collectives. Hyde (1989, pp. 172–3) also reported on the 'contradictions of co-operative settings', where the realities of high commitment, sense of ownership and 'group think' can act as barriers to inclusion. Brown (1992, pp. 163) observes that greater attention to internal relationships can mean a neglect of networking activities and information seeking.

Networking appears to be integral to rural practice. Lynn claims that networking approaches are consistent with rural life, which is characterised by dense over-lapping ties—'the nexus between locality and networks is mutually reinforcing as a definer of community' (Lynn 1990b, p. 21). The evidence of this study identifies women working to extend their lateral ties within the community, seeking to encompass women with diverse perspectives and to be multiply connected, not perceived only as feminist. At the same time they reported strong bonds between themselves, facilitated by the merged boundaries characterising their lives both as women and as active participants in the interlinked community services sector and by their developing historical connections. On the one hand the strength of connection in a regional centre can create the potential for developing vision, support and energy important in feminist, change-oriented practice. Paradoxically the visibility of everyday life, combined with the intensity of connection may exaggerate the stereotypes and tensions and create the potential for polarisation, as suggested in the women's stories.

The key question for feminist practice in smaller, conservative communities appears to be the same question identified by Adamson, Brisken and McPhail (1988). How can feminist practice both maintain its vision and yet also engage with the breadth of women in their everyday lives? The insights gained from this study and from reflecting on the literature suggest that feminist practice in smaller communities needs to balance the importance of engagement with the breadth of local networks in relation to the importance of developing and maintaining women-specific network links, important for providing the strength, vision and support necessary for change-oriented practice. However, it may be that the balance is easier in a major rural centre, highlighting the need for more research in small communities.

(3) Providing service to women as well as working for change

Writers on feminist community practice have grappled with the difficulty of relating the purpose of social change with particular ways of working and sites for action. For example, whether personal change was an appropriate or sufficient goal; linking broader political change with a focus on individual women, women's groups and traditionally female arenas; and the co-opting of social change goals as activism is diverted to service within the funding requirements (Schechter 1982; Hyde 1989; Lane 1990; Dixon 1993; Fried 1993; Weeks 1994b).

The Albury-Wodonga study shows that women's community practice was directed both at addressing the current needs of women as well as working for broader change. Four major activities were identified: providing service and programs to individual groups of women; planning, lobbying for and developing new services and programs responsive to women's needs and the particular context; developing community and professional education programs; and advocating for policy and practice changes in local and non-local arenas. These major areas of activity support and build on Weeks' (1994a) conceptualisation of the triple purpose of feminist women's services.

The study was not designed as an evaluation project and hence cannot be used to assess the change outcomes and the relative effectiveness and success of different strategies in different sites. In this sense it cannot address the question of 'how much' change, nor whether this constituted 'substantial social change'. Useful insights can, however, be gained by reflecting on the themes of practice in relation to the literature. Within the framework of feminist practice proposed by Adamson, Briskin and McPhail (1988, pp. 178–84) responding to women's current needs through a range of services and programs can be understood as a 'mainstreaming' practice in which the purpose is 'to be concrete and immediately relevant to women's lives' and to engage with large numbers of women in the change effort. According to these authors, the risk of mainstreaming is institutionalisation, where feminist challenge is redefined and the scope of the vision for change is limited.

In this study a legitimate mandate was named as important, and women spoke of stretching the boundaries of that mandate. This suggests that it is possible to engage in mainstreaming, while keeping a broader vision of change. On the other hand, the risk of institutionalisation was evident in the expressed concern about 'band-aiding' practice, or the possibility that the impact of neighbourhood services or Mobile Child Care could be reinforcing, rather than liberating, women's current domestic status.

Programs such as assertiveness, parenting skills or self-esteem programs are open to the same critique. The efforts of community workers to engage with women's lives, as well as respond to the issues viewed as important, reflect this tension. Balancing the four types of activities named above may be one way to maintain the strategic tension between mainstreaming and marginalisation.

The importance of women's networks and networking practices in maintaining lateral ties and coalition building allowed women in this study to provide services and programs while continuing also to engage in action on a broader scale.

(4) Linking local activity to the broader movement

The accounts of women's community involvement in this study suggest a practice that had strong locality focus and commitment. They focused on Albury-Wodonga, not just on their neighbourhoods, in spite of crossing the state borders and running up against different statutory and organisational policies and practices. Perhaps the locality focus was reinforced by 'living in the country' and marginalisation from the capital cities. However, this did not exclude a sense of identification with the broader women's movement. Indeed women's accounts of their activities suggest the opposite, in spite of the barriers of distance. Women maintained links outside the local area by participation and membership in statewide and national organisations, through attendance at conferences and workshops and by inviting key women leaders to visit the local area. They developed local initiatives within national spheres of action, for example, by running a local 'National Agenda for Women' consultation and organising a national education conference.

Rural practice writers urge the formation of local and regional coalitions across interest groups, newcomers and old-timers, and across people with different ideological positions (Martinez-Brawley 1986, 1987; Collingridge and Dunn 1993). By focusing on rural difference, disadvantage and powerlessness, the commonalities can be overlooked. Similarly the possibilities of networks with urban colleagues may also be overlooked. The evidence from this study is that coalitions among local people as well as coalitions across the rural/urban divide, can enrich and strengthen local efforts for change.

Conclusion

How is feminist community practice in a major rural centre best conceptualised? What can the experiences of women in a major rural centre contribute to understanding the broader picture of feminist community practice? La Nauze suggests that feminist community practice is most usefully understood as a conceptual framework guiding women's change-oriented practice, rather than as an expression of the identity of individual women. Furthermore, she argues that feminist community practice in a regional centre is most usefully conceptualised with a generic feminist practice framework, rather than as a separate category of activity. The evidence from this study suggests that the concepts of context and paradox and/or tension, when combined with the articulation of practice principles, provide promise for conceptualising a feminist community practice which has relevance beyond the bounds of a metropolitan context.

Context

The generic rural practice literature and the small number of reports on feminist practice in rural areas have highlighted the significance of context in developing and understanding practice. This study re-emphasises this. Adopting contextual sensitivity points to the importance of flexibility, responsiveness and openness to different organisational forms and bases of practice. It points to the importance of understanding local networks and power relations and of strategic practice that is cognisant of those networks.

La Nauze argues, however, that this does not necessarily equate with developing separate models of practice, nor does it imply accepting the concept of rurality underpinning organising. Because the context of the regional centre was between the poles of rural and urban she was particularly watchful of how women described their practice in relation to this issue. Women were concerned with issues of women's everyday lives, such as health, family planning, and child care, which are reflective of women's lives across the nation. In addition, the commonalities of practice and the local, statewide, national network connections highlighted in this study suggest that conceptualising the importance of context, rather than theorising rurality and difference, is the most useful approach. The approach to the particularities of context is thus strategic rather than categorical. This parallels the shift in thinking from earlier concepts of core and margins in minority women's participation in the women's movement.

Paradox and tension

Concepts such as ambiguity, paradox, dual purpose, managing tensions and contradictory outcomes could be considered hallmarks of the feminist practice literature. The tensions identified in this study include: developing strong connections, yet maintaining diversity; the strength yet vulnerability associated with blurred personal and professional boundaries; and the tension between a focus on individual women's needs while pursuing broader goals of change. Another tension was the local and national links, networking and definitions of issues. The approach of Adamson, Brisken and McPhail in conceptualising feminist practice around tensions is therefore particularly useful. As a key practice concept it mediates between the concrete particularities of women's experiences and opportunities for change, and the generality of principles of and for practice. It has promise for being change-oriented and context connected, rather than rule bound.

Practice principles

In this study the practice principles were inter-woven around four themes. Creating a women-centred focus around different sites and issues suggests the inclusion of contextual sensitivity as a practice principle. The study also gives support to the principle of applying a gender lens to analysis of issues of concern for practice. Third, creating women-friendly spaces and co-operative ways of working were repeatedly reported. Networking, connection and connectedness also stood out as central to feminist community practice in Albury-Wodonga.

Providing service to women while working for broader change was confirmed as a practice principle in this study. The final practice principle identified is linking local activities with the broader women's movement.

When combined with contextual sensitivity, these practice principles facilitate managing the tension of engaging in the concrete realities of change, while recognising and addressing broader structural changes. They also resonate with the principle of sisterhood within cultural diversity—developing practice around the consciousness of being women, yet recognising the diversity of women's experiences.

References

Acklesberg, M. A. 1988, 'Communities, resistance and women's activism: some implications for a democratic polity', in *Women and the Politics of Empowerment*, Bookman, A. & Morgen, S. (eds), Temple University Press, Philadelphia, pp. 297–313.

Adamson, N., Brisken, L. & McPhail, M. 1988, *Feminist Organising for Change: The Contemporary Canadian Women's Movement*, Oxford University Press, Toronto.

Alston, M. 1990, 'Feminism and Farm Women', in *Australian Social Work* , vol. 43, no. 1, pp. 23–7.

Balbo, L. 1987, 'Crazy Quilts: rethinking the welfare state debate from a woman's point of view', in Anne Showstack Sassoon, (ed.), *Women and the Welfare State*, Harvester Wheatesheaf, London.

Bookman, A. & Morgen, S. 1988, *Women and the Politics of Empowerment*, Temple University Press, Philadelphia.

Brandwein, R. A. 1987, 'Women and Community Organisation', in Burden, N.S. & Gottlieb, N. (eds), *The Woman Client*, Tavistock Publications, New York, pp. 111–25.

Brisken, L. 1991, 'Feminist practice: a new approach to evaluating feminist strategy', in Wine, J.D. & Ristock, J. (eds), *Women and Social Change: Feminist Activism in Canada*, James Lorimer and Co, Toronto.

Brown, H. 1992, *Women Organising*, Routledge, London.

Collingridge, M. & Dunn, P. 1993, 'Rural Australia: people, policies and services' in Inglis, J. & Hogen, L. (eds), *Beyond Swings and Roundabouts*, Pluto Press, Sydney.

Curthoys, A. 1992, 'Doing it for themselves. The Women's Movement since 1970', in Saunders, K. & Evans, R. (eds), *Gender Relations in Australia: Domination and Negotiation*, Harcourt Brace Janovitch, Marrickville, pp. 425–47.

Dallow, R. 1992, 'The role of women in agriculture and rural settings', in *The Australian Journal of Rural Health* vol. 1, no. 1, pp. 3–9.

Dixon, J. 1993, 'Feminist community work's ambivalence with politics', in *Australian Social Work* , vol. 46, no. 1, pp. 22–7.

Dominelli, L. 1990, *Women and Community Action*, Venture Press, Birmingham.

Dominelli, L. 1995, 'Women in the Community: feminist principles and organising in community work', in *Community Development Journal*, vol. 30, no. 2, pp. 133–43.

Dominelli, L. & McLeod, E. 1989, *Feminist Social Work*, Macmillan, London.

Dunn, P. 1989, 'Rural Australia: are you standing in it?', in *Rural Research Bulletin*, no. 2, pp. 12–13.

Franklin, M., Short, L. & Teather, E. K. (eds) 1994, *Country Women at the Crossroads: Perspectives on the lives of rural Australian women in the 1990s*, University of New England Press, Armidale.

Fried, A. 1994, 'It's hard to change what we want to change: Rape Crisis centres as organisations', in *Gender and Society*, vol. 8, no. 4, pp. 562–83.

Gilkes, C. T. 1988, 'Building in many places: multiple commitments and ideologies in Black Women's Community Work', Bookman, A. & Morgen, S. (eds), in *Women and the Politics of Empowerment*, Temple University Press, Philadelphia, pp. 53–76.

Graveline, M. J., Fitzpatrick, K. & Mark, B. 1991, 'Networking in Northern Manitoba', in Wine, J.D. & Ristock, J. (eds), *Women and Social Change: Feminist Activism in Canada*, James Lorimer and Co, Toronto.

Gutierrez, L. M. & Lewis, E. A. 1994, 'Community Organising with Women of Color: a feminist approach', in *Journal of Community Practice*, vol. 1, no. 2, pp. 23–86.

Hawkeshurst, D. & Morrow, S. 1984, *Living our Visions: Building Feminist Community*, Fourth World Press, Arizona.

Hyde, C. 1989, 'A feminist model for macro-practice: promises and problems', in *Administration in Social Work*, vol. 13, nos 3/4, pp. 145–81.

Hyde, C. 1994, 'Commitment to Social Change: voices from the feminist movement', in *Journal of Community Practice*, vol. 1, no. 2, pp. 45–63.

James, K. 1982 (ed.), *Women in Rural Australia*, University of Queensland Press, St Lucia.

La Nauze, H. 1996, *Conceptualising Feminist Practice in a Major Rural Centre*, unpublished Master of Social Work thesis, University of Melbourne.

Lane, M. 1990, 'Community work, social change and women', in Petruchenia, J. & Thorpe, R. (eds), *Social Change and Social Welfare Practice*, Hale and Iremonger, Sydney.

Lynn, M. 1990a, 'Rural social work: applying Martinez-Brawley's tenets to Gippsland', in *Australian Social Work*, vol. 43. no. 1, pp. 15–21.

Lynn, M. 1990b, *Developing a Rural Social Work Practice Model*, unpublished Master of Social Work thesis, Monash University, Clayton.

Martinez-Brawley, E. 1982, *Rural Social and Community Work in the United States and Britain*, Praeger, New York.

Metzendorf, D. 1990, *The Evolution of Feminist Organisations: an organisational study*, UMI Dissertations Service, Ann Arbor, Michigan.

Miles, A. 1991, 'Reflections on integrative feminism and rural women', in Wine, J.D. & Ristock, J. (eds), *Women and Social Change: Feminist Activism in Canada*, James Lorimer and Co, Toronto.

Mitchell, J. 1994, 'Grass roots and government initiative: Victorian Rural Women's Network', in Franklin, M., Short, L. & Teather, E. K. (eds), *Country Women at the Crossroads: Perspectives on the lives of rural Australian women in the 1990s*, University of New England Press, Armidale.

Raymond, J. 1986, *A Passion for Friends: Towards a Philosophy of Female Affection*, Women's Press, London.

Ristock, J. 1990, 'Canadian feminist social service collectives: caring and contradictions', in Albrecht, L. & Brewer, R. M. (eds), *Bridges of Power: Women's Multicultural Alliances*, New Society Publishers, Philadelphia, pp. 172–81.

Rowbotham, S. 1992, *Women in Movement: Feminism and Social Action*, Routledge, London.

Schechter, S. 1982, *Women and Male Violence: The Visions and Struggles of the Battered Wives Movement*, South End Press, Boston.

Teather, E. K. 1992, 'Remote rural women's ideologies, spaces and networks: Country Women's Association of New South Wales, 1922–1992' in *Aust. & NZ Journal of Sociology* , vol. 28, no. 3, pp. 369–87.

Weeks, W. 1994a, *Women Working Together: lessons from feminist women's services*, Longman, Melbourne.

Weeks, W. 1994b, ' Feminist principles for community work', in *Women in Welfare Education*, no. 1, pp. 19–44.

Weil, M. 1986, 'Women, community and organising', in van den Bergh, N. & Cooper, L. B., *Feminist Visions of Social Work*, NASW, Silver Springs, pp. 187–210.

8

Community-embedded rural social care practice

Brian Cheers

Introduction

Over the last 20 years, urban-derived social care structures have lurched into rural Australia, only to get bushed in foreign environments. Although the number of rural practitioners—social workers, community developers, social planners, psychologists and the like—has increased considerably during this period, major recruitment and retention difficulties continue to disrupt service continuity and effectiveness (Cheers 1998, pp. 191–3). For instance, Lonne (in progress) has found that 67% of a national sample of social workers resigned from their rural positions earlier than they had anticipated, 39% within the first 12 months. Reasons include agency recruitment policies, lack of organisational support, poor preparation for rural practice through education and training programs and the dearth of useful practice literature (Cheers 1998, pp. 192–3).

'Social care' consists of all the formal and informal arrangements within society, other than the market, which provide material, social and emotional resources to people (Cheers 1998, pp. 17–18). Mainstream Australian social care literature and education come at rural practice from the wrong angle. Inevitably, rural practice, and practitioners, are embedded in the social, cultural, economic, political, environmental and spiritual processes of 'human community'. The practitioner works and lives within rather than outside the myriad structures and processes comprising his or her community and its interaction with the outside world. Though central, the practitioner is still only one player amongst the many people and organisations involved in providing informal and formal social care for residents.

Foundations

A community-embedded framework provides a different way of looking at rural practice—a new angle on where the practitioner, and practice, fit within a community. The framework is reflected in rural practitioners' stories from around the world (for example Collier 1984; Martinez-Brawley 1986; Hart 1995), draws on established knowledge about rural life (Cheers 1998, pp. 61–90) and is supported by the few empirical studies of rural practice (Whittington 1985; York, Denton and Moran 1989; Puckett & Frederico 1992).

Community-embedded practice puts social care, and practitioners, back into the real world. Ultimately, social care is an *expression*—or *function*—of 'human community'. 'Human community' is what we humans create, and continually re-create, through social interaction. This process is perhaps more vivid in rural than urban communities for, in a rural locality, the limited pool of people produces a particular community through daily interaction across all arenas—culture, social structure, economy, politics, religion and the natural environment (Wilkinson 1991, p. 16). Social care is expressed through both formal structures (such as human service organisations) and informal interaction. From this angle, then, practitioners must take their place, albeit humbly, within the rich mosaic of all social care arrangements. They are no longer aliens visiting from 'planet welfare'.

Community-embedded practice has crystallised from rural, rather than twentieth-century urban, practice because rural practitioners are a long way—geographically, administratively and culturally—from the rarefied atmosphere of large city welfare offices. They swim constantly in the sea of community processes, structures and interaction which provide the context, form and tools for their work. The social worker in the Barra district on the North-west Scottish Isles is a good example.

> [Her] responsibility ... (is) ... to coordinate and energise local community informal systems and resources. The idea is that the patch worker will become known to those she serves, will capitalize on their strengths and generally tailor services to needs in very personal ways. In the Barra 'patch', the social worker employed local home helpers from the community. She had developed a cadre of workers whom she had trained. Because she knew the elderly and the home helpers, she was able to place them close to their homes and with compatible personalities. What the elderly got was someone who looked after

them in a personal way, who stopped by their houses even when they were not scheduled to work, etc. The home helpers often coordinated with other neighbours. All this resulted in a close and very supportive network of care. The social worker knew the mothers of young children who were feeling overwhelmed. She knew who needed a break from children but might enjoy caring for an elderly person a few hours a week; she knew who could cope with young children and who couldn't, etc.

(Martinez-Brawley 1989, p. 12)

This way of working has a strong philosophical base. The propensity to care for each other is deeply embedded in human nature and society (Bookchin 1995, pp. 21–34). Social care expresses three fundamental concerns—or 'products'—of human community:

- establishing and preserving human rights for material, social and emotional well-being;
- distributing resources to ensure the preservation of human rights; and
- commitment to, and responsibility for, others.

Most of us, in other words, go out of our way to nurture human community and support the rights of others while pursuing our own interests. This dialectic of social commitment and self-interest reflects two fundamental needs of human nature:

- for social belongingness; and
- to assert one's individuality.

From these we get a moral dialectic—that it is good to be *both* self-determining *as well as* socially committed to, and responsible for, others. We have, in other words, the right to pursue self-interest *and* a duty towards others. Because of our very nature, we try endlessly to balance these, most of the time imperfectly.

The dialectic is perhaps more vivid in rural, than urban, communities. At the individual level, there is substantial evidence that most rural people are committed to both self-interest *and* community well-being (Martinez-Brawley 1990; Cheers 1998, p. 66). At the collective level, rural communities can provide social belongingness and, through this, a sense of personal security, which provide the crucial foundation for the development and expression of one's individuality (Cheers 1998, p. 66).

By supporting *both* individualism *and* social cohesion as two facets of the same process, social care brings the dialectic together in the pursuit of 'social integration'. In its dialectic sense, then, 'social integration' is what I think we are on about.

Principles

Community-embedded practice should not be seen as a diluted, eclectic version of specialised work—it is qualitatively different and has an integrity of its own. It is an attitude that the practitioner has towards living and working in a rural community, an attitude which values social care as the dual responsibility of ordinary people arising from the mutuality of everyday community living *and* of formal service organisations. Practitioners are part of the network of mutuality which binds communities together, their expertise taking its place alongside the social care wisdom of other residents. They enter into, and understand, local cultural and linguistic frameworks, which may well be at odds with those into which they have been socialised personally and professionally (Martinez-Brawley 1990, p. 84; Zapf 1993, pp. 701–2).

Community-embedded practitioners weave themselves into the fabric of everyday community life. They are out in the community, being visible, becoming known, learning of people in need, working their way into social and political networks and connecting people with each other. They are finding out about current and emerging social issues, participating in regional development, working with power brokers, organising committees and so on. This is all good preventive work because, where the practitioner is strengthening local bonds and facilitating the caring that people give to each other, the community is well placed to anticipate and respond to personal and community issues before they become major problems. Other residents are, for example, more likely to provide support and child-care relief for a low-income sole mother with preschool children before she becomes overwhelmed by her situation.

Community-embedded practitioners focus on, and contribute to, the well-being of the whole community. They respond to local needs and priorities—ensuring, for example, that home-care services receive higher priority than residential facilities in a community where most aged people want to remain in their own homes. Practitioners recognise, as do rural people generally, that individual well-being depends largely on the state of the community as a whole and its various interrelated sectors—economy, politics, culture, ecology, spirituality, social care, education and health care. This is why they relate with, and contribute to, other 'sectors' and encourage people in these to contribute to social care. For example, while a practitioner is conducting a social impact assessment for an economic development committee a local business executive might be providing leadership for a community youth centre.

Focusing on whole communities, practitioners frequently intervene through community-wide processes to resolve individual and family problems. For instance, I once knew a young woman who was miserable and failing at school because she felt ostracised by her peer group. This was related to her new step-father being regarded as deviant by the town's residents. I told her this—which gave her a different perspective. I also mentioned the problem to her teacher and the local nurse who was an informal adviser for some of the local young women. The teacher subsequently encouraged her participation in peer-group interaction at school, and the nurse encouraged her closest former friends to renew the friendships.

A whole-community focus also means that practitioners may be 'community animateurs' (Martinez-Brawley 1986, p. 365, 1990, p. 41). 'Community animation' has three components: energising, conscientisation and politicisation. 'Energising' involves encouraging people to contribute to social action and social development initiatives. This is especially important in communities with low morale resulting from recession, population depletion and service withdrawals, and in some rapidly expanding communities, such as retirement and tourism centres, where some groups are alienated. 'Conscientisation' involves creating and increasing community members' awareness of their shared marginalised, disadvantaged and disempowered situation. 'Politicisation' builds on this, involving the practitioner in generating resident political action. Although community animation is most clearly associated with social action and community development, it can also occur through practice with individuals and families. For example, through counselling, disempowered women in a patriarchal community can be freed from the shackles of their socialisation, become aware of their oppression and encouraged to unite to challenge local social and economic structures.

The community-embedded practitioner is located at the intersection of vertical and horizontal ties (Martinez-Brawley, 1990, p. 13; Cheers 1998, pp. 97–100). Vertical ties are those that connect the community and its residents to structures extending 'upwards' through the wider society. For example, community-based organisations are 'tied' to government funding departments and state-wide peak welfare bodies. Horizontal ties, on the other hand, connect local people and organisations with each other and link residents with their informal social and support networks, both within and outside the community. The practitioner relates the horizontal and vertical arenas to each other, harnessing their respective resources for community and individual well-being. This might involve, for example, co-ordinating local and non-local services, linking people with informal networks and interpreting local needs to funding bodies.

Community-embedded practice is indigenous to the cultural and linguistic frameworks of local sub-populations which provide meaning to social issues and suggest how they should be handled (Martinez-Brawley undated, p. 6). For example, incarceration in detention centres will not help young Aboriginal offenders whose cultures understand their behaviour to be the result of alienation from their own communities. It would be more useful to reconnect them with their cultures through re-absorption into their communities, linking them with indigenous role-models and facilitating their participation in cultural activities.

This is perhaps less obvious, though still important, in non-indigenous rural cultures. For instance, I once had a rather poetic conversation with a male pastoralist while hanging over the back of a Toyota. He said:

> Look mate, when I have problems I ask a gum tree what it thinks. If I don't get the answer I want I go to the next one. I just keep going down the line until I hear something that makes sense.

A few days later we continued the conversation after he had consulted his eucalypt counsellors. One of them had given him a clue which, after some discussion, became a solution to his predicament. Men in his culture do not often talk about their personal issues directly and avoid eye contact while doing so. 'Going bush' to try to sort them out alone is quite common; and they do some 'serious' talking with each other while hanging over the back of a Toyota, a fence or something similar.

Because of the dearth of local specialists, and because they are embedded in all aspects of community life, rural practitioners tend to be generalists (Collier 1984, pp. 58–65; Cheers 1992). This fits well with rural cultures where people are generalists in their everyday lives. The practitioner works across fields and methods—she or he will be a caseworker, counsellor, group worker, community worker, policy developer, social planner and researcher. The same practitioner, for instance, may counsel a suicidal young man, organise home care for an aged woman, chair a management committee and develop a social plan as a component of local area planning.

As they practise their 'craft', community-embedded practitioners focus on *whole* people and *whole* families. The perspective resists the movement away from:

> a craft … paradigm in which we were interested in global results [towards] a highly bureaucratic and industrial model in which we focus on partialized well-being … Remember the craftsperson? The cabinet-maker who cared about the quality and beauty of the total product rather than about the successful assembly of various bits into a perfectly symmetrical but boring structure? Remember the social worker who cared about the whole family in the community milieu, not just his or her client? [Now] the child welfare worker cares about the children; the … agency on aging worker looks after grandmother and the mental health office is concerned about mother's depression. Perhaps the unemployment office is working with dad, but no one is really looking at or serving the whole family in the context of its own networks in the local town. We are doing assembly line social work.
>
> (Martinez-Brawley 1989, p .6)

As generalists with a holistic focus, community-embedded practitioners need a diverse knowledge base. They have to know about all fields and methods of practice as well as related disciplines such as economics, politics, rural sociology, geography and local area planning. They need both 'formal' knowledge—found in books, journals and courses—and 'informal knowledge'—practice wisdom, personal and professional experience and the insights of other residents. The practitioner's knowledge and skills are socially produced, generated through her or his ongoing interaction with the community and its members. These are real only as they exist within the practitioner as 'potentialities' to be actualised in forms that she or he shapes in response to the immediate context. The community-embedded practitioner is an aware, feeling, thinking, reflecting, reacting and creating human being who makes decisions according to her or his ideological frameworks, knowledge, expertise, personality and understanding of the situation at hand within its community context. In this way, the practitioner's 'knowledge base' is continually created and re-created as she or he participates in the multicoloured, intermingling flows of community life. She or he is an 'artisan' whose craft expresses her or his own meanings in interaction with the rich mosaic that is community.

In keeping with rural cultures, community-embedded practice is 'sensible', 'practical' and 'improvisational'. Just as rural people tend to do what obviously needs doing so, too, professional practice must also 'make sense' in the situation. The community expects the practitioner to 'muck in' on the practical tasks—to help organise the fete, work on a street stall and sell raffle tickets at the pub. These are not necessary evils taking up valuable time that would be better spent exercising more sophisticated skills. Through activities such as these, practitioners are becoming involved in community life, gaining credibility with other residents and generating the support of key community leaders. They are gaining access to local networks, information about the community, and people who can contribute to service provision, agency management and social development.

Rural cultures also value improvisation—in a rural community, if you don't know how to do something, and there is no-one else around who does, then you simply have to do your best. Practitioners, too, are expected to devise novel solutions, regardless of the limitations of their training, organisations or professional literature. Just as the lack of local specialised expertise has bred many bush mechanics and lawyers so, too, has it produced many bush social planners, community developers, researchers and therapists.

The flexibility and genericism of community-embedded practice, the many chance meetings of practitioners with other residents and their participation in community life mean that practice frequently happens through informal interaction. Early in my career, while sharing the streets of inner-city Sydney with skid-row alcoholics, I learned that the content of interaction with 'clients' was more important than its location, whether it was planned, or how 'formal' it was in language and behaviour. Similarly, during more recent rural travels, opportunities to help people have arisen while fishing with a young Aborigine on Cape York Peninsula, panning for gold with a prospector, and helping a young man fix his car.

Inevitably, community-embedded practitioners are highly visible and accessible through, for example, telephone calls at home and chance meetings in supermarkets, on street corners and at football games (Cheers 1998, pp. 229–30). This provides many opportunities to help people, obtain useful information, establish community acceptance and connect with key community leaders. In one town, for instance, 'pub talk' gave me the clues and the confidence I needed to raise the issue of domestic violence with an abused woman. However, to avoid burn-out, practitioners also need to maintain some personal-professional boundaries.

Organisational and professional boundaries also tend to be fuzzy in community-embedded practice—'child protection' workers might also do community development and teachers, family counselling. In rural communities, this boundary blurring occurs for three reasons. First, role-definitions in small, community-based organisations are usually more flexible than in large, bureaucratic agencies, partly because of community expectations. Second, locally-based rural practitioners frequently provide continuing services for specialised, non-local organisations, regardless of professional or organisational role definitions. Third, lacking an array of local specialised services, practitioners use each other's special aptitudes and expertise, regardless of formal qualifications.

Community-embedded practice is located within, and needs some support from, community power structures (Cheers 1998, pp. 235–40). Consequently, practitioners need to know how power is structured and decisions made, the relative influence of various 'power actors' in relation to particular issues, what the local interest groups, factions and coalitions are, who belongs to them, and their respective spheres of influence. They also need to know which issues unite, and which divide, their communities.

The practitioner should understand the pace of social change that the community will accept. Change usually happens slowly and incrementally in traditional communities with stable populations, strong local kin networks and enduring structures and institutions. In these, the practitioner might initially address some narrower issues—such as developing sports facilities for young people—working gradually towards small cumulative changes, while postponing the broader, more controversial issues—such as resolving youth-police conflict—until later. In contrast, communities with unconsolidated social structures, such as those experiencing rapid social change (for example tourist centres and declining communities), may be open to more rapid and pervasive change.

How much support a practitioner can anticipate from local power structures is related to many factors, including the project's scope, how controversial it is, its potential contribution to the general public good, and how much power and resources can be marshalled. In general, projects touching a wide cross-section of the community, such as establishing a residents' action group, will attract either broad support or widespread resistance. For these, the practitioner needs the support of the most powerful local influentials and those who span a wide spectrum of interests. In contrast, narrower issues, such as establishing a women's shelter, require the support of power actors with more specialised interests and spheres of influence. Furthermore, controversial issues, such as resisting a proposed tourism development require a higher level of support than those that are ideologically 'safe', although such support is more difficult to muster. On the other hand, issues that are clearly in the general public good, such as establishing a community health centre, will normally attract widespread support.

Practitioners should establish strong working relationships with key 'power actors' and generate sympathy for social justice issues across a wide cross-section of residents. This can be done, for example, by keeping issues in the public consciousness through media activities and public meetings, and ensuring they are on various committee agendas. Other strategies include educating people about social justice issues, briefing local influentials on specific issues and what can be done about them, and involving residents in social care work. Local influentials can also be invited to join community-based management committees, help with media work, act as political lobbyists and provide consultation on management, budgeting and strategic planning.

Many roles are available to the practitioner when working with community power structures. In different situations, it might be more effective to oppose, confront, collaborate with, or attempt to persuade, power actors. Practitioners might also: co-opt influentials into projects; build coalitions with, and amongst, special interest groups; and form coalitions between neighbouring towns and regions. Where there is conflict with or amongst power actors, the practitioner might seek out common ground and issues that are open to negotiation, bargaining and compromise. For instance, a shire chair might agree to allocate council property to an emergency accommodation program, provided that the practitioner does not publicly support local opposition to a new mining development.

Finally, the ability of the practitioner to influence local events, or even their 'clients', will be significantly reduced if they have not *joined* with the community and its various power actors, opinion-leaders and sub-populations (Cheers 1998, pp. 240–3). Rural communities tend to establish boundaries between themselves and the outside world, dividing the social universe into 'us' and 'them'. Through *joining*, the practitioner crosses this boundary to become 'one of us', though not necessarily a full-fledged community member. Within the systems of meaning provided by local cultures, he or she becomes a familiar, non-threatening person rather than an unknown 'foreigner' to be treated with caution and suspicion.

The creative practitioner will find many ways to join with a community and its residents. A commitment to the community can be demonstrated by becoming involved in committees, participating in recreational activities and important social institutions such as the 'family night' at the pub, attending major community events such as rodeos, and shopping and relaxing locally. Identifying with social custom and adopting local behaviour patterns and lifestyle preferences that feel comfortable is another way. No doubt my preference for wearing a cowboy hat and sleeping in a swag has helped me join with many communities in Northern Australia. During the early period in a new community it is especially important to identify with locally cohesive issues, while staying away from divisive ones. For example, I once joined with a bitterly divided town by commenting on, and identifying with, residents' shared commitment to their children's education, demonstrated by their support for the local school. I attended some Parents and Citizens Association meetings. At the same time, I studiously avoided commenting on economic development issues, as these were central to the town's factional disputes.

Conclusion

Community-embedded practice has grown out of rural contexts. It provides practitioners with new ways of thinking about their place in a rural community. But it is far more than this. It is also an antidote for the late twentieth-century escape into rampant individualism, self-interest, materialism, managerialism and the modernist view of human life as the contextless, disengaged flight of a desperately lonely 'astronaut in a space capsule' (Midgley 1989). Philosophically, and morally, the framework is based on the dialectics of human existence—those of individuality *and* social belonging, of self-interest *and* social duty. Through its support of 'social integration', and as an expression of human community, social care also embraces this dialectic.

References

Bookchin, M. 1985, *The Philosophy of Social Ecology: Essays on Dialectical Naturalism*, Second Edition, Blackrose Books, Montreal.

Cheers, B. 1992, 'Rural Social Work and Social Welfare in the Australian Context', in *Australian Social Work*, vol. 45, no. 2, pp. 11–21.

Cheers, B. 1998, *Welfare Bushed: Social Care in Rural Australia*, Ashgate, Birmingham.

Collier, K. 1984, *Social Work with Rural Peoples: Theory and Practice*, New Star Books, Vancouver.

Hart, J. 1995, 'The Challenge of Remote Area Social Work: A Pacific Island Experience', in *Australian Social Work*. vol. 48, no. 2, pp. 39–45.

Lonne, R. E. in progress, 'Retention of Rural Social Workers', PhD Thesis, James Cook University, Townsville.

Martinez-Brawley, E. E. undated, *Social Services in Spain: The Case of Rural Catalonia*, Department of Sociology, The Pennsylvania State University, University Park.

Martinez-Brawley, E. E. 1986, 'Community-oriented Social Work in a Rural and Remote Hebridean Patch', in *International Social Work*, no. 29, pp. 349–72.

Martinez-Brawley, E. E. 1989, 'Community Oriented Social Work: Some International Perspectives', unpublished paper, Department of Sociology, Pennsylvania State University, State College PA.

Martinez-Brawley, E. E. 1990, *Perspectives on the Small Community: Humanistic Views for Practitioners*, NASW Press, Silver Spring, MD.

Midgley, M. 1989, *Wisdom, Information and Wonder: What is Knowledge For?*, Routledge, London.

Puckett, T.C. & Frederico, M. 1992, 'Examining Rural Social Welfare Practice: Differences and Similarities between Rural and Urban Settings', in *Australian Social Work*, vol. 45, no. 2, pp. 3–10.

Whittington, B. 1985, 'The Challenge of Family Work in a Rural Community', in *The Social Worker/Le Travailleur Social*, no. 53, pp. 104–7.

Wilkinson, K. P. 1991, *The Community in Rural America*, Greenwood, New York.

York, R., Denton, R. & Moran, J. 1989, 'Rural and Urban Social Work Practice: Is there a Difference?', in *Social Casework*, no. 70, pp. 201–9.

Zapf, M.K. 1993, 'Remote Practice and Culture Shock: Social Workers Moving to Isolated Northern Regions', in *Social Work*, no. 38, pp. 694–704.

Section 2
Creative practice

Introduction

Creativity is expressed in human relationships, in programs that create hope, in the use of media to communicate from different speaking positions, in facilitating lived experience as the medium for learning, in bringing together ideas or people who were previously categorised separately, in challenging oppression and changing systems. Our sample of creative practices is a drop in the ocean of innovation arising as a response to need that is newly recognised or reconceptualised, or where the means are made possible by technology or essential because of crisis. Chapters in Section 4 may equally have been placed here, but we chose to have them highlight the aspect of diversity.

The rural environment demands creative responses because there is a dearth of resources and usually a lack of choice if services do exist. Programs that are introduced centrally require local adaptation if they are to function effectively, and some issues are peculiarly rural or they present differently in rural communities. Centrally driven models rarely take sufficient account of distance, and the way that distance alters consideration of time, cost and outcomes in rural programs. To the extent that social life is organised differently in the country and values are more homogeneous, both contestable assertions to some but accepted by many as orthodoxy, practices reflect these differences in being more holistic, more network-focused, less readily aligned with radical perspectives, more consensual.

This section opens with an emerging and critical issue for the 1990s, youth suicide. Heidi Green and Michael Brown explore a project in New South Wales that beautifully captures the elements of rural practice in being generalist, focused on whole persons in their community context, rather than specialist and symptom or problem-focused. It is an optimistic story of creating meaning and connection, and restoring young people to a central place in community.

Fran Crawford deals with a complementary issue of young social work students in Perth, whose learning about rural communities and appropriate practice is a constructed rather than a lived experience. Locating the development of the educational process, within an historical and policy context, Fran produces a framework of nine 'meaning-making' Rs of working rurally and remotely that resonate with the content of other chapters.

Three chapters provide contrasting approaches to working with women in rural communities. Helen La Nauze and Shirley Rutherford analyse the development of programs to address domestic violence in a provincial city. Their discussion is located within the political contexts of federal policy advance and retreat, and of a conservative community where their feminist analysis and practice needs to be negotiated. They identify the tensions to be addressed in working with and through local networks to achieve change. Jan Brand and Ann Kesting also work from a woman-centred perspective in combining their discipline approaches to provide a more integrated service to women who need both clinical and social systems intervention. Their practice is subjectively informed by feminist values, rather than deliberatively negotiated with their community or those who use their service. Peter Munn's work with women takes its theoretical positioning more from ecological systems theory than gender analysis, reminding us that gender can be part of the active framing or the assumptive background.

David Barlow's case study of a community radio station demonstrates the powerful community development and individual growth potential of such a medium, owned, operated, managed and controlled at a local level, and communicating the soul of the community.

All chapters emerge from unique settings, but present ideas that could be adapted creatively wherever there are people who are attracted to them.

9

The story of Project X
A framework for preventing youth suicide

Heidi Green & Michael Brown

Introduction

Just as the key to a species' survival in the natural world is its ability to adapt to local
habitats, so the key to human survival will probably be the local community.

(David Suzuki 1997, p. 8)

People who would be known and respected as elders in other cultures and in
other times seem to increasingly bemoan the destruction of family and the loss of
community in Australian (and other 'Western') societies. It may indeed be true
that human civilisation is at a low ebb in the value placed on community. The
sense of loss is absent for young people; this is just the way things are. The sense
of alienation is still hard to deal with and defiance, rebellion and rejection are for
many the easiest way of dealing with day-to-day realities. To many (too many),
opting out is another solution. Too many of our young people opt out; too many
opt out irreversibly through suicide. While generally a suicide takes one life, it is
obvious that large numbers of people are affected through linkages that are the
warp and weft of community structure.

Introducing Kyogle

Kyogle is a town in the Northern Rivers area of New South Wales. The community, including the mayor, a local business and the high school, have all boasted that Kyogle is the best address in the world. The population consists of a harmonious mixture of lifestyles, with deep but rarely engaged differences in values. Youth-related crime and incidents related to depression and self-harm are low, but appear to be increasing, parallel to Australia-wide trends.

In 1996, the local government council considered an address by the local high school principal, urging them to take an active role in youth issues. The address was met with silence. There was no debate, there was no resolution, there was no action. This followed an intensive debate on whether council should authorise the expenditure of $45 on signage at the local showground (expenditure denied). This example is typical of the alienation of youth issues from the institutional structures in many towns and communities. Kyogle has a rural economic base that has declined. Many long-term locals bemoan that the sense of progress, pride and purpose, which even thirty years ago inspired and integrated the community, has evaporated. This type of loss can cause both structural anomie and structural egoism (Durkheim 1951), that is, an inbuilt absence of shared purpose, direction and values, and a related absence of vigorous cross-generational attention, connection and interplay. The collapse of these basic community-building processes has meant that the community knows itself less, cares for itself less and less effectively, and is becoming indifferent, fearful and adversarial towards its own youth.

A close analysis of the dynamics of the institutions of Kyogle revealed that the institutions of culture, the organisations that make up the town, were growing more separated and specialised, and more aged and age-exclusive. Service clubs, church groups and other clubs were active but largely independent of each other. This 'balkanisation' created a hollow centre in the town into which more and more young people fell. They belonged to nothing, and without the intergenerational communication and interplay that was once a feature of country towns, feelings of impotence, mutual resentment and distrust had developed. There was a collapse in the opportunities for each generation, but particularly young people, to create social capital and build a cohesive network of friendship and support. There was some expressed cynicism and despair in both generations, and a sense of being stuck. Without cross-generational interplay it is hard for young people to develop both an acknowledged, mature social identity and a sense of worth based on a history of contribution and displays of prowess acknowledged by friendly adults.

Over time, the activities of many of these institutions had also been declining in appeal, particularly to young people. Paradoxically, the activities seemed to be more embedded and depended on by their declining number of adherents, comforted in the increasing strangeness. Churches, sporting organisations, service clubs and general interest clubs were included in this general condition. The memberships had developed a cosy enclave style, small groups with established friendships sharing their common beliefs and routines, the demands of administration and the compensating status benefits of belonging and bearing office.

Apart from traditional sports, there was no youth infrastructure beyond the school facilities or the pubs. The town has always been a net exporter of its youth, but now, with very high youth unemployment everywhere and the complete decline of the unskilled jobs sector, youth are staying home longer or going and coming back, finding poverty and boredom in their own community a bit friendlier than in strange towns. There is a filtering effect where the high achieving, high socio-economic status youth can go and, by tertiary studies, make a go of it, and the residual youth, needing more stepping stones to make the vital crossing into meaningful integrated adult community and economic life, are not getting this facilitation. A post-school youth subculture has developed, feared and abandoned by the ageing adult institutions of culture and local government.

It is not fashionable to seek counselling, develop relationship skills or to talk seriously with kith or kin within this fairly typical rural community. Not only will families avoid seeking professional service delivery help, the 1996 Queensland *Young People at Risk* research shows that youth will not talk about precipitating events to available welfare and school professionals either (Raphael 1996).

Kyogle has traditionally had a low provision of youth-related community services. The most obvious (and common) solution to leap to in this context is to seek and demand an increase in service provision. Project X, however, is not about service provision. It is about increasing the capacity of the community to look after its members. By channelling their energies, the young people of Kyogle have created a vibrant youth organisation for the town. Such is the change in attitude that Kyogle council now asks young people's opinion and most committees include a youth representative. The relationship between the young people and the police has also greatly improved over the life of the project. Linkages in the community are increasing as a direct result of youth action and it is hoped (and believed) that this will improve the mental health of members of the community.

Framing the need

The project was initiated and developed by a young woman, who had intimately experienced a variety of aspects of life 'on the street' and had returned to school as a mature age student, and the high school principal. These two people (the authors of this chapter) regarded the school as a key community agency for youth, and discussed with young people ways of increasing their joy of life, and ways of increasing the resilience of young people in regard to depressive and suicidal episodes in themselves and others. Commonwealth funding under the Youth Suicide Prevention Initiative helped facilitate the project. The project is about 'diligent, unspectacular work in the population which mitigates those factors which lead, among other things to suicide' (Rosenman 1998, p. 102). The authors believe that this was (and must again become) a feature of community processes that have partially collapsed. Perhaps as a consequence of this apparent collapse of community processes, Australia has one of the highest youth suicide rates in the industrialised world, and males living in rural areas have a consistently higher rate of suicide than their urban counterparts (Mental Health Branch 1997, p. 13). The rate of suicide among young males increased by 50% between 1986 and 1992 (Mental Health Branch 1997, p. 13).

Young women are also showing signs of crisis, with females *attempting* suicide four times as often as males. 'Approximately 10% of our country's young people attempt suicide at least once' (Edwards and Pfaff 1996, p. 1).

The necessity to re-establish linkages between youth and the rest of the community became a common theme in discussions held to address the concerns. In conversations with existing community groups, their reason for being was reinforced and they were encouraged to value, develop and establish links with other organisations, groups and individuals that supplemented and complemented their own aims. The role of youth, as a participant in, and recipient of, their activities, was stressed.

Put simply, how does a community grow and nurture wise, loving, joyful youth? The culture must itself become wiser and clearer about the importance of consciously cultivating itself and its new generation. The acceptance of the legitimacy of a young woman in seeking to change community perceptions and practice in the name of improved mental health was at times a slow and tough battle. The results are promising.

> *The need for community and its rituals is an ancient need. It has been built into the human psyche over hundreds and thousands of years. If it is frustrated, we feel 'alienated' and fall prey to psychiatric and psychosomatic ills.*
>
> (Stevens 1996)

The project aimed to build a more supportive, skilled town using a community development approach involving young people. This strengthening of the community's care, involvement and attentiveness towards young people was intended to reduce youth suicide, including suicidal ideation, attempts, and re-attempts; provide a better response to these attempts; and empower youth to create their own events and desired outcomes.

Primary prevention, as conceived and developed in this project, is about raising the social health of a community by clarifying and altering the culture of the community. Rather than seeking to intercept the level of 'deathwish' arising in the community, the approach has been to encourage and elaborate the level of 'lifewish'. The link to appropriate theory is primarily through the work of Durkheim (1951). Durkheim showed that suicide was a social fact. Distinct communities have distinctly stable suicide rates. These rates increase when social change disrupts the stability of social relations, by which kith and kin systems are formed and maintained, and the clarity, acceptance and transmission of social roles, norms and values. Durkheim also showed how suicides could be divided into two main categories—egoistic and anomic. Egoistic suicides are related to loss of connection, status and relationships, and anomic suicides are related to loss of values, meaning and purpose.

Project X

The project was advised by a reference group, comprising twenty-nine volunteers nominated and co-opted from key organisations such as police, Department of Community Services, Mental Health, Department of Education and Training, Youth and Family Services, local council, North Coast Children's Home, Community Health and Juvenile Justice. Parents who had lost children through suicide, an Aboriginal elder and a researcher in the field of youth suicide were also members of the reference group. Management of the project is now conducted by a small core group of young people, each of whom had a 'shadow' adult drawn from the reference group. Over the 12 months of the project, there was a total of 74 people who had direct involvement with the project; 41 of these were young people. It was considered important to have a high level of participation, input and involvement in the decision-making processes from those we were trying directly to help. During the course of the project, many volunteers were co-opted. A work experience student from the local TAFE assisted with the project, and the project relied on extensive support from the community to run activities and programs.

The project consisted of (and continues to function with) four strands. The first strand is typical of youth programs and concentrates on 'something to do'. *'Life Sux (But So Does The Pub)'* involves young people in planning, constructing and attending drug and alcohol-free activities for young people. Concerts, camping, music, skating, adventure training and similar activities are organised by young people. Participation in, and celebration of, the joy of life and interaction with others is promoted. The desire to achieve something for the common good can be seen in the building of the town's skateboard ramp last year. A project worth $7–8000 cost only $60, following donations in time and materials by local people.

The second strand deals with the break down in communication between the generations. *'Wise Old People'* encourages young people to spend time with their elders and for both groups to learn from each other whilst participating in activities together.

'Family Home Support' (the third strand) covers all aspects of a young

person's living arrangements. 'Over 80% of young homeless males have experienced mental disorder at some stage of their lives' (Herrman et al. 1990, p. 199) and mental disorder is closely associated with many (if not all) suicidal episodes. This strand includes co-mediation, crisis housing, medium-term housing and tenancy advice. Co-mediation (following the Regional Extended Family Services model developed in Victoria) is a support service for the young person who is still at home (or has recently left home) to help reconcile differences between them and their family. Crisis accommodation is available with trained families for situations where short-term accommodation is available where a family crisis occurs. Supported medium-term accommodation is available for young people who need to move out of home but are not quite ready to live totally independently. Tenancy support is available to help young people and real estate agents understand about youth issues and the rights and responsibilities of a tenant.

The fourth strand, *'Harm Minimisation'*, seeks to further develop the prevention of life threatening behaviours. Parenting and self-esteem were identified by young people as being important issues to them, and it was decided to include them in the project. Young people have written material to assist parents in the discussion of issues affecting young people. Support for their peers is provided through a self-esteem program written and delivered by young people with 'wise-old' facilitators.

Young people need to feel empowered in life and through this project many young people have been heard saying: 'I finally feel as though I can make a difference'; 'They actually listened to what I had to say—it was amazing'; 'Through something that I have said they changed the way they were going to do something'. Suddenly young people were wanting to sit on 'boring' management committees because they realised that they could make a difference and that people would listen to them. Young people in Kyogle set about creating a Youth Centre—a place of their own. Youth Centres are structured avenues for young people to be able to share confidences and access other support. Young people rarely approach professionals for help when they feel unhappy. They are most likely to seek help from friends, partners and family members (Raphael, 1996 vol. 2, pp. 108–9). The success in obtaining a community youth centre building from Kyogle council was another success, where the previously anti-youth institutions of town showed their faith in the ability of youth to make a difference. The building was then extended and repainted by young people with their 'wise old' mentors. It will house a resource and referral centre for youth, staffed by workers and volunteers, and will run a variety of developmental and recreational activities integrated in a youth centre program. Young people show older people how to use the Internet and regularly meet with other members of the community to continue the development of the four strands started by Project X.

The project's funding through the Suicide Prevention Initiative ended in April 1998. However, the project successfully secured funding to continue operation and implementation of the four strands through the employment of a Youth Development Officer under the Area Assistance Scheme, and a paid Executive Officer funded through the 1997 New South Wales Health Country Communities Competition, which the project won. The community and other agencies became supportive in meeting the housing needs of young people. North Coast Community Housing Company head-leased a five-bedroom house to be used as the medium-term accommodation house. The Department of Community Services provided funding for the establishment of a crisis service. Areas that had been the most problematic in the project became areas of success.

The Kyogle community is becoming entrepreneurial about recreating itself. There is a definite increase in the perception and identification of opportunities by community members and community groups. This renewal has been led and facilitated by youth. The difficulty in obtaining quantitative evidence to prove that community development interventions are effective is well documented (Raphael, 1996 vol. 2, p. 11). There is no statistically valid way to demonstrate proof of the project's effectiveness. It is a fact that no young person in the local government area committed suicide during the 18 months from the start of the project. Suicidal parents who came to the attention of people associated with the project were also given rapid and effective support, which combined professional service delivery and kith and kin intervention strategy responses. All the young people at risk who came to the attention of the workers and management committee were provided with rapid responses, referral, and ongoing support.

Consultation was the key to success. Spin-offs from large community meetings, surveys of youth and meetings with existing community groups generated new mini-projects and activities that were 'owned' by sectors of the community and delivered by youth (with help from their wise old people). The down-side of consultation is that many of the participants in meetings seemed to regard the consultation as the end of the process. Other 'barrow-pushers' used the consultation process as an opportunity to criticise. However, activities generated by youth following consultation seemed to evoke a pleasant expression of surprise to accompany the normal expressions of satisfaction articulated by those witnessing a change which they had been part of suggesting.

Young people and adults have worked together to make the town that they share and live in a better place for the community as a whole, using a youth approach. Watching the change in the elders, who had previously acted as though all young people were nuisances and only caused trouble to them, were now working with and greeting young people in the street and seeing them as positive and caring members of their community. They worked together, solved problems together and made friendships with each other that, for some, have continued to be an important part of their lives.

The four strands of what was Project X are organised by the youth organisation (with over 50 members) and adult support to assist youth and the community to co-create new or modified structures of community activity with these clear aims:

1   To produce and distribute more joy, uplift and inspiration (the opposite of depression) and to teach the skills of creating desired inner states and managing, digesting and learning from undesired inner states. Undesired inner states of depression and sadness can be converted into joy and excitement. This conversion occurs through activities that can include friendships, relationships, making music, play, sport, adventure and service. These activities require skill, and are in sharp contrast to the unskilled activities of drug-taking, fighting, risk-taking, alcohol consumption and passive viewing of television and video that can result in blocked and depressive inner states.

2   To facilitate more connections between people, between institutions and between generations. This deliberate building of the fabric of kith and kin relations is achieved by organised activity—interplay—and it provides pathways along which the emotional states, relationships and wisdom needs are transmitted, and back along which the community can transmit empathy, connection, love and wisdom.

The elders of the community can become clear that their core work is around noticing and nurturing the interplay that binds their community together. Youth can become clear that they are valuable and valued in their community.

Protect the vigour and diversity of local communities. The social unit that will have the greatest stability and resilience into the future is the local community, which provides individuals and families with a sense of place and belonging, fellowship and support, purpose and meaning. The local community provides a common history and culture, shared values and a shared future.

(Suzuki 1997, pp. 213–14)

References

Durkheim, E. 1951, *Suicide: A study in sociology*, The Press, Illinois.

Edwards, S. J. & Pfaff, J. J. 1996, *The 4R's—Managing Youth Suicidal Behaviour: A guide for general practitioners and community health personnel*, Commonwealth Department of Health and Family Services, Canberra.

Herrman, et al. 1990, p. 199 cited in Hearn, R., 1993, *Locked Up, Locked Out: The denial and criminalisation of young people's mental health crisis.*, VICSERV, Victoria, pp. 27–31.

Mental Health Branch 1997, *Youth suicide in Australia: A background monograph*, 2nd edition, Commonwealth Department of Health and Family Services, Canberra.

Raphael, B. 1996, *Young People at Risk Research and Evaluation Program*, University of Queensland. Herston.

Rosenman, S. J. 1998, 'Preventing suicide: what will work and what will not', in *Medical Journal of Australia*, 169, pp. 100–2.

Stevens, A. 1996, 'A Basic Need', in *Resurgence Magazine*, Jan/Feb.

Suzuki, D. T. 1997, *The Sacred Balance: Rediscovering our place in nature*, Allen & Unwin, St Leonards.

University of Queensland, Department of Psychiatry, 1996, *Young People At Risk Research and Evaluation*, Volume 2, Evaluation Report.

10

Rural social work education
Connecting professional, personal and place

Fran Crawford

Introduction

How are practitioners best prepared for rural social work? Establishing social work programs in rural settings (Condliffe 1991; Young 1997) and providing on-going professional education support to rural practitioners are two approaches that have proved successful across Australia. This chapter examines the design and implementation of a Rural Social Work elective subject within a city-based four-year Bachelor of Social Work program.

The core of the elective is a three- to four-day field trip to a country town followed by the collaborative writing of a community profile. Students prepare for the trip by reading relevant rural social work literature and information on the town itself. During the visit they immerse themselves intensively in the human service interactions of the town, interviewing key players and accompanying them in their work. Returning to the city, they reflect on what they have learned and what they will write up together for return to the townspeople concerned. A personal outcome for participants is a clearer sense of whether rural practice is for them.

The process contributes to students uncovering some of the local knowledge required for working in rural contexts. Such local knowledge is clearly not separate from the extra-local. The lives of residents are deeply implicated in wider cultural workings, and concepts of marginality and difference as central to identity and practice become apparent. With this understanding students begin to reflect on the usefulness of a critical, post-structural and feminist framing of the social world (Denzin 1997). Grounding these ideas in an actual place, students look at the what and how of social work in action. The 'gemeinschaft' holism of a rural community, and the possibilities this offers a community aware practitioner, is seen to incorporate the simultaneously inclusionary and exclusionary workings of power dynamics.

In an era of downsizing services, declining agricultural fortunes and increasingly fly in-fly out mining operations, being rural and/or remote has worked its way into shaping the identity of interacting individuals in all Western Australian country settlements. Community members have been keen to meet with our group, to celebrate achievements and to discuss issues seen as peripheral to centralised human service decision-makers' concerns. Students ponder why being marginalised does not lead to a sense of connection with differently marginalised 'others', and why being marginalised does not always disempower, but can be a source of solidarity in taking action for improvement. As participants debrief with fellow students and local human service practitioners, they begin to reflect on their own subjectivity in making particular connections across the wide range of 'private troubles/public issues' (Wright-Mills 1957) always unveiled on any field trip.

This discussion aims to unpack this shifting awareness of self and others in regard to working rurally. It names a set of processes central to effective place-aware professional practice, concluding by suggesting that these may serve as pointers, enabling practitioners more generally to orient for action in a postmodern era of uncertainty and difference.

How the Rural Social Work elective came into being

In the late 1980s, a senior officer of the State Welfare Department took action on the chronic failure of his organisation to recruit qualified social workers to staff country offices. Like me, he had long experience of the satisfactions of rural social work. He believed students would choose to work in the country if they could be exposed to what was involved. At the time, social work education was not readily available to rural residents, and not many urban students had experience of country life. In discussions with members of the School of Social Work at Curtin University of Technology, resources were offered to enable students to spend time in a country town, to be introduced to the network of human service practitioners that existed.

Academics at Curtin, including myself, were receptive to this initiative, conscious of the need to develop Australian-based understandings of the dynamics of rural social work. At this time other agencies besides the State Welfare Department were beginning to locate their services outside Perth, and were seeking assistance in providing their staff with the necessary knowledge and skills. In the profession, at a national level, there was a naming of support for rural social work as a priority area for development.

A cameo of the history, geography and economics of the state of Western Australia will further contextualise the above scenario. I write from a state where, prior to 1965, there was no social work education available locally and where my own first appointment as a rural social worker in 1976 was greeted in 'the' newspaper with the headline 'First Social Worker for Broome'. There are historic reasons for this relatively late development of social work and then of rural social work.

Western Australia, by far the largest state, has approximately 10% of the total population of Australia. Eight out ten Western Australians live in the capital Perth and its immediate surrounds. This carries forward a long standing theme in our history of being a settlement with but a precarious hold on the territory it occupies. Perth is indisputably the centre, and life in the peripheral settlements has been largely oriented and directed from there. This mirrors the pattern of relationship that Perth, the most isolated capital in the world, has to the rest of Australia and indeed the pattern of Australia's historical relationship to London and Europe. It is the pattern of modernism inscribed deeply at all these levels by our modernist history. The 'facts' listed above have been taken for granted as the objective, centralised and normative way of the world. At the same time, resistance from the margins is evident at all these levels of interaction. As Australia moves closer to Republic status, rural West Australians express their desire for more local control of their affairs, and for human services practitioners who will respect local knowledge, differences and culture.

With dreams of building a community for gentry, the first British settlers came in 1829 (Stannage 1981). Imaginings that the resident Aboriginal population, conservatively estimated then at 60 000 across the state (Docherty 1992), would prove biddable servants were short-lived. After what settlers called the Battle of Pinjarra in 1834, and Aboriginal people describe as a massacre, the development of these two populations proceeded along relatively separate paths. They shared the centrality of government in shaping and structuring their futures.

By the middle of the nineteenth century when the non-Aboriginal population had slowly climbed to 6000, the leaders of the tiny colony begged the British government to send convicts to solve their labour crisis. By 1868, when transportation ceased, 10 000 male convicts had arrived with public monies from Britain for the necessary infrastructure. By 1890, the non-Aboriginal population had reached 46 000 and agriculture in the region had established its potential.

Then in 1892 came the first big mining boom for the state. Gold was discovered in the Kalgoorlie region. By the beginning of the twentieth century,

180 000 non-Aboriginals (or 10% of the present population) lived alongside a much reduced Aboriginal population. A major imbalance between the sexes in the non-Aboriginal population, brought about by both the convict system and the gold rush, persisted until well into the twentieth century and continues to mark gendered and racial patterns of interaction in the state, particularly in country areas.

Agricultural lands were further opened with governmental support to feed the mining population and then after the First World War, through the Returned Soldier's Settlement Scheme, to supply overseas markets. Right through this century up until the 1970s, apart from the Depression and cyclical downturns in market opportunities, the growth and development of rural Western Australia was steadily upwards. Understandably this created great faith among those so advantaged in the modernist myth of progress. That faith has been severely tested by the recent experiences of rural residents.

Though mining and agriculture have always provided the bulk of the state's income, relatively few people live in the country who are directly involved in production. This proportion has reduced over time, making it less viable to distribute goods and services equitably across the state in an era of 'user pays'. In agricultural lands there has been a depletion of population with losses to salt, the economic imperative of 'get big or get out' among producers and the downsizing or even cancellation (as with rail) of government services with the knock-on effect this has on businesses in small towns. To drive through many Western Australian wheat belt towns is to see a line of boarded-up shops.

In the mining areas, recent developments have similarly caused a depletion in numbers. In the 1960s and 1970s in the Pilbara, a huge amount of government funded infrastructure was provided to mining companies to build towns to house their workers and families. The value of 'populating the bush' to bring about development and progress was then unquestioned. Now, overwhelmingly, mining companies choose 'fly in-fly out' operations. Decision-makers see the disadvantages of being away from support services (including work for partners) in Perth as outweighing the advantages of full-time family life if it has to be in the bush. Mining is a short-term extractive industry, and it does not make sense to put down expensive housing so far from the centre. It is apparent that, given a choice, most Western Australians prefer to base themselves in Perth.

These recent developments in agricultural and mining areas mean that rural people are now more aware and demanding than ever of their 'fair share' of human services and more resentful of what they see as the prosperity of the centre built on the endeavours of rural residents.

Through the first seventy years of this century, 'welfare' was not a word that either miners or farmers readily applied in regard to themselves. Among miners with strong unionisation the talk was of rights and conditions. Farmers and pastoralists in turn saw themselves as central to the welfare of the country as a whole and the governmental subsidies they received as an integral and necessary part of this enterprise. 'Welfare' was, in contrast, a word strongly associated by many rural residents with Aboriginal people. The 'Welfare' was believed to refer to the Native Welfare Department. This remained the case even two decades after that department was subsumed, along with the Child Welfare Department, into a general state welfare department. Though the *Community Welfare Act* of 1972 clearly established that it was the responsibility of the state to support the welfare needs of all residents, for many the idea of going to 'welfare' remained laden with cultural baggage.

Officially in 1972 all Native Welfare offices in country towns became Community Welfare offices, along with the fewer Child Welfare offices. The uniformity of signs announcing this masked the complexity of issues now to be addressed by human services practitioners. Native Welfare disappeared at a time when Aboriginal people throughout the state were becoming more conscious and articulate as to the interconnections with and differences from each other and the wider community in the matters of voting, land, mining and family rights. Resisting the continuing 'welfarisation' of their lives 'for their own good' (Haebich 1988) was a commonly expressed aim of Aboriginal people. Escape did not come lightly, as the bureaucratic machinery of the centralised state system remained deeply inscribed in the everyday lives of Aboriginal people. Ongoing wardship responsibilities and juvenile justice cases were key formal roles, but in many communities access to alternative sources of human service support was only just beginning. These were often developed by Aboriginal people, sometimes with the support of human services practitioners.

Aboriginal people's ties to the land largely were not generated by mining or farming, so an infrastructure of modern social supports had not been established alongside economic development as it had for other rural residents. Yet many Aboriginal people's traditional social supports had been disrupted and destroyed by these same economic activities. How could staff at the local level, both non-Aboriginal and Aboriginal, male and female, rural and non-rural be supported in shifting some of the ingrained dynamics that perpetuated old patterns of disempowerment? Part of addressing this issue was the immediate genesis of the Rural Social Work subject.

Additionally, in this environment of change and contesting demands on its monolithic bureaucratic structure, the state welfare department decentralised and funded others to deliver services rurally. In the hard hit agricultural areas mobile counselling services were initiated. This to some degree overcame resistance to seeking assistance by its being relatively anonymous and going to meet clients on their own territory. The fact that counselling was often given in the name of financial counselling proved another fruitful way of 'starting where the client is'. As well, church-based welfare agencies were encouraged and funded to set up new rural services (the era of old-style missionising having gone). Local government and community initiatives were encouraged in concert with federal policy and resources. Sensitive to complaints from non-Aboriginal rural electors, local offices were directed by central management to make it clear that their services were available to all. Then, too, other government departments took seriously issues of access and equity as regards their country constituents, while the Departments of Agriculture and Economic Development were recognising the importance of acknowledging the social while addressing the economic.

The text above is but a proportion of the rich context I set out to describe. Our educational assignment was preparing students to effectively negotiate this complex field, and it became my task to craft a curriculum within which student learning could happen effectively.

My connection with rural social work

My first position as a social worker in 1976 was with the state welfare department in Broome in the North West. This followed a final placement in nearby Derby, where my supervisor was dedicated to actioning rural social work as a form of community work. He flexibly incorporated different ways of working according to context and the cultures of those with whom he worked (Crawford 1997). A Perthite with strong ties to the country through visiting relatives, like most Western Australians I had no desire to go bush long term. When offered a country position prior to placement, I was angry at being taken as only good enough for the country.

After my Derby experiences I asked for the Broome position. Over my next seven years, I became a rural social worker with lots of annealing along the way (Crawford 1992). My frequent and private refrain was 'This should have been covered in the course'. Seeing the outcomes wrought by well-intentioned but ill-prepared practitioners, including myself, was a strong motivation in putting some of the collaborative knowledge gained in interaction with clients, colleagues and citizens into a text focusing on working with Aboriginal people (Crawford, 1989). This closely followed leaving Broome in the early 1980s.

Now I found myself invited to cover 'everything' needed in a rural social work course! Closure was not likely given my own positioning in the field and the constant changes. From reflected experience my orientation to the task was on preparing students to learn in the field in an ongoing way. For this they needed to value a university course as a preparation for life-long learning. The intended aim of the course was to learn how to think and research critically within the value dimensions of social work and in a grounded place. In my experience there was certainly no one right way of doing rural social work but instead many examples of better and worse practice.

The content of the course

As I set out on my preparations the social work literature that resonated most strongly for me was the writing of Emilia Martinez-Brawley, an American who wrote with a strong focus on culture and context. She visited Australia in the late 1980s and spoke of the importance of reflective practitioners striving to achieve best practice in context (Martinez-Brawley 1987, Lynn 1990). Her writings map the long tradition of locality-focused social work in America, stretching back to Jane Addams. They then suffer a severe dampening of influence after the *Social Security Act* of 1933 brought widespread adherence in curriculums to the centralised certainties of technical rational planning to meet social needs. She cohesively argued that while the dominant voice of positivism had textual authority in social work education, in the world of rural action other knowledges such as relational, spiritual and local were effectively deployed in achieving the aims of social work.

The curriculum developed from a grounding in Martinez-Brawley's (1982) four tenets of rural social work. Understood as philosophical anchorage points rather than technical rules, the first of these tenets was that the rural practitioner needed to be a generalist. The practitioner is required to hold the whole community context in mind in addressing any part of it. Openness rather than certainty in understanding client's issues was the mark of a generalist, implying a working with people in coming to solutions. The second tenet was that rural social work would be both conscientising and politicising for the practitioner, with a constant need to check out developing awareness with the client constituency. Practising a necessary community awareness was the third tenet while the last stressed a highly indigenous connection with and respect for local culture and local determination of policy planning and implementation.

By building on these ideas, lectures, reading and videos provided content on the histories and cultures of farmers and pastoralists, miners and Aboriginal people. Particular attention was paid to the way in which different cultures shaped possibilities of gender, class, race, disability and age. Students were geared to observe and question what happens in the spaces of connection between these cultures, and to explore auto-ethnographic writings that depict the insider's view of rural cultural settings (Chi 1991, Facey 1981, Ward 1987, Zubrycki 1991).

A third area of content was literature on working in community (Kelly & Sewell 1988). This included the growing Australian literature on rural/remote practice, especially those that address practitioner reflexivity (Crago, Sturmey & Monson 1996, Hart 1995).

The final area of focus was local documents and videos, as well as the latest Australian census figures for the particular area. Community histories and promotional videos are useful artefacts to provide the means for students to start thinking about who has voice, and who is absent. They can compare and contrast these representations with their other interpretive research.

The conduct of the course

Working with these tenets requires a constant reflection on and working between professional, personal and place of practice concerns. Students were asked at the beginning of the course to choose an area of professional interest such as health, domestic violence, working with Aboriginal people, farming families in crisis or working with the aged. They were also assigned an area to research for the community profile such as geography, history, economics or demography. Through all this they were asked to work collaboratively with the group and at the same time reflect, preferably through a journal, on their own positioning in the process.

Because of the days in the field, there is a minimum of organising seminars. The field trip is scheduled for the mid-semester break. In the five times the unit has run, accommodation has ranged from billeting, Curtin facilities (at Muresk), a government hostel and a church conference facility. There have been local practitioners willing to facilitate our maximum utilisation of time on the ground. Armed with address and contact numbers students are able to set up interviews from Perth. Time is also scheduled for us to meet as a group, with key local human services practitioners. Always we have been provided with space and time by local practitioners. Students are usually surprised at how much they learn in a relatively short time and at how they can weave the different strands of information they gather into a relatively clear snapshot of a town.

Returning to Perth shifts the project into another phase. How would the students write up what they have learned so that it could be usefully returned in a public form to its diverse source? As they say, it is one thing to write an essay for the lecturer to mark. It is a complex and political leap to write publicly in ways that will do justice to the input of so many concerned constituents. Many students report feeling frozen at the idea of entering the public domain with their writing. Will they be good enough? Do they give away the chance to convey what may have been their strongest learning because they know it will upset people who had been hospitable? Are there ways of conveying information so that it is heard rather than resisted? Whose story moved them to action? What does this say about them as individuals? Can they keep the dialogue going so that townspeople don't feel used by a group of university students there for a jaunt? How? How are they going to hold this together as a team? All these questions and more have to be processed in the completion of the community profile.

Reflecting on the work involved for all of us in the conduct of this course, and in an extension of the original four tenets, nine processes are identified as being involved in achieving effective outcomes in rural social work.

Meaning-making Rs of working rurally and remotely

These nine meaning-making Rs have been adapted from the work of Shulamit Reinharz (1983).

Realities

While we all live on the same planet there are multiple human 'realities' lived out, most of which overlap and interplay but not always as the players would want. People's troubles are not often usefully understood by their degree of deviance from a centrally established norm. Context and culture make for differences and part of the practitioner's task is to work in these differences while also making connections to bring about differing realities desired by their constituents.

Regionalising

The multiple realities we work with in any rural setting are not likely to be a random sample of all the human possibilities available universally. Rather, they are likely to be deeply inscribed with the particularities and cultural baggage of the site in which they occur. To work with child abuse in a downsizing mining settlement, it is important to understand how everyday lives are lived out in tension with the intervention possibilities available in the area. 'Knowing your patch' is part and parcel of 'starting where the client is'. (See Scott (1993) for an example of these skills in operation at a national level.)

Researching

Part of knowing your patch is researching it. Hard data such as population numbers and incomes are only part of this research. Building a community profile is the ongoing research task of the rural practitioner at many simultaneous levels, and one not likely to come to closure in a text. Every trip to the supermarket is likely to produce more information to be stored. Emerging from this will be a growing awareness that as you have been researching 'others', they have been researching you.

Rapporting

The processes of communicating. The processes of active listening. In a rural community, this needs to be achieved among a wide range of people and it can be counter-productive to have set ideas on the nature of policemen, Aboriginal people and farmers.

Relationship building

The nature of the relationship between the practitioner and those worked with is a key shaper of the outcomes achieved in any rural social work. It is not humanly possible to work equally and neutrally with all constituents but it is critical to be aware of the nature of your relationships in the town and reflect on their patterning.

Reflecting

Reflection on both practice processes and the meanings to be made of them are essential. Part of this is reflecting on the plays of power and on the question of 'whose interests are being served by the conduct and outcomes of my practice?'

Reflexivity

This refers to yourself in action, and your reaction to circumstances. It involves reflective awareness of the effect that you, personally, have on shaping the process and outcome of interaction and the effect of that process on the multiple aspects of yourself. Through doing, what have you learned about your many selves, your strengths, weaknesses, taken-for-granted values and assumptions and positioning in the world as a gendered/racialised being? How does knowing connect back to action?

Resonance

Practitioners identify differentially with the practice possibilities of social work and are likely to feel concern for some issues more than for others. To work fruitfully with this practitioners need to be aware of their own values and positionings and at the same time be able to connect to these in clients. Practice is for the benefit of the targeted group of people involved and not for the abstract notion of 'science's sake'. Far better then if the practitioner resonates with the concerns of the 'critical reference group', than takes pride in a positioning of neutrality and objectivity.

Rigour

The planning, action, presentation and reflection of the practice process must be thorough and coherent. Although aspects of practice will emerge out of process, this openness should not be confused with 'letting it happen'. Focused and ongoing consideration of process and outcome is needed to do justice to the potential in rural social work.

Risk-taking

A sense of not being in control is often involved. Some models of social work offer control, objectivity and disengagement from the world of the client. Practising with people in their everyday worlds is not often like that. What do you do when you walk into the pub and people at the tables look away from you? What do you do when you are invited to a client's wedding? Working with rather than on people involves both dialogue and risk.

Conclusion

This has been my story of educating others to become rural social work practitioners, scripted very much by my own experience of *doing* rural social work. As a profession we continue to mediate between human stories of trouble and systems of addressing what are identified as public issues. This is often a messy business, oppressive for practitioner and client, and not always addressed well from a framing of knowledge which suggests that if we needed to know this territory it would have been in the course.

Increasingly social work scholars are articulating the usefulness of an interpretive framing of knowledge in our postmodern times (Martinez-Brawley & Zorita 1998). It is interesting to note that ways of working locally have persisted, despite efforts to instil normative foundational truths of practice. These ways of rural social work are readily cast as postmodern, with the slant that they are firmly grounded in the action component said to be missing from that theoretical perspective (Denzin 1997). Interestingly, graduates have reported that the content covered in the rural course was equally useful for community-minded urban practice. Reflecting on this, it can be asserted that practice principles of rural social work speak powerfully from the margins on the possibilities for practice in urban settings.

> Social work is a collage of perspectives and opportunities ... If social work is to live up to its own identity, it must openly and unapologetically acknowledge that in nurturing and caring, the rational is not more important than the intuitive, the systematic is not more valid and truthful than the asymptomatic ... Truth itself is evasive and knowledge is relative and situated, that is related to the knower and ... bound by place and time.
>
> (Martinez-Brawley & Zorita 1998, p. 210)

References

Chi, J. 1991, *Brun nue dae*, Currency Press and Magabala Books, Paddington.

Condliffe, P. 1991, 'Bringing social work education to the bush: Addressing the rural decline?' in *Australian Social Work*, vol. 44, no. 2, pp. 11–18.

Crago, H, Sturmey, R. & Monson, J. 1996, 'Myth and reality in rural counselling: Toward a new model for training rural/remote area helping professionals', in *Australian & NZ Journal of Family Therapy*, vol. 17, no. 2, pp. 61–74.

Crawford, F. R. 1989, *Jalinardi ways: Whitefellas working in Aboriginal communities*, Curtin University Press, Perth.

Crawford, F. R. 1992, 'Meaning of "community" in thought and action', in Coppin, M. (ed.), *Community work: Solution of illusion?*, Kookynie Press, Kalgoorlie, pp. 118–22.

Crawford, F. R. 1997, 'No continuing city: A postmodern story of social work', in *Australian Social Work*, vol. 50, no. 1, pp. 23–30.

Denzin, N. K. 1997, *Interpretive ethnography: Ethnographic practices for the twentyfirst century*, Sage, Oakbrook.

Docherty, J. C. 1992, *Historical dictionary of Australia*, The Scarecrow Press, Metuchen, NJ and London.

Facey, A. B. 1981, *A fortunate life*, Fremantle Arts Centre Press, Fremantle.

Haebich, A. 1988, *For their own good: Aborigines and government in the southwest of Western Australia, 1900–1940*, University of Western Australia Press, Nedlands.

Hart, J. 1995, 'The challenge of remote area social work: A Pacific island experience', in *Australian Social Work*, vol. 48, no. 2, pp. 39–45.

Kelly, A., & Sewell, S. 1988, *With head, heart and hand: Dimensions of community building*, Brisbane: Boolarong, Brisbane.

Lynn, M. 1990, 'Rural social work: applying Martinez-Brawley's tenets to Gippsland', in *Australian Social Work*, vol. 43, no. 1, pp. 15–21.

Martinez-Brawley, E. 1987, 'Young people in country towns: Tasks for rural social work and community workers across nations, in *Australian Social Work*, vol. 40, no. 1, pp. 23–31.

Martinez-Brawley, E. & Zorita, P. M. 1998, 'At the edge of the frame: Beyond science and art in social work', in *British Journal of Social Work*, 28, pp. 197–212.

Mills, C. W. 1959, *The sociological imagination*, Oxford University Press, New York.

Reinharz, S. 1983, ' Implementing new paradigm research: A model for training and practice', in Reason, P. & Rowan, J. (eds), *Human Inquiry: A sourcebook of new paradigm research*, Wiley, Chichester.

Scott, D. 1993, 'International technology transfer in family preservation: Differences between Australian and US contexts', in *Children Australia*, vol. 18, no. 2, pp. 17–28.

Stannage, C. T. (ed.) 1981, *A new history of Western Australia*, University of Western Australia Press, Perth.

Ward, G. 1987, *Wandering girl*, Magabala Books, Broome.

O'Sullivan, D., Ross, D. & Young, S. 1997, 'A framework for the use of competencies in rural social work field practice placements', in *Australian Social Work*, vol. 50, no. 1.

Zubrycki, T. (producer and director) 1991, Bran Nue Dae: A film about the musical by Jimmy Chi and "Kuckles", Bran Nue Dae Productions Aboriginal Corporation, Broome.

11

Women's work against violence
Community responses in a rural setting[*]

Helen La Nauze & Shirley Rutherford

Introduction

'Let's Lift the Lid', an innovative and integrated community response to violence and in particular to violence against women, was launched in Albury-Wodonga in 1994. The program had been successful in winning funds through a New South Wales competition for Healthy Country Communities. Its launch marked a significant breakthrough in establishing violence against women as a priority issue requiring a comprehensive, strategic response.

Violence is an issue of women's lives that country women, be they of town or farm, share with city women. Nonetheless, country women's experiences of violence and the strategic responses of women to address violence in non-metropolitan areas of Australia have received only limited attention in the literature.

---

[*] This chapter was first published as an article in *Women Against Violence: An Australian Feminist Journal*, 2, June 1997. As part of an endeavour to promote Helen La Nauze's writing widely, it will also appear in a forthcoming edition of *Issues Facing Australian Families*, edited by Wendy Weeks and Marjorie Quinn.

Lyla Coorey (1988) identified the particular vulnerability of women experiencing domestic violence in country areas. Her research reported, inter alia, that high visibility, small town interrelationships between the men together with hostile attitudes, the lack of political organisation among rural women and the limited availability of a range of services, were barriers for women from rural towns who wished to escape violent situations and establish themselves independently. Kate Baxter (1992) claimed that city-based models for sexual assault services in New South Wales were not necessarily transferable to rural areas and workers often had to 'start from scratch' to develop more appropriate models. She also identified that workers in rural areas had to engage in the process of challenging community attitudes that were often very conservative and resistant to change.

In this chapter, we aim to give voice to the experiences of some women from a rural area by tracing the development of responses to violence against women in the rural centre of Albury-Wodonga. The focus of the chapter is primarily on violence against women in their own homes—or 'domestic violence'—but this is not an exclusive focus. Indeed, the thrust of the 'Let's Lift the Lid' program was to broaden the understanding of and integrate responses to violence against women.

By telling the story, we highlight the unfolding of local initiatives within the broader context of statewide and national developments. Additionally, we identify three key lessons about working within a conservative major rural centre. We argue the importance of maintaining a feminist analysis; the need to be sensitive to the local context, while remaining cognisant of the broader context; and the importance of working with local networks.

The chapter draws on our experiences as feminist community workers within the town and, in particular, Shirley's experience in the development of the 'Let's Lift the Lid' project. It also draws on research undertaken by Helen to explore the nature of feminist community practice in the town (La Nauze 1996). Additional interviews and document research were undertaken to fill gaps in our knowledge and to check our assumptions and interpretations.

Albury-Wodonga, a cross-border growth centre

Albury-Wodonga is situated on the Murray River, the border between New South Wales and Victoria. Wodonga, on the Victorian side, is approximately 300 kilometres north-east of Melbourne. Albury is approximately 600 kilometres south-west of Sydney. The centres are linked with the two capital cities by road, rail and air. The 'twin cities' straddle, and are separated by, the physical and political boundaries. The river and flood plain stretch for approximately three kilometres between the centres, while the state border means that a variety of policy and service provision differences intervene in the way in which people and organisations conduct their lives. It is a centre that has undergone significant growth for more than two decades. This growth is consistent with a general trend for some provincial centres to grow at the expense of surrounding rural areas as well as with the stimulus provided by the 1973 declaration of Albury-Wodonga as a 'national growth centre' (Albury-Wodonga Development Corporation 1974).

Locating Albury-Wodonga as 'rural' is perhaps contentious. Indeed, the term 'rural' is contested. Although Australian and international literature recognise the ambiguity and lack of consensus around the term, it is common, to accept a broad, pragmatic definition of rural as 'non-metropolitan' (Dunn, 1989; Lynn 1990). The Victorian Rural Women's Network adopts a similar approach, including all women outside the metropolitan areas of Melbourne and Geelong in its definition (Mitchell 1994). Nonetheless, as non-metropolitan Australia is diverse in population density, remoteness and on other dimensions, we have chosen to identify the context as that of a 'major rural centre', allowing for greater specificity.

In a recent study, Albury-Wodonga was alternatively described by the small sample of women participants as 'rural', 'country town', 'small community' and even 'country city'. Nonetheless, participants explicitly assumed that 'it was different from capital cities', and implied that they sometimes felt marginal to the mainstream of urban/metropolitan life (La Nauze 1996, p. 64).

An emerging awareness of violence against women: The establishment of a local women's refuge

This story of the struggle to develop adequate responses to violence in Albury-Wodonga begins with events in the 1970s. This was a period of national rapid social change resulting from the 'conjunction of an active women's movement and a reforming Labor government' (Curthoys 1992, p. 436). Both the women's movement and the Whitlam government of 1972–75 provided an important context for the national emergence of awareness and action against violence against women (Melville 1993). This national backdrop, combined with the conservative nature of the Albury-Wodonga community, provided a context within which local developments took place.

Albury-Wodonga women were quick to join the national trends by developing their own responses. They formed their own branch of Women's Electoral Lobby (WEL) in 1972. Border WEL undertook a number of local initiatives, including steps to place violence on the local public agenda. Members of WEL were aware of and had visited refuges in Sydney; they had also undertaken local research which had identified, inter alia, the need to provide crisis accommodation for women and children. They organised a local forum for International Women's Year (1975), but clashes between Right to Life Supporters and Border WEL members (Bruce 1975) dashed any hopes of support for a co-ordinated initiative to establish a women's refuge or other women's service.

Border WEL, however, convinced of the need for such a service, decided to establish a women's refuge centre to provide support and accommodation 'for women and girls who are the victims of wife-bashing and other assaults' (*Border Morning Mail*, 6 Feb. 1975). Members developed a system of offering shelter in their own homes and prepared a submission to the Federal Department of Health for funding.

At the same time, a voluntary welfare group, the Community Service Centre, had also been assisting women and children with emergency accommodation, often by using a local hotel. At the instigation of the WEL women, women at the Community Service Centre became involved with the plan to develop a refuge. Several women recollected that the WEL women were finding the voluntary system in their own homes enormously stressful and sought the assistance of the Community Service Centre in auspicing a refuge. The WEL women who were initially involved with the voluntary scheme did not continue with the project.

The first refuge was established with the assistance of the Albury-Wodonga Development Corporation (AWDC), a statutory authority created by the Whitlam government to plan and develop the 'National Growth Centre'. On the advice of their social planner, the AWDC offered a house to the Emergency Housing sub-committee of the Regional Council for Social Development. The refuge, which was staffed entirely by volunteers, was called Albury Crisis House. Its initial focus and purpose were not specifically about women who were experiencing violence. Rather, a crisis house was seen as 'a home where a woman and her child [could] come whilst they recover from the physical and emotional traumas of a breakdown in their lives' (First Annual Report of the Albury Crisis House, n.d.). The women from the Crisis House committee lobbied federal politicians and were successful in attracting federal funding as a women's refuge in 1977. In 1978 the name was changed from a crisis house to a 'women's refuge'.

A safe space for women

The decade of the 1980s included a number of significant developments for women in Albury-Wodonga. A number of women's networks were established and women were involved in taking action in areas such as education, health, child care, discrimination and the local media. Women's health issues were particularly prominent and some bitter public struggles ensued, often impacting heavily on the lives of local activist women (La Nauze 1996).

Within this context, the Refuge workers and committee advanced the local responses to violence against women in several ways. They maintained a stable organisation which successfully provided a safe place for women, despite a local climate that was often hostile to women's services and feminist understandings. They expanded their program through local initiatives, such as a voluntary follow-up program known as the Friends Program, as well as through statewide-funded developments such as a child support program and the employment of a non-English speaking background worker. They were also successful in maintaining the support of traditional organisations such as churches and service clubs.

Ludo McFerran (1990, p.2) claims that the Women's Refuge Movement in NSW played an important political role in organising 'many ... politically inexperienced groups into a powerful and political refuge movement'. This claim is borne out by experiences at the Albury-Wodonga Women's Refuge. Significant involvement with the statewide movement was developed. Local women joined statewide activities and the Albury refuge became the auspice body for the NSW Women's Refuge Working Party in 1983. The Working Party included delegates from all regions of the state working on issues related to women and domestic violence, children's issues and housing. In 1986 it also became the auspice for the NSW Women's Refuge Referral and Resource Centre (Albury-Wodonga Women's Refuge Ltd 1996).

Involvement in the statewide movement substantially influenced the practice and understandings of the Albury Refuge. In particular, the Refuge came to clearly identify its role as focusing on domestic violence. It became an autonomous organisation with women only membership, and adopted some organisational structures which incorporated notions of collectivity.

The Refuge was also involved in several community initiatives. In 1984 women from the refuge participated in an Albury Domestic Violence Group and, with the Albury Community Health Centre and Sexual Assault Service, conducted a domestic violence phone-in. In 1987, at the invitation of the Albury police, it convened the establishment of a local Domestic Violence Committee (Albury-Wodonga Women's Refuge, Ltd 1996).

The Sexual Assault Service had developed as a separate local initiative in the early 1980s. The service, at first known as the Help Centre, was developed as a local response to the identified issue of sexual assault. It was established as a hospital-based service but staffed by volunteers. Later, the NSW Women's Health Policy Review in 1984 identified the lack of access to services for women in rural areas. Albury was one of the areas targeted for a fully funded Sexual Assault Service (Women's Co-ordination Unit, NSW Premier's Department 1988).

Despite these developments, for much of the 1980s the issue of violence remained largely separate from the official public domain and, indeed, often separate from other women's action within the town. The refuge workers and committee maintained strong links with the traditional and often conservative networks of the town but did not develop links with the women's networks. The women's networks, on the other hand, did not develop a significant focus on violence against women. For example, there was an extensive network of neighbourhood houses and community-based education and support services offering feminist-oriented women's programs (La Nauze, 1996). Nonetheless, as one of the workers reflected recently:

in [those] days we never would have had domestic violence or adult survivors of sexual assault as an issue. We wouldn't even have talked about it … [We] never dreamt that in all of those places women were coming who were being abused … We knew that women were powerless … we talked a lot about economic powerlessness, the powerlessness of not having any transport, about having no access to get to information and places … We didn't talk about being black and blue…

Furthermore, a locally initiated consultation for the National Agenda for Women did not identify violence as an issue about which women were concerned (McGowan 1986).

Developing a complex and diversified response

Towards the end of the decade there were signs that violence against women was beginning to be seen as an issue that required strategies beyond the provision of safe space for women. Nationally, a 'groundswell of public concern' had developed, resulting in a strong focus on violence in the first National Agenda for Women in 1988 and the establishment of the National Committee Against Violence Against Women (Weeks and Gilmore 1996). Locally, a number of developments occurred.

Staff at the Albury-Wodonga Women's Centre, opened in 1986, were soon confronted with the reality of violence in may women's daily lives. They began to incorporate an explicit focus on domestic violence within their program. This included convening information seminars in Wodonga (Albury-Wodonga Women's Inc 1990) which contributed to a growing awareness of violence against women and to local effort to seek a Wodonga-based service.

Initial efforts were directed towards gaining a funded Refuge in Wodonga, but women in Victoria at the time were looking at developing outreach models for services for women experiencing violence. Wodonga thus became the location for one of the Victorian pilot outreach programs. The service began in 1992 auspiced by Upper Murray Family Care, a major non-government organisation providing a range of family support services. The program workers played a significant role supporting women living with or escaping violence as well as engaging in community action and initiatives such as the development and implementation of 'Let's Lift the Lid'.

In the 1990s, staff of the Albury Community Health Service became significantly involved in the issue of violence against women through its health promotion program. Until 1992, the service focus on disease and clinical service delivery has been essentially reactive, framed by funding limitations, historic practice and statewide disease priorities. 'Community development' was acknowledged as important but the organisation lacked a coherent conceptual base to underpin its practice. Community development was mistakenly equated with delivering service from a community-based venue.

In 1992, a needs assessment was undertaken to provide a planning base for the redevelopment of health promotion activities. It aimed to identify the perceived health issues, examine demographic patterns, assess the viability of inter-agency networks and determine how the Albury Community Health Service could develop effective, responsive ways of working at the local level. Although it was initially assumed that poverty and low income would emerge as the major issues, it became clear that the consequences of violence, particularly violence against women, was an even greater issue confronting most government and non-government services.

The needs assessment identified that the lives of women affected by violence were often fragmented into 'welfare packages' of crisis accommodation, income support, counselling or emergency assistance. Although diverse services ranging from the women's refuge to, for example, neighbourhood houses, accommodation services, police, legal services of early childhood services were all attempting to deal with the consequences and indicators of violence, violence per se was not always identified and named. Often there was no evidence of a clean construction of violence against women as a social or justice issue. Instead, workers' practice and approaches were defined, named and constrained by the nature of the services they provided. Services were working in isolation, constrained by tightly targeted funding and stringent accountability criteria and there was plenty of scope for personal value judgments and well-intentioned but paternalistic welfare responses. Thus women who were experiencing violence were receiving a range of services that were failing to recognise and address the violence in their lives. The fact that many women continued to live in danger of abuse and assault was treated as an apparently unchangeable reality that the workers and the women faced every day.

In response to these findings, the Albury Community Health Service reviewed its policy and objectives in early 1993 and began to refocus service delivery, introducing a focus on violence and collaborative and co-operative ways of working with other services. A range of initiatives followed, such as women's health clinics at the Women's Centre and a neighbourhood house on a public housing estate; joint facilitation by Women's Centre and Women's Refuge staff of mutual help groups for women living with or escaping violence; and flexible, women centred, community based 'Living with Kids' programs for women who had experienced domestic violence. Male Community Health staff worked with the police, probation and parole and Family Court staff to develop a men's group and work began on the redevelopment of the Albury Domestic Violence Committee. These activities and the co-ordinated approach contributed to more adequate responses to violence by raising consciousness of violence, diversifying service responses and reducing the isolation and image of the Community Health Centre as a specialist resource.

Initiatives from other services developed concurrently. In 1992, the Women's Centre co-operated with other services to establish a volunteer Domestic Court

Support Program to support women who had applied for protection orders in New South Wales and Victorian courts. By 1993, work had begun on increasing the credibility and profile of the court supporters. In 1993, the Women's Refuge successfully submitted to the Office for the Status of Women for funding to undertake a Rural Community Awareness Program. This project enabled the Refuge staff to prepare an information package and to speak to groups in isolated rural communities.

The announcement in April 1993 of the Healthy Country Communities competition provided the impetus to crystallise and formalise the comprehensive and collaborative approach to violence against women. However, it involved the need to present violence as an issue within the traditional disease-focused health promotion strategic priorities that formed the basis of the competition. While there was significant discomfort with entering a statewide competition to address violence, pragmatic workers were brought together under the auspices of the then ailing Domestic Violence Committee to prepare a proposal for submission for a regional prize and a further proposal for a more substantial statewide prize. The 'Let's Lift the Lid' program thus emerged.

The first component of the proposed program focused on professional development and training and the second identified a major public and community awareness program. The Domestic Violence committee was expanded to include representatives from a range of services and became the 'Let's Lift the Lid' steering committee. The proposal was selected for the regional award following a public presentation, and subsequently awarded the inaugural statewide prize following another public presentation in Sydney. This award was significant as it recognised violence as a public health issue and as a legitimate focus for the previously narrowly focused health promotion program. The funding provided an organisational framework and paid workers, which supported ongoing development and established community legitimacy. A sub-committee structure addressed professional development, community education and legal issues.

The complexity of the issues contributing to and arising from violence against women was an ongoing challenge to the diverse committee, but an agreement developed that understanding and practice within a feminist framework were central to effective change in the service system. It was also agreed that raising community awareness was essential to changing the low visibility and current level of tolerance of domestic violence.

During 1994 and 1995 a community-wide media and education campaign was developed and service responses were enhanced. Significant developments included:

- establishment of a widely representative reference group including women's services, other community services and the police service;
- training more than eighty (80) workers to understand domestic violence

issues and to develop professional practice that was non-judgmental, effective and women-centred;

- a survey of general practitioners which was conducted by Community Health and Albury Base Hospital medical staff to assess knowledge, awareness and responses to women who experience domestic violence;

- preparation of posters and related television advertisements, focusing on the prevalence and impact of domestic violence;

- preparation and dissemination to general practitioners and other professional workers of locally relevant information in the form of pamphlets, cards and a referral reference;

- education for solicitors, court staff and general practitioners, including a conference sponsored by the Women General Practitioner's Network;

- on-going development of group work programs;

- expansion of the Court Support Volunteers program, including engaging the active support of police and court staff;

- the development of school-based education at primary and secondary levels;

- the development of an ongoing Men Against Violence Group.

For some, 'Let's Lift the Lid' was understood as a campaign while others saw it as a vehicle for expanded service delivery. These alternative understandings are certainly valid for some of the activities but do not address the breadth of intent and outcomes of the project. Indeed, a key element of the program was the consciousness raising and politicising of the diverse participants through their co-operative engagement with the task.

Struggling to avoid full circle

'Let's Lift the Lid' has sought to develop a complex response to complex issues and demands by placing the issue of violence against women on the local public agenda, changing understandings of violence against women and developing women-centred, responsive approaches across a broad range of relevant and diverse services in the town. Change of that order, however, requires, inter alia, sustained and viable researching. Recent attempts to secure further funding to both continue these efforts and build upon them have not been successful. The program currently rests on the support of services such as the Women's Refuge, the Albury Community Health Service, which is operating within a regional context of savage funding cuts and the Women's Centre, which receives meagre funding from the Victorian government to support the Volunteer Court Support Program. In a recent publication, Wendy Weeks and Kate Gilmore (1996, p. 152) commented that 'the issue of violence against women has become unpopular in Canberra', thus reflecting local concern about the absence of sustained and appropriate levels of funding.

A further confronting issue, triggered particularly by the violent death in 1996 of a young woman in Albury, has been the activation of a competing popularist construction of violence as violent acts in public places. Responses that have been canvassed in the local media, and by a predominantly male and business oriented group, argue for more policing and changes to current hotel and club practices. They are notable for the absence of any gender analysis or recognition of violence in the private as well as public domain.

What lessons can be learned?

How can the experiences of women in Albury-Wodonga contribute to an understanding of the struggle against violence against women? What are the key lessons to be gained?

We have chosen three aspects of the story that we believe are key to working within conservative rural towns. These are: the importance of a feminist analysis; understanding and working within the local context while remaining cognisant of the broader context; working with local networks.

The importance of a feminist analysis

Underpinning the development of the 'Let's Lift the Lid' program was a feminist analysis of social issues in general and violence in particular. This analysis ensured that women's lived experiences were heard, thus enabling the issue of violence to be recognised and named in the health promotion needs assessment. Understanding the connections between the different aspects of women's lives enabled strategic responses which recognised violence as a legitimate health promotion issue. This understanding also ensured that the responses to that identified issue were complex and diverse, traversing legal, social and educational systems within the town.

In rural areas it is common to meet ambivalence and hostility to feminism (see, for example, Alston 1990, Piner 1990, Hogan 1994). Hogan, who has written about working within women in agriculture, notes that workers are often gatekeepers and are faced with a 'constant challenge to balance the costs against the gain of working with a feminist perspective' (Hogan 1994, p. 34). We argue that it is important to focus on ensuring that a feminist analysis underpins the responses to violence against women, whether this is in rural or metropolitan areas. The questions of whether and how to identify publicly with feminism per se are perhaps strategic questions to which there is no single response. Women in rural areas will no doubt continue to grapple with this dilemma both collectively and individually.

Understanding and working within the local context while remaining cognisant of the broader context

The Albury-Wodonga story has demonstrated the interweaving of national and statewide developments and local initiatives. The broader developments provided a context of awareness about the issue, together with government policies and machinery and women's organisations and networks that women used to enhance local initiatives and access resources to develop local responses. However, strategic local developments, cognisant of opportunities and constraints within the local context, were necessary to place the issue on the local agenda and ensure that responses were grounded in that context. Central to that approach is the importance of working with diverse local networks.

Working with diverse local networks

In Albury/Wodonga, responses to women experiencing violence have had to be developed within the context of a politically conservative town which at times has demonstrated public hostility to the changing position of women. Arguably, the Refuge has successfully managed to sustain a service for women and by women in this climate by, inter alia, maintaining strong links with the more conservative networks in the area.

Rural human service workers are often urged to work with local networks and to develop coalitions across disparate groups and ideologies (Martinez-Brawley 1987, Lynn 1990, Cheers, 1992). Margaret Lynn (1990) argues that rural networks are dense and overlapping. They can operate to maintain the strength of conservative social values and power relations, and workers must join with these networks in order to raise awareness and politicise broader social issues. The challenge is how to seek broad-based change without being constrained by those networks. 'Let's Lift the Lid', clearly underpinned by a feminist analysis of violence, nonetheless was a program that encompassed workers and organisations with a range of understandings. The task for the key workers was not just program development but also that of consciousness raising and politicising the local welfare, legal, police and medical network through the program development process.

References

Albury Crisis House (n.d.), First Annual Report of the Albury Crisis House, unpublished report, Albury-Wodonga.

Albury-Wodonga Development Corporation 1964, First Annual Report, Albury-Wodonga.

Albury-Wodonga Women's Refuge Ltd 1996, 'Refuge Time-Line 20 Years', unpublished paper, Albury-Wodonga.

Alston M. 1990, 'Feminism and Farm Women', in *Australian Social Work*, vol. 43, no 1, pp. 23–7.

Baxter K. 1992, 'Starting from Scratch: Sexual Assault Services in Rural Areas', in Breckinridge, J. and Carmody, M. (eds), *Crimes of Violence: Australian Responses to Rape and Child Sexual Assault*, Allen and Unwin, Sydney, pp. 174–81.

Bruce, J. 1975, 'Year Women Meet, and Clash', *Border Morning Mail*, 4 Feb.

Cheers, B. 1992, 'Rural Social Work and Social Welfare in the Australian Context', *Australian Social Work*, vol. 45, no 2, pp. 11–21.

Coorey, L. 1988, *Domestic Violence and the Police. Who is Being Protected?* University of Sydney Printing Service, Sydney.

Curthoys, A. 1992 'Doing it for Themselves. The Women's Movement Since 1970', in Saunders, K. and Evans, R. (eds), *Gender Relations in Australia. Domination and Negotiation*, Harcourt Brace Jovanovich (Australia), Marrickville, NSW, pp. 425–47.

Dunn, P. 1989, 'Rural Australia: Are You Standing in it?', in *Rural Research Bulletin* 2, pp. 12–13.

Hogan, E. 1994, 'Making Women Visible: Reflections on Working with Women in Agriculture in Australia', in Franklin, M., Short, L. & Teather, E. K. (eds) 1994, *Country Women at the Crossroads. Perspectives on the lives of rural Australian Women in the 1990s*, University of New England Press, Armidale, pp. 31–7.

La Nauze, H. 1996, 'Conceptualising Feminist Community Practice in a Major Rural Centre', unpublished Master of Social Work thesis, University of Melbourne, Parkville.

Lynn, M. 1990, 'Developing a Rural Social Work Practice Model', unpublished Master of Social Work thesis, Monash University, Clayton.

McGowan, C. 1986, *National Agenda for Women*, Albury-Wodonga and Districts Consultation.

McFerran, L. 1990, 'Interpretation of a Frontline State: Australian Women's Refuges and the State', in Watson, S. (ed.), *Playing the State: Australian Feminist Interventions*, Allen and Unwin, Sydney, pp. 191–205.

Martinez-Brawley, E. 1987, 'Young People in Country Towns: Tasks for Rural Social and Community Workers', in *Australian Social Work*, vol. 40, no. 1.

Melville, R. 1993, 'Turbulent Environments: Women's Refuges, Collectivity and the State', unpublished Doctoral thesis, University of New South Wales, Sydney.

Mitchell, J. 1994, 'Grass Roots and Government Initiative: Victoria's Rural Women's Network', in Franklin, M., Short, L. & Teather, E. K. (eds) 1994, *Country Women at the Crossroads: Perspectives on the Lives of Rural Australian Women in the 1990s*, University of New England Press, Armidale, pp. 140–50.

Poiner, G. 1990, *The Good Old Rule: Gender and Other Relationships in a Rural Community*, Sydney University Press, Melbourne.

The Women's Centre, Albury-Wodonga (Inc.) 1990, Annual Report, 1989–1990, Albury-Wodonga.

Weeks, W. and Gilmore, K. 1996, 'How Violence Against Women Became an Issue on the National Policy Agenda', in Dalton, T., Draper, M., Weeks, W. & Wiseman, J., *Making Social Policy in Australia*, Allen and Unwin, St. Leonards, NSW, pp. 141–53.

Women's Co-ordination Unit, NSW Premier's Department 1988, NSW Sexual Assault Committee Report to the Honourable Barrie Unsworth, M.P., Premier of NSW, January 1985–87, Government Printer, Sydney.

12

Co-ordinating services in a forgotten mining town

Peter Munn

Introduction

This chapter discusses the service co-ordination model adopted in late 1993 to provide services to Tarcoola, a small remote town approximately 700 kilometres from Adelaide. Access to Tarcoola is by an unsealed road which can be impassible in wet weather. The closest regional community is Port Augusta some 400 kilometres from Tarcoola.

Australian National, the Commonwealth government-owned long distance railway operation, moved its employees from Tarcoola in 1997, which led to the closure of most of the facilities available to people living there. Whilst the town is now closed there is much to learn from the approach adopted by human service practitioners to working in a small remote location.

Introducing Tarcoola

Facilities in Tarcoola in 1993 included a hotel (meals and accommodation), a hospital, public phone, post office, police station and general store. The population varied between 70 and 120 people, depending upon whether the male railway workers were home or whether they were repairing the railway line as far as 1000 kilometres away from town. The women in the town could be without their partners for a time period ranging from 5 to 21 days.

The homes for railway employed workers tended to have a 'sameness' and whilst they had been established for years still had the look of being temporary accommodation. Some people living in these houses had tried to establish gardens but in outback South Australia the dry climate and redness of soil makes this extremely difficult. These houses were separated by a wide unsealed road from the houses where the professional workers were located. People from the neighbouring pastoral stations bought their food and fuel supplies from Tarcoola.

Women were often 'stuck' in Tarcoola. There were very limited opportunities to gain a break from their children and they took the major responsibility for child-rearing as their husbands were frequently out of town. This placed considerable pressure on them regarding disciplining of their children. For much of their time they were the 'sole' parent. There were no child care facilities available to them.

The children experienced more freedom than in larger communities. They were free to wander about the town with little fear of becoming lost. When the family visited larger cities, however, the children often had difficulty adjusting to the traffic. Several stories were shared by the women of children having no comprehension of the basic rules for crossing the road in larger communities.

People within Tarcoola were often living with the uncertainty of closure. The distances travelled by the railway employees from their home base indicated they could be moved to larger communities. In general, the people were isolated, had minimal social support services, partners were separated for long periods of time and there were few visitors because of the remoteness. One woman summarised their position as 'being stuck doing nothing except yelling at the children'.

My role was one of acting as a consultant to enhance the co-ordination process in Tarcoola. This involved interviewing the women and all the service providers. As someone from outside the community I felt a sense of desperation to help the residents as they appeared to be 'forgotten' by people living in urban, rural and many other remote locations. It was easy to become entangled with the lives of the women and want to seek out resources for them to be able to function more effectively. At the same time there was the realisation that only very limited resources would be allocated by human service organisations to meet their needs. In departing Tarcoola on my final visit I experienced a real sense of depression knowing that whilst services had been enhanced the women's physical and emotional isolation from the outside world remained.

Factors affecting service delivery in rural and remote Australia

Regional Australia has special characteristics affecting the extent and quality of service delivery. Location factors influencing service delivery include geographical isolation from major centres, population of the town and regions, distances to be travelled to major centres, the economic base of the town and other services available.

People in rural and remote areas are clearly disadvantaged with respect to the level of health and welfare services available as compared to people living in urban areas (Smith 1989; Cheers 1994). Many communities lack the population to have locally based services within their community, or alternatively do not have the range of services offered in urban communities.

Accessibility of services is a crucial issue and is related to the geographical proximity of the service to the user, the waiting time to receive assistance and the cost of the service (Cheers 1992). For many communities their size limits service availability. Visiting services have limited accessibility and yet, in remote areas, they may be the only service available to the community.

In rural and remote Australia human services practitioners require skills and knowledge in case work, group work, community organisation, planning, community and regional development as well as social action (Munn 1993). This range of work requires the employment of 'generalist' or specialist/generalist workers. Being sensitive to their users was identified by Martinez-Brawley and Delevan (1991) in their in-depth study of service provision in Pennsylvania as the top priority of service administrators towards their work.

Lastly, and specifically with regard to the needs of people living in remote locations, the attitude of service providers and administrators towards meeting their needs is crucial to what services are developed at the local level. Jean Martin (1978) discusses the concept of the 'active contemporary definer'. She argues that disadvantaged people need someone who is prepared to stand up and argue for development of services. This concept is particularly relevant for working in remote communities as they lack the economic, political, social and media power of urbanised communities.

Services delivery co-ordination in Tarcoola in 1993

For the purposes of this study co-ordination is defined as:

> *planning and commitment between organisations to the ongoing process of joint action in sharing and exchanging information and resources to assist organisational and service delivery functioning for the purpose of enhancing the achievement of the goals of the individual organisation or their collective goals.*

(Munn 1998, p.62)

A team of professionals, mainly from Port Augusta, was established to help improve the delivery of services to Tarcoola. Feedback from the local clinical nurse and from residents indicated services were fragmented and organised to suit the service providers rather than the service users. The first meeting of this group in the later part of 1992 focused on their working relationship and assessment of need (Weetman 1993). I was invited to join this team as a consultant to help establish an effective method of delivering co-ordinated services to Tarcoola. The team developed the aim of enhancing the well-being of people in Tarcoola and helping to promote a stronger and healthier community.

Human service organisations involved in the co-ordination project

The organisation initiating the project was the Remote Inland Children's Exercise (RICE) which is a well-respected organisation providing support to people living in remote locations. The RICE family counsellor was instrumental in establishing the Outreach Team. It was his commitment and enthusiasm for improving service delivery that initiated the establishment of the Outreach Team exercise. RICE was responsible for conducting what was known as the School of the Air program, which provided children on remote stations the opportunity to talk to a teacher by two-way radio. The teacher was located in Port Augusta. It also provided many supports for people in outback locations through visits to many isolated people either by car or by train.

The Department for Family and Community Services (FACS), a statutory government department responsible for family and children's issues, particularly child protection, visited Tarcoola once every three months before this project. It had statutory responsibilities to meet during its visits. This organisation agreed to visit monthly and to expand its role into adult education as well as meeting statutory obligations.

The nursing staff at the Tarcoola Hospital provided a pivotal role in facilitating and providing health and welfare services. They recognised that they had an important role in being the broker between the Port Augusta based organisations and their service users. They needed to advocate on behalf of their service users with the Port Augusta based human service organisations.

The Port Augusta Community Health Services Division had established an effective community development approach, through forming teams with a mix of disciplines in providing outreach work. This had helped to break down professional barriers. They saw the Tarcoola project as positive, and saw their role as responding to the needs given to them by the local nursing staff at the Tarcoola Hospital.

The Port Augusta Family Centre, a non-government organisation, provided a 'hands on' service to facilitate the skills of people in need of assistance. They were a practically based organisation offering training, games, craft, activities and child care support. They helped initiate the parents group.

The Child Adolescent and Family Health Services (CAFHS) had been visiting Tarcoola once per month for 10 years. It provided an effective service operating a clinic as well as beginning to provide an educative service to women with young children. The Royal Flying Doctor Service flew the CAFHS nurse to Tarcoola as part of a mobile team visiting remote locations.

The contribution of Australian National to this project was important. It provided transport to several of the service delivery groups in this exercise. Australian National provided RICE and other human service organisations with a carriage on one of their trains that visited isolated communities such as Tarcoola and Cooke. This train was affectionately known as the 'tea and sugar' train.

Acacia Women's Health Centre, a small non-government organisation, saw their role as providing an educative service to the nursing staff at the Tarcoola Hospital. They were prepared to help organise a health expo in Tarcoola once per year. Given the size of the community a yearly two-day commitment was viewed by this organisation as appropriate.

The goal of the human service organisations was to help co-operate with the residents of Tarcoola in the development of a healthier and stronger community. They wanted to provide the community with a model of co-operative action, help establish effective liaison and working relationships with the residents, provide one-to-one counselling when the need existed, institute a parents group and generally provide information and assistance to initiate a process of community empowerment.

Factors affecting service co-ordination in Tarcoola

There were initial difficulties in organisations working together. Representatives from each organisation needed to understand the importance of each others' role within the team. Each representative needed to determine whether the objectives for this team were congruent and within the goals of their organisation. These sensitivities are understandable given that working together can be perceived as a threat to organisational autonomy (Whetten 1977; Halpert 1982; Weiss 1987).

Similarly, issues of 'turf protection' needed to be addressed as there were some areas of overlap between organisations. Representatives of each organisation were able to talk through these issues and make decisions on who should be given responsibility for performing functions. Whilst 'turf protection' existed to a small extent, the team was able to minimise its effect and representatives from all organisations were able to respect each others' territory.

Professional differences emerged as an issue for the group early in its life. The team members handled the potential for conflict by accepting there were differences and rather than regarding this as a limiting factor, built on the complementarity of each other, for example, one organisation being responsible for the theoretical input on parenting whilst another provides the 'hands on' input.

For service providers 'external' to Tarcoola they had many other areas of work. The pressure of work meant that less time for some service providers was given to the team than they would have liked. There was also some tension for these service providers as they faced pressure in their own organisations to reduce their time to this project.

The needs of service users

Users had expressed a sense of dissatisfaction with the lack of commitment from human service organisations external to the community. There was a feeling that they were not worthy enough to be given services. As one resident stated, 'we just don't seem to be important to anyone outside of Tarcoola'. Another comment made was 'unless someone has been reported to welfare we hardly see anyone outside of RICE and the Royal Flying Doctor Service'.

As part of the co-ordination and outreach process, service users were consulted regarding their needs and established a list of their requirements. Their needs were not overly demanding. They saw the two locally based clinical nurses as essential, a need for a parents group to be held weekly, child care provision for the parents group, monthly social work visits from the RICE counsellor, a yearly health expo, CAFHS clinical visits on a monthly basis and FACS was to visit as part of a mobile team visit on a three-monthly basis.

In the initial planning by the service co-ordination team there was a desire to link-up as many services to arrive at Tarcoola on the same day. The women expressed concern at this approach, as they argued it would result in their being overloaded with services for the day and then minimal 'external' services for the remainder of each month. As a result of this feedback the service co-ordination team adjusted their service provisions to Tarcoola such that services were available on a fortnightly basis. A timetable was formulated between the organisational team members and agreed to by the women in Tarcoola. This consultation was critical as it helped to empower the women in making a contribution to help meet their needs as service users.

The service provided

Women in the town were comfortable in using the hospital, and saw the support provided by the clinical nurses as critical to the well-being of women and children. A trusting relationship existed, and they viewed the nurses as their friends. The barriers between the professional nurses and service users were seen as minimal, allowing the nurses to gain a depth of understanding of the issues facing the women. Through the assistance of the nurses, I was able to interview several of the women about their service needs. The women were keen to share their need for parenting skills, and saw the establishment of the parents group as extremely positive.

The parents group was used by twelve women and ran for two sessions every three weeks during school terms. Each session ran for two hours, with the purpose of building self-esteem and helping to address the feelings of isolation felt by these parents in raising their children. Topics addressed in the parents group include the relationship between spouses, styles of parenting, age and stages of human development, behavioural and parental discipline. Various techniques were used to share the information within the group including the use of hand-outs, exercise sheets, videos, role-play, brainstorming and experiential games. The group was considered to be very useful by users. It provided an opportunity for sharing about themselves in a supportive environment. The women gained knowledge in the range of options available to disciplining their children.

The women were extremely appreciative of the child care provided while they were at the parents group. The children enjoyed the stimulation and were willing to learn from the exercises covered. It was seen as an opportunity for assisting with motor skills and social development.

The positive attitude of service providers was clearly evident in the outreach team. Whilst there was some uncertainty as to how they would relate to each other, there was also a sense of enthusiasm about sharing information with service users. This positiveness by service providers is considered essential by several writers if service co-ordination is to be effective (Gans & Horton 1975; Botsch 1988; Glisson & James 1992).

Similarly, several writers (Gans & Horton 1975; Halpert 1982) argue that service administrators having a positive attitude facilitates service co-ordination. With this outreach project administrators tended to be supportive, yet were aware of the time and energy given to this exercise. There was some concern expressed that giving time to this exercise may affect the time given to other areas.

Being receptive to the needs of the service users and providing services that are accessible are often highly valued in remote communities (Weetman 1993). Services were provided within the local community, co-ordinated through the nursing staff at the local hospital. By having this co-ordinated approach there was a decrease in fragmentation and duplication of service delivery. In fact the establishment of a team to assist in co-ordinating service delivery can be seen as an attempt to be sensitive and responsive to local needs. The willingness to meet with local service providers and residents was a clear example of responsiveness of needs.

Outcomes of the Tarcoola project

The service users were able to gain access to a greater range of co-ordinated services. They were able to establish a schedule of visits from the 'external' service providers that enabled them to achieve the best outcomes from the limited services available. This helped to increase their self-esteem and gave them a greater sense of control over their lives.

Service providers were now aware of what other organisations were able to offer, and thus were able to enhance resource options to their service users. Networking between the service providers in the different organisations was improved.

The improved service delivery to Tarcoola enabled service providers to be aware of the services available to the town. As a result of this awareness there was less overlap of services. They felt positive about their role in enhancing service delivery in Tarcoola.

An evaluation was carried out three months after the completion of the project. The evaluation was a simple exercise, where some of the service providers and users were asked to describe their thoughts and feelings after the event. Service providers indicated that they had achieved several positive outcomes. Firstly, there was a much greater appreciation of the needs of a small remote community. Secondly, both informal and formal networks with workers in the other participating organisations had been enhanced. Thirdly, the service providers thought that they had been received more positively by service users. Fourthly, a plan had been determined for organising visits which meant that staff could be aware in advance of their movements. Lastly, it helped to promote cultural change within organisations since people in the different organisations had greater knowledge of each other which enhanced their willingness to work together.

Service users, as indicated above, discussed their enhanced self-esteem. They indicated that there was also some breakdown of the tension between women who lived in the town and those who lived on the pastoral stations. One extremely positive outcome was their commitment to help one family move elsewhere because of the domestic violence to both the wife and children. They were uncertain that they would have given the support to the woman to move without the skills and knowledge gained from the parents group. The perpetrator was also informed that he was no longer wanted in Tarcoola.

There were some less positive aspects. Some service providers experienced tensions in their own organisations, as it was considered they devoted too much time to this project. Although service users were aware that much more could be gained from education yet there were extremely limited opportunities or facilities to meet this need. They recognised that to gain access to services they would have to move to larger communities.

Conclusion

The attempt to enhance service delivery to Tarcoola was an extremely beneficial exercise. It clearly demonstrated the need for human services organisations to work together to provide effective services. In the initial stages there were some difficulties in relation to funding, staffing and other 'teething problems' that occur when organisations attempt to establish working links. The outreach team was able to meet its objectives through the establishment of the parents group, offering child care, and enhancing local community involvement in meeting needs through the work of the local nurses coupled with greater awareness of needs from service providers 'external' to Tarcoola.

The parents group established as a result of the team project helped a number of people from different backgrounds to come together and share concerns, especially in relation to disciplining children. This outlet was invaluable in helping to break down barriers between the women. It provided them with 'time-out' from children, who also benefited substantially as willing participants in the child care activities.

Responding to the needs of the women in Tarcoola was important. A semi-formal structure of services was established to ensure that services were more efficiently co-ordinated. All service providers and service users were committed to this semi-formal structure.

The team approach identified the potential for human services to work together in remote areas. It provided an organisational framework that could be expanded upon to other remote areas. It provided a 'best practice' approach to remote areas (that is practice procedures, frameworks for service delivery, utilisation of professional people). Each service provider, with the support of their organisation, was focused towards enhancing service delivery to Tarcoola.

Whilst the decision of Australian National in 1997 to move the railway workers to the larger regional communities effectively closed most services in the town the model adopted in Tarcoola is one that could be used in other small remote communities.

References

Botsch, C. 1988, *Professionalism as a Barrier to Human Services Integration: A study of Service Providers' Attitudes*, Doctoral Thesis, University of South Carolina.

Cheers, B. 1992, 'Rural Social Work and Social Welfare in the Australian Context', in *Australian Social Work*, vol. 45, no. 2, pp. 1–21.

Cheers, B. 1994, 'Rural Social Work and Social Welfare in the Australian Context: A Rejoinder to Munn', in *Australian Social Work*, vol. 47, no. 1, pp. 55–8.

Gans, S.P. and Horton, G.T. 1975, Integration of Human Services The State and Municipal Levels, Praeger Publishers, New York.

Glisson, C & James, L. 1992, ' The Interorganizational Coordination of Services to Children in State Custody', in *Administration in Social Work*, vol. 16, no. 3/4, pp. 65–80.

Halpert, B. 1982, 'Antecedents' in Rodgers, D, & Whetten, D. A. (eds), *Interorganizational Coordination: Theory, Research and Implementation*, Iowa State University, Iowa.

Kennedy, R. 1997, 'Approaches to Coordination in Council of Social Service of New South Wales', in *Consultation and coordination in human service planning*, Pro Grafica, Petersham.

Martin, J. 1978, *The Migrant Presence*, George Allen and Sons, Sydney.

Martinez-Brawley, E.E. & Delevan, S.M. 1991, *Considerations on Integrative Structures. Conditions and Alternative Models for Country Human Services Delivery*, Centre for Rural Pennsylvania, University Park.

Munn, P. 1993, 'Reflections on Brian Cheers' Analysis for Rural Social Work in The Australian Context', in *Australian Social Work*, vol. 46, no. 4, pp. 49–51.

Munn, P. 1998, 'Service Coordination in Rural South Australia', PhD work-in-progress, Centre for Rural and Remote Area Studies, Whyalla.

Smith, B. 1989, 'Welfare Service Delivery: Options for Remote Areas', paper presented at Remote Area Social Welfare Practitioners Conference, Coober Pedy, South Australia.

Weetman, N. 1993, 'Coordination of Service Delivery to Remote Areas: The Outreach Team Project—SALTBUSH', (Progress Report), Remote and Isolated Children's Exercise Inc, unpublished.

Weiss, J.A. 1987, 'Pathways to Cooperation Among Public Agencies', in *Journal of Policy Analysis and Management*, vol. 7, no. 1, pp. 94–117.

Whetten, D.A. 1977, ' Towards a Contingency Model For Designing Inter-Organisational Delivery Systems', in Burack, E.H, & Negandhi, A.R. (eds), *Organisation Design: Theoretical Perspectives and Empirical Findings*, Kent State University Press, Kent.

13

By the people for the people

A rural community radio station

David Barlow

Introduction

Until the early 1970s, radio in Australia was delivered by a two-sector broadcasting system consisting of the ABC (as the national public service broadcaster) and the commercial services. Dissatisfaction with the programming offered by both sectors prompted a movement for a new form of radio. Not unlike overseas experience, criticism focused on the style and approach of the two dominant models and in particular the exclusion, distortion or marginalisation of minority interests and issues, resulting in a lack of adequate programming for all sections of the community (Lewis 1984, p. 140). Those advocating change included educationalists, ethnic groups, trade unionists, religious groups, music buffs, members of Aboriginal and Torres Strait Islander communities and a myriad of other individuals and community organisations (see, for example, Bear 1980, p. 25; Law 1986, p. 3; Mayer 1976, p. 166).

The first licences for community (then known as public) radio stations were issued between 1972 and 1975 during the Whitlam Australian Labor Party government (Harding 1979 p. 10), but it was not until 1978 under Malcolm

Fraser's Liberal-Country Party Coalition government that the new sector was enshrined in legislation (Harding 1979, p. 92). Since that time the community broadcasting sector has continued to expand. Of the current 216 licensed community radio stations,[1] 150 are located in rural and remote communities, and with 100 of the 170-plus aspirant broadcasting groups expecting to be licensed in the next year or so, Australia will have in excess of 300 community radio stations by the new millennium (Community Broadcasting Foundation 1996, p. 7).

At a time when the nation is expecting a deluge of new radio and other media services via satellite, microwave, cable and the Internet, and ABC and commercial radio services are turning to syndication and networking to reduce costs—and, by implication, local presence and local content[2]—continuing interest in radio for purposes of community development rather than commercial gain is to be welcomed. Constituted as community media rather than mass media, community radio stations share many of the characteristics of non-government community organisations, that is: a local focus, providing information and services for a specific locality; community ownership; a non-profit orientation; reliance on a number of funding sources; dependence on volunteers as unpaid workers and fund-raisers; the provision of services that can be accessed without charge; and a commitment to some form of community improvement and individual empowerment (Barlow 1995, p. 240).

This chapter draws on the study of a rural community radio station to illustrate the potential of a community controlled, locally oriented, community communications medium. Data was acquired by way of in-depth interviews (Minichiello, Aroni, Timewell & Alexander 1990, p. 87), documentary sources, direct observation and participation by the writer in some activities at the radio station. Interviews were conducted with a variety of participants associated with the station using a semi-structured interview schedule developed around themes of access and participation, diversity and plurality, independence, non-profit and non-commercial, and alternative, deemed the 'key elements' of community broadcasting (Barlow forthcoming).

A recursive approach to questioning (Minichiello et al. 1990, p. 112) was used and all interviews were taped and later transcribed. NU.DIST—Non-numerical Unstructured Data Indexing Searching and Theorising—software (Qualitative Solutions & Research Pty Ltd 1995) was used to help organise the data, but analysis and coding was carried out manually and 'off-line'. As access to the research site was dependent on an agreement of anonymity, the names of the radio station, location and respondents have been disguised.

The radio station in context

Seaview and Hilldene are small rural communities located near a state border and equidistant from two capital cities. For local residents, travel to either capital city involves a road journey of at least seven hours as there are no rail services in the area. With a population of 200, Hilldene is a three business community, containing a service station, pub and shop. Farming and logging are its major industries but both are in decline. Situated on the coast, Seaview is a community of 1000 people, which swells substantially during peak holiday periods. The only road access into Seaview is from Hilldene, a journey of 23 kilometres. It has been the pattern for years that Hilldene residents drive to Seaview for a number of local services, but due to the limited size of the two communities a 90-minute journey to larger centres of population is necessary if major consumer items are required.

Seaview has a resident doctor and dentist, but the nearest hospital requires a two-hour drive and the recently moved shire offices, previously located in Seaview, now involve a three-hour journey. Limited allied health and welfare services are supplemented by visiting workers. Seaview and Hilldene also rely on a mobile library service and there are no public transport services in or between the two towns. Apart from some light industry, Seaview's economy is reliant on tourism. Both communities receive ABC television and radio services along with two commercial television channels, but reception of commercial radio services is patchy with none physically located in the area. In addition to the usual major daily newspapers, there is a weekly local community newspaper published by the post-primary school.

Radio station SHB-FM is managed and operated by Seaview and Hilldene Broadcasting (SHB), a community-based non-profit organisation established with the express purpose of developing a local radio station. The current organisational structure consists of an annually elected Board of Directors, which formulates and ratifies station policy, and a Management Committee responsible for day-to-day operations. SHB-FM broadcasts on weekdays between 7 a.m. and 1 p.m. and on a 24-hour basis at weekends. Although the majority of programs are locally generated, the station does use a satellite 'feed' overnight at weekends. With no paid staff, SHB-FM is an all-voluntary operation, relying on approximately 50 'on-air' presenters plus another ten people acting in a variety of support roles. The station survives primarily on revenue generated from business sponsor announcements supplemented by fund-raising and donations. SHB-FM is situated in Seaview and the signal relayed to Hilldene. In keeping with its commitment to ensure community access and participation in the management and operation of the station, SHB-FM constantly seeks more presenters, business sponsors and others willing to be involved in fund-raising and other non-broadcasting roles. There is even a sense of obligation about accepting anyone requesting involvement in the station.

A cursory overview of those interviewed for the study gives some indication of the diversity of backgrounds and how they became involved with the station. Ranging in age from 11 to 75 years, both genders were equally represented. In addition to those engaged in home duties, at school, retired or unemployed, the interviewees included a landscape gardener, cruise boat crew member, neighbourhood house worker, teacher, minister of religion, small business operator, supermarket employee and a professional musician. How they came to be involved with SHB-FM varied from receiving a personal invitation on the basis of their technical or entrepreneurial skills, responding to requests for assistance by the station in the local newspaper, making a casual enquiry while holidaying in the area, or simply being 'roped in' by friends or relatives already associated with the station. Motivation ranged from seeking a new interest or hobby, the possibility of a media career, wanting to contribute to community life, seeking self-improvement and/or an enhanced self-image, or simply enjoying music and the thrill of playing it for others. Whatever the motivation, none had previously aspired to being a radio broadcaster nor imagined themselves in such a position, but were nevertheless enjoying the experience.

A community pulse

The nature of SHB-FM's relationship with the communities of Seaview and Hilldene suggests an unusual intimacy. With all involved in the radio station residing, studying and working—paid or unpaid—in Seaview and Hilldene, SHB-FM acts as a form of 'community pulse'. This is very much what the station's pioneers envisaged, but their original motivation was provoked by events in 1983 when bush fires threatened to engulf the community of Seaview. Establishing a radio station that could operate as a local communications centre and update residents on evacuation procedures in cases of emergency was seen as a way of compensating for a lack of localised electronic media. While the absence of other local radio services is now seen as a competitive advantage, all involved remain acutely aware of the station's history and hope it will be never be required to fulfil its original purpose. SHB-FM's primary role today is to provide entertainment and information programming for the populations of Seaview and Hilldene.

SHB-FM's 'spoken-word' (as opposed to music) programs include two news and current affairs shows plus programs offered by the neighbourhood house, a local church, the school, and a group consisting of members of local sports clubs, all of which are broadcast weekly. The daily breakfast shows also include news and current affairs segments along with community announcements interspersed with music. The remainder of the station's programs are essentially music based. A brief overview of some of the information oriented programs provides an indication of their breadth and focus.

The neighbourhood house often involves visiting health and welfare workers in their programs. Examples have included interviews with a visiting bush nurse promoting a 'spot check' day for skin cancer, a family services worker outlining services available to women and children, and a representative from the Department of Social Security informing about changes to family and child benefits. Staff at the neighbourhood house stress the importance of these programs, indicating that the radio bridges local concerns about anonymity and confidentiality by providing information to people who are (or feel) unable to access services in person. It is often the case that such programs are followed by telephone calls from people seeking clarification or help with the matters discussed.

The school program is co-ordinated by a teachers aide, whose role is to facilitate the preparation of programs by students in school and then co-ordinate the live broadcast from the station. Each weekly program includes story telling, a book and video review, a report on local sports, plus a selection of music. Students from grades 1–6 are involved in designing and contributing to the program, but the broadcast is executed by those in grades 5 and 6 and heard by all contributors tuned in at school. It is customary for the broadcasters to receive a cheer when they return to the classroom.

Although prepared and presented by the minister and his wife from the Uniting Church, the church program garners information from all religious denominations in the area. Contemporary social issues are discussed with the aid of resource material supplied by Christian organisations and complemented by a variety of Christian and popular music. As a result of feedback through a variety of sources, the presenters of each of the above programs acknowledge their surprise about the number and variety of people listening.

The two weekly news and current affairs shows concentrate on matters of general public interest, the rationale being that ABC and commercial radio and television services very seldom address such issues. Referring specifically to the 'local' ABC radio, most respondents were keen to point out that the nearest station broadcasts from a town at least four hours drive from Seaview and Hilldene and condenses news from a vast geographic region into a few daily five-minute timeslots. Even when issues of local relevance are included, they are very seldom followed up. This is contrasted with SHB-FM, which is 'able to keep issues alive … and have them debated over several weeks' (presenter and member of the board of directors). Amongst a range of topics, these two programs have included on-air debates about the impact of changes to local government boundaries, involved local politicians and government bureaucrats in studio discussions about the reduction of fish species in local waterways, and broadcast recorded coverage of local council meetings. In addition to its formal programs, the station's capacity to update and disseminate a range of information, both substantial and otherwise, is aided by its central location and welcoming aura:

> … *people ring up or trot up the stairs with something saying we have got this*
> *happening can you announce it, or the shop is going to be closed for a couple of hours …*
> *or [there is] a raffle to raise money to send a couple of kids to Tasmania to be in a soccer*
> *team, so all the presenters will go through in their own time slot and promote that raffle*
> *and the cause, and so things like that are happening all the time.*
>
> (presenter)

In the tourist season the radio station is used to provide details on lost and found children, announcements about caravan and camping grounds and advice on dangerous areas for boating. Locals also use it to locate their lost pets. With some justification, one respondent was moved to suggest that the station is 'slowly becoming a backbone of the community' (presenter and member of the management committee).

Catalysing growth

Whilst all involved with SHB-FM hasten to focus on concrete achievements, such as the 'home built' studio and almost exclusively 'home grown' programming provided by an all-voluntary organisation, there is acknowledgment of less tangible outcomes which might be considered 'by-products' of a process that encourages and sustains the involvement of local people.

SHB-FM has provided local residents with an opportunity to swap their previous passive media habits for active involvement. Even with an open invitation to become involved, a number of respondents admitted their initial reluctance due to a belief that they did not have the 'right voice' for radio or the required technical knowledge and skills. Since overcoming these and other hurdles and becoming involved in preparing and broadcasting radio programs, all respondents are emphatic about the benefits. Most reported increases in self-confidence and self-esteem and a strong sense of satisfaction in overcoming the technical challenges of the studio, in particular, 'the [control] panel'—seen by many as the real monster! One respondent recalled her first experience, 'I was quite enjoying it … even though I was still shaking. I found at the end I was getting a real buzz because it was so hard to do and accomplish' (presenter). The consensus is that once a few programs have been completed initial apprehension is replaced by a noticeable increase in on-air confidence, which in turn leads to more sophisticated presentation skills.

Contrary to the experience of some participants whose involvement in the station is in addition to an already busy schedule involving paid employment, social and family life and other community activities, SHB-FM has provided others with an opportunity to find meaning in lives where it has been lacking. Now undertaking a number of roles at the station, one respondent acknowledged participation had increased his self-confidence and circle of friends, as well as allowing him a chance 'to show the Pension Board that I am capable of working' (presenter). For this person and other participants, the station provides a role that is valued by the community, even to the extent of generating mini-celebrity status, and, in some instances, allows fellow citizens an opportunity to re-evaluate previous negative stereotyping. SHB-FM also provides an opportunity for people of all ages who are simply looking for a hobby or a more satisfying social life. One respondent, who develops his music collection through visits to Op (portunity) Shops, reflected on his own experience and that of his colleagues:

*'SHB-FM is good for people like myself ... sometimes it gives me the shits and all that,
but it gives me something to do and I know that there are lots of other presenters [who
feel the same way], they have really dived into it, they are loving it.*

(presenter and member of the board of directors)

A number of respondents commented on how involvement with SHB-FM
has assisted with the acquisition or enhancement of social and vocational skills.
The most oft quoted example was the school program. Now somewhat of an 'old
hand' at eleven years of age, having commenced broadcasting at nine, one
respondent described the process employed by her and her co-presenter:

*When we do our book reviews we usually work them out and write them up on the
computer at school. Sometimes we change it on-air as we go depending on how it is
going. Our scripts for the show are also typed up on the computer.*

(presenter)

Participation in the radio station was suggested as a precursor to
developments in other life spheres. Referring to an all-women program in which
she participated, one respondent likened the radio experience to a stepping stone:
'I have watched women just blossom in working with the radio station. It
improves their confidence and everything, and then they take steps to do other
things' (presenter). Others believed the analytical and communications skills
developed through the process of preparing and delivering programs enhanced
performance at interviews and improved chances of obtaining employment or
accessing tertiary education.

The station was also seen as helping reduce the isolation of listeners, not
only through the provision of information and entertainment, but by way of its
'personalised voice' which was often contrasted with the anonymity of other
radio stations. The words of one respondent encapsulate the views of others:

*Have you ever realised that listening to the voice of somebody you actually know is really
nice on the radio. Like a lot of people say, I just like turning on SHB-FM because it is the
voice of somebody that I know, and so I think that I might be filling a role for people who
are living isolated lives. If they know you from down the street and they turn on the
radio and you are there, it is like you are in their living room, not an anonymous face,
you are Jan with three kids who works at the neighbourhood house and yes, I have seen
her cook fish and chips and all that sort of thing.*

(presenter)

There was also a sense of the radio station acting as a community forum, its
voice attracting the participation of people from all echelons of the two
communities, and in doing so, developing and strengthening individual and
community networks. Reliance on local people as program makers and
presenters, it was suggested, also contributes to the oral history of the area,
increases awareness about hitherto unknown human resources and broadens
people's horizons.

Conclusion

With the ABC unlikely to be in a position to increase the quality and quantity of public service broadcasting at the sub-regional level and commercial networks unable (and/or unwilling) to fill the void for different reasons, the following comments about the role of localised non-profit community media are pertinent:

> *The need for locally oriented media to confront oligopolist and transnational cultural industries will become more urgent in the coming years. Non-commercial and locally oriented media as social and cultural tools—and not as mass media in local disguise— can play an important part in strengthening local identity and self-respect.*

(Prehn 1992, p. 266).

SHB-FM epitomises the thrust of this message. In all conversations before and after interviews and during the interviews themselves, there was never an occasion when the radio station was discussed as a discrete entity. All remarks, observations and analysis considered SHB-FM in the context of its two host communities, perhaps best illustrated through the words of one respondent, 'it's not just what the radio does for the community, but what the community does for the radio' (presenter and member of the board of directors). Maintaining and strengthening this mutually beneficial relationship between radio and community is viewed by participants as essential if SHB-FM is to improve the quality of community life, a goal identified in its original licence application.

The natural affiliation between community broadcasters and locality has always been cited as a strength of this third sector of radio since it was highlighted by the Minister for Post and Telecommunications when introducing the initial legislation. Community broadcasters, he suggested, 'should have a better appreciation of the interests, hence needs of their broadcasting communities than anyone else, including government' (Staley 1978, p. 2). The current federal Coalition government in 1998 appears keen to maintain and strengthen the relationship between community broadcasters and other community-based organisations. A recent policy initiative has encouraged the sector's involvement in the 'information age' by suggesting community broadcasting stations as 'access points' for community information and government services made available via the Internet's World Wide Web (WWW) information retrieval system (Department of Communications and the Arts 1997, pp. 25–6). To facilitate such an eventuality, the government has provided funding to the community broadcasting sector which should result in most community radio stations having an Internet connection within the next few months.[3] The government has also encouraged community broadcasters to look towards organisations in the community sector as potential partners for community-oriented ventures (Department of Communications and the Arts 1997, p. 25). Aware of these initiatives, ACOSS is also encouraging community sector organisations to consider how they might become more involved with community broadcasting groups for the betterment of individuals and communities (Australian Council of Social Service 1996, p. 102).

Whether it be through radio, video, print, or a convergence of all three media in 'online' form via the Internet, publicly owned and operated community media organisations are clearly in a position to play a key role in rural and remote communities in the context of what is fast becoming a commercially oriented multi-channel global media and communications environment.

Notes

1   This includes the 83 stations established under the Broadcasting for Remote Aboriginal Communities (BRACS) program (see, for example, Meadows 1992).

2   Developments of this nature have implications for rural and remote communities. For instance, mergers between commercial radio organisations have resulted in fewer owners and larger networks and the decline of solus stations in regional Australia is expected to continue as they are 'swallowed' by multi-station groups (Peters 1996, p. 8). With syndicated music, news and current affairs programs (most of which are produced in metropolitan centres) available at a fraction of the cost of local production, some are forecasting a proliferation of automated radio stations linked by satellite to city-based program providers, leading to a loss of diversity and an erosion of locality (see, for example, Randall 1993, p. 3). Evidence of some of these trends can be observed by the John Laws radio program which is received in 74% of Australia's 96 radio markets, 75 of which are in regional areas (Communications Update, 1997, p. 7), and the Sky News service (owned by Sydney-based commercial radio station 2UE) which is distributed by satellite into 91% of Australia's metropolitan and regional radio markets (Communications Update, 1997, p. 7).

3   The now partly implemented infrastructure package involves a grant of $1.5 m over three years to develop a Community Access Network (CAN), Community Broadcasting Database (CBD) and upgrade the current community broadcasting satellite, ComRadSat. The CBD will enable on-line access to management, marketing, training, audience survey and technical resource information about the sector, while the CAN will allow community broadcasters access to the CBD, a multimedia capacity and the ability to provide community information services.

References

Australian Council of Social Service 1996, *Electronic Communication and the Community Sector*, ACOSS Paper no. 81, September.

Barlow, D.M. 1995, 'Effective Partnerships Between Community Groups and Radio', in McDonald, D.J. & Cleave, L.R. (eds), *Partnerships that work?*, proceedings of the 1995 Regional Social Services Conference, 20–23 November, 1995, Christchurch, New Zealand, Department of Social Work, University of Canterbury.

Barlow, D.M. (forthcoming), *The Promise, Performance and Future of Community Broadcasting in Australia*, PhD thesis, Department of Media Studies, School of Arts and Media, Faculty of Humanities and Social Science, La Trobe University, Bundoora, Victoria.

Bear, A. 1980, 'The Development of Ethnic Broadcasting in Relation to Public Broadcasting', in *Media Information Australia*, February, no. 15, pp. 24–7.

Communications Update 1997, 'Media Ownership in 1996', in *Communications Update*, issue 129, February, pp. 6–8.

Community Broadcasting Foundation 1996, *Discussion Papers on New Funding Initiatives*, Community Broadcasting Foundation, Fitzroy.

Department of Communications and the Arts 1997, *A New Funding Model and Future Strategy for the Community Broadcasting Sector*, Discussion Paper, Department of Communications and the Arts, March.

Harding, R. 1979, *Outside Interference—The Politics of Australian Broadcasting*, Sun Books, Melbourne.

Law, M. 1986, 'Public Radio: where is it headed and will it get there?', in *Media Information Australia*, August, no. 41, pp. 31–5.

Lewis, P.M. 1984, 'Community Radio: the Montreal Conference and after', in *Media Culture and Society*, no. 6, pp. 137–50.

Mayer, H. 1976, 'What should (and could) we do about the media?', in Major, G. (ed.), *Mass Media in Australia*, Hodder and Stoughton, Sydney, pp. 164–264.

McKay, S. 1996, 'Closure Cuts the Choice of News', *The Age*, 16 January, p. 3.

Meadows, M. 1992, *A Watering Can in the Desert: Issues in Indigenous Broadcasting Policy in Australia.*, Institute for Cultural Policy Studies, Faculty of Humanities, Griffiths University, Queensland.

Minichiello, V., Aroni, R., Timewell, E., & Alexander, L. 1990, *In-Depth Interviewing—Researching People*, Longman Cheshire, Melbourne.

Peters, B. 1996, 'Radio: Calm Before the Storm', in *Communications Update*, issue 118, February, p. 8.

Prehn, O. 1992, 'From Small Scale Utopianism to Large Scale Pragmatism', in Jankowski, N., Prehn O., & Stappers, J. (eds), *The People's Voice: Local Radio and Television in Europe*, Academia Research Monograph 6, John Libbey, London, pp. 247–66.

Randall, L. 1993, 'Syndication Steadily Erodes Localism', in *Communications Update*, issue 85, February, p. 26.

Staley, A.A. 1978, *Development of Public Broadcasting*, Ministerial Statement, Commonwealth Government Printer, Canberra.

Qualitative Solutions & Research Pty Ltd 1995, *Workshop Manual for Q.S.R. NUD.IST qualitative data analysis software*, Qualitative Solutions & Research Pty Ltd, Melbourne, Australia.

14

Sharing the space and blurring the boundaries*

Jan Brand & Ann Kesting

Introduction

This chapter describes a client-centred, collaborative and team-focused service delivery system developed for women in a rural environment. Illustrated by case examples, a model utilised by two workers co-located at the Murray Mallee Community Health Service in Murray Bridge, South Australia, has been designed to provide the best possible service to respond to the local milieu, drawing on the expertise of two seemingly divergent disciplines.

The authors work within a context of limited resources, long distances, and a traditional rural culture. The challenge for us was to determine how two workers, from seemingly opposing philosophies and disciplines, could develop a team approach to providing an efficient and effective rural service within a feminist framework. Ann Kesting is a Community Mental Health nurse and Jan Brand is a Women's Health social worker and counsellor. Both are employed in

---

* This chapter is an expanded version of an article with the same title, which appeared in *Stateing Women's Health*, vol. 7, no. 3, 1997

case management capacities. Jan has thirteen years experience in social work and community development in remote and rural areas, and takes a broad view of the woman in society. Ann, a community-based nurse for the past 15 years, takes a broad view of the health of an individual, incorporating both clinical and social views of health.

The Murray Mallee and the service

The Murray Mallee has a population of 29 471 (ABS 1996) and covers an area of 21 132 square kilometres. Its agricultural base is mainly broadacre farming with some diversification. The main townships are Pinnaroo, Lameroo, Meningie and Karoonda, each with estimated populations of 600. The main service town is Murray Bridge, with a population of 12 831. Travelling time to Pinnaroo (furthest point) from Murray Bridge, round trip, is an estimated four hours on sealed roads.

We are approximately one hour's drive from Adelaide, with limited public transport. Murray Bridge and the Murray Mallee fall into a rural 'never-land' where we are not far enough away to have designated remote services, but too far for easy and convenient access to Adelaide services and resources. Murray Bridge has a high percentage of Housing Trust (public housing) areas.

The Murray Mallee area does not have a mobile mental health crisis response team as does the metropolitan area. We have access to a 24 hours per day, 7 days per week, toll free, adult mental health service number staffed mainly by nurses, with access to a psychiatrist as required. We have a part-time clinical service delivery mental health team.

We now have easy access to video-conferencing (telemedicine) for a psychiatric assessment by a consultant psychiatrist from Adelaide, which has been a real boon. No more treks to Adelaide for psychiatric assessment, with its waiting around and dislocation from local familiar networks, when a women is under stress.

This system was established by South Australian Rural and Remote Mental Health Service. Access by Women's Health has been a major breakthrough, with telemedicine offering a realistic choice of service to women. Urgent assessment can be scheduled for the same day, or next day at latest. There is a choice of a female psychiatrist. With mutual clients, both the mental and women's health workers are able to sit in on the session, providing support from both disciplines and then mutually developing strategies, in consultation with the client.

Telemedicine has been particularly successful with adult survivors of child sexual assault, where any involvement in the mental health services is often short-term intervention. Flashbacks of experiences can be distressing and confusing, requiring assessment in relation to possible psychotic episodes.

Jan, as the half-time Women's Health Counsellor, provides a counselling service on a one-to-one basis, usually based at Murray Mallee Community Health

Service, Murray Bridge, but she also provides an outreach service if requested to do so. With long distances to travel, both for workers and clients, efficient and focused use of resources, both human and material, is paramount in providing a quality service to a client.

Clients and cases are shared. A mental health client may require women's health intervention, or a women's health client may require a psychiatric assessment; or the presenting issues in a case may be so complex that the only efficient way to handle them is for more than one worker to be involved.

Working as a team

In our approach, with the emphasis on collaborative team work, we believe we have developed a response which can broaden our skills base and gain understanding of quality service provision to our clients. In so doing, we need to put aside the delineation between disciplines, and look at the skills required in order that the client has access to the best we can offer. As Darlington (1996, p. 121) states:

> approaches are recommended which emphasise collaboration between worker and client and which truly regard a woman as an expert, both on her own experience and on what is best for her.

Collaboration gives us the opportunity of sharing our client's space and blurring our discipline boundaries.

There are five key elements in our collaborative practice:

- sharing a similar philosophical base;
- clarity of tasks and division of labour;
- communication;
- respecting clients by taking time to listen to women's stories;
- clarity about achievable and realistic goals.

Sharing a similar philosophy

We both believe in early intervention and education in order that a woman can make informed choices. 'The client remains the expert of her own life' (Keddy 1996, p. 389). In our response we, as workers, are 'creating a process in which the use of such skills as validation, empowerment and demystification increases their [the women's] sense of having options for themselves' (Goodrich, Rampage, Ellman, Halstead 1988, p. 28).

We believe we are developing a process of understanding that respects the differences between our disciplines. This forms a common philosophy supported by a common language that draws on both disciplines, is underpinned by feminist and primary health care principles of self-determination and social justice, and recognises the need for our own support and nurturing and a genuine concern for the well-being of other women. Within this framework, Jan had to confront issues around the use of medication, and working in a rural community that does not have access to an institutionally secure environment when a client is at risk. In many ways, this can be seen as being in direct conflict with feminist notions of empowerment and control by the client, and our supporting her to develop her own coping capacities.

Ann was also confronted with issues relating to relinquishing power and giving back control to the client. This issue is identified by Peplau (1995, cited in Hall 1996, p. 23), 'that instead of seeing symptoms as indicators of disease, nurses would do better to see them as problem-solving actions that have a highly individual meaning and purpose'. Peplau also reiterates Hall's advice for mental health nurses to put aside professionally learned thinking about who is the healer and give back to people their right to heal themselves in consultation with a nurse (Peplau 1995, Hall 1996).

The clinical and social issues in the following scenario, demonstrate feminist principles with practitioners working together.

Approximately three years ago 'Mary', a young woman with a diagnosed psychiatric disability, who had suffered many losses and was in a state of grief, contacted the mental health team. Was she acutely mentally ill, or was she overwhelmed with grief? Was this a medical issue or a social one? Or did one feed into the other? By being labelled already as seriously mentally ill, where was the primary focus for our intervention? Later it was revealed that Mary had been sexually abused as a child. Choices were presented to Mary: increase her medication so that it masked her past experiences or try to work through the issues that were overwhelming her and perhaps resolve some of them.

Mary decided to confront her issues, and so for a short period of time Jan became Mary's primary worker in a therapeutic relationship as a counsellor. Although Mary had a history of child sexual abuse, we focused on supporting her to gain self-respect and self-confidence, whilst she continued to take her regular medication for her mental illness. This enabled Mary to move on and become less reliant on the mental health system. She has since spoken at a Women and Mental Health seminar, and has read her poetry at 'Arts in Action' venues.

That is how it all began, as a joint venture between the Community Mental Health nurse and the Women's Health counsellor: a melding of the various views of health, to the benefit of women.

Clarity of tasks and division of labour

The need for clarity is highlighted by the example of 'Barbara', with whom we both worked. Barbara lived on a farm one hour's drive from Murray Bridge. Because of the distance involved, Ann and Jan travelled together on the first visit, and this provided an opportunity for a joint assessment. The services were immediately available, and strategies put in place without protracted appointments with one worker and then another. This provided a less fragmented approach to service delivery, and a more efficient use of worker time.

Initially, we did not agree on an appropriate response to Barbara, who, on referral, had a diagnosis of depression with suicidal thoughts. As Barbara was assessed at the home visit to be in a high risk situation, Anne's immediate response was to argue that Barbara be transported to a place of safety, that is, admission to hospital. Barbara also saw this as her preferred but temporary option, and wished to have delayed admission in order to sort out her domestic situation. This situation involved the care of her six children, which combined with a complex range of other issues confronting Barbara.

Jan, coming from a women's health and social work framework, acknowledged Barbara's previous abusive experiences of institutions and was concerned in regard to the effect for her of a premature hospital admission. Ann acknowledged these factors, but believed that Barbara's safety was the paramount issue as she was presenting as a risk to herself. Under Section A of the *South Australian Mental Health Act*, this constitutes grounds for detention for appropriate medical assessment and treatment.

Barbara saw herself as being completely powerless within her environment. Given her history of abuse and oppression by institutions and within relationships, it was imperative that we employed strategies that enabled and assisted Barbara to make decisions that acknowledged her as the expert of her own life, whilst also acknowledging that some situations were beyond her control.

Barbara expressed strong concerns in relation to the care and well-being of her six children. A plan was developed in conjunction with her partner for the care of the children if she were to be admitted to hospital. By engaging Barbara and her husband in the logistics of organising the children, and the anticipation of imminent safety and sanctuary in hospital, Barbara agreed that she could maintain control with daily phone support and access to the 24 hour adult mental health services contact number until admission.

A delayed planned admission was not within the normal processes of the admitting hospital, and therefore Ann played a strong advocacy role. 'We must experience some power, some organizational and interdisciplinary esteem and meaningful authority, in order to make these qualities available for those with whom we work' (Labonte 1997, p. 64).

Because of its complexity and the associated high-risk conditions, this case was considered beyond the scope of any one system. In collaboration with Barbara, we structured a case management plan that divided the issues and developed strategies, enabling everyone to be clear about their roles and responsibilities, including Barbara. For more efficient use of resources, because of both the distance and complexity involved, we relied heavily on the telephone to communicate to Barbara and other key people.

Much of the process involved knowing and using the local rural community networks. The women from the Lutheran Guild were more than prepared to help with the washing, preparing casseroles for the family and providing respite for the parents. It was a case of ringing up Helen who would speak to Joan, and along through the community networks. And if they could not help then they knew who would. We believe that rural workers are much more embedded in the local networks and know how to relate to their community in a way that does not happen in the city. The constraint to this way of working is the need for confidentiality, so being very clear with your client about the process you wish to undertake and getting their permission is paramount to the successful use of community networks.

Supporting Barbara in finding a way through the complexity of problems, and engaging her in this process, provided a learning experience for her. It had the effect of lowering her stress as she developed the ability to unravel her problems and lessen her feelings of being overwhelmed by them. This problem-solving process, which shared knowledge rather than withholding it, enabled Barbara to develop positive coping skills that she was able to integrate into her on-going life skills.

Initially we spent a lot of time with Barbara and her family, as well as utilising case conferences and co-ordinating the services used. After about six weeks, we were able to decrease our involvement as some problems were resolved and the family felt able to use the services with which they wished to continue.

Barbara's case highlighted for us how, together, the services of Mental Health and Women's Health could offer a more comprehensive approach. This enabled her mental health status to be monitored, but also recognised the gender-specific principles and social constructs to be taken into account and responded to when working with Barbara. Clarifying tasks lessened the potentially conflicting aspects of a social versus clinical response.

Barbara had been oppressed and disadvantaged all her life, firstly by the system and then in her marriage. This needed to be acknowledged through Jan as the Women's Health social worker and by Ann as her advocate when back in the 'system'.

Effective communication

The co-location of both the Mental Health and Women's Health teams at Murray Mallee Community Health Service, Murray Bridge, certainly helped the process of communication. Communication is easier if meetings can be informal as well as formal.

Community Health also provided a common ground of organisational support in regard to primary health care principles embedded in social justice ideology. 'Health is rooted in our social experiences ... it is this holistic concept of health that many people working in community health use to distinguish their work from medicine' (Labonte 1997, p64). These concepts are also at the root of feminist service provision.

What has also helped is that we each have a complementary style of interacting, and a shared sense of humour. This has also included being open in our communication and willing to abide by the ground rules of trusting, sharing and learning, and respecting each other, for critical feedback to be of benefit. We held many discussions and conversations as to how to gain clarity in our common interpretations of feminist principles, and how they related to our particular disciplines and were then translated in our work.

Respecting clients by taking time to listen to women's stories

It was clear right from the start that we would not be agreeing on everything in relation to a client's support, so what became obvious very early on was the fourth key—taking time to listen to women's stories, which became the common ground for developing strategies.

Once accepting the premise that 'the client remains the expert of her own life' (Darlington 1996), we, as practitioners, needed to actively listen, then to translate, using our knowledge base, skills and resources, to develop appropriate strategies that were neither disempowering nor paternalistic. We elicited responses from our client using our particular discipline base, skills framework, assessments and style. This blending of knowledge from our respective disciplines was combined with an understanding of our limitations, factors of distance, the need for confidentiality, and the availability of human and material resources within a rural community. The development of appropriate and realistic responses arose from the merging of our knowledge with what women told us about their immediate needs and their perceptions of their world.

For example, we have found that in rural communities isolation is often at the basis of a woman's depression. So setting aside time to listen to a woman's story is critical to our joint practice. It may become apparent that it would be more appropriate to find creative ways of assisting her with transport in order to increase her social contacts, than to rely solely on medication to alleviate her depression. As quoted in the *Expanding Possibilities: Women and depression project*, auspiced by Statewide Women's Health, Adelaide: 'You're given Prozac with no looking at what is going on in your life' (Morgan 1997, p.16). During this time we also encourage women to reflect on their position in society, and to become more informed about alternatives.

This combination of information provided a richer picture of a client and her needs. We had to be clear about our own agenda to the client and to ourselves. It was all about 'starting where the client is'. This made it much easier to make decisions about intervention strategies, when the expressed and felt needs of the client were the focus for developing strategies.

Clarity about achievable and realistic goals

Once a crisis situation has diminished it is vital that long-term plans are negotiated and set in place to lessen the danger of re-occurrence. We have found that post-crisis, women are looking to make long-term plans, especially if they have gained a greater sense of control through learning problem-solving skills and have a heightened sense of self-worth.

'Sonia' had a history of severe childhood abuse and rape. She decided, through a process of dealing with some of her abuse, that she was ready to confront one of her underlying causes of her panic and anxiety—a fear of fire, which was directly related to her abuse.

After an initial assessment via the teleconferencing facility, Sonia was admitted to the Anxiety Disorders Unit at a General Metropolitan Hospital as a planned admission. Through cognitive behavioural techniques used in their exposure program, which lasted nine weeks, she learned long-term strategies. This was a big step for Sonia who had previously survived by moving from one crisis to the next.

During this time both workers stayed in touch with Sonia, and Jan, as case manager, engaged in the final debriefing and information process, given by the hospital, to support Sonia on her return home.

Conclusion

With the greater interaction of Women's Health with Mental Health in Murray Mallee, a better understanding has evolved of the role of psychiatric medicine, and there has been greater recognition by other professionals from a medical model of the value of a strong social and feminist framework, particularly when working with abused women.

We believe the use of collaborative service outcomes has been positive for both workers and clients. For the workers, although there was an initial intensive involvement there was also an early withdrawal from the case, leaving the client describing herself as more self-reliant. Women have appreciated the clarity of our roles and the safety that this provided by having access to either service. As Sonia said, 'All bases were covered'.

More work needs to be done on evaluation of this process. We have relied on qualitative informal feedback from clients concerned as well as looking at the frequency of service usage, including re-admission rates, which appear to be reduced. Because this collaborative team response is still new to our organisation, it would seem appropriate to develop an evaluation process that engages women who have not requested a service for some time.

For workers the outcomes have been that we each have a deeper understanding and appreciation of the other's work. We have more imagination and motivation to tackle what needs to be done, and to be involved in these processes of change. Amongst an array of confusing and often contradictory interests of clients and services both Ann and Jan have been delighted to see clients move on in their lives, gaining in confidence and creativity.

To work effectively together, we have both had significant shifts in our thinking. For Ann, as a nurse, who works with people who are marginalised by virtue of their mental illness, it has highlighted the value of a collaborative response using a gender-based perspective in order to better advocate for these women as individuals, within a feminist framework. From a social worker and women's health perspective, Jan has acknowledged, with great difficulty, the place that medication may have to support some women.

Every woman has the right to feel safe and secure, and to develop a quality of life that is unique for her. This does not detract from the ongoing need to continue the debate in regard to establishing egalitarian social relationships for women and to continue to reframe women's experience within the social context. It is imperative that we as workers do not pathologise gender-based problems but continue to view them as a social construct.

By working closely with the client, and having strong communication between mental and women's health workers, we are sharing our space and blurring the boundaries for the benefit of the women with whom we work.

References

Astbury, J. 1996, *Crazy for you: The making of women's madness*, Oxford University Press, Australia.

Brand, J. and Kesting, A. 1997, 'Sharing the Space and Blurring the Boundaries', in *Stateing Women's Health*, Aug–Oct, vol. 7, no. 3, pp. 20–21.

Darlington, Y. 1996, *Moving on: Women's experiences of childhood sexual abuse and beyond*, The Federation Press, Sydney.

Dominelli, L. & McLeod, E. 1989, *Feminist Social Work*, MacMillan Education Ltd, London.

England, H. 1986, *Social Work As Art*, Allen & Unwin, UK.

Goodrich T. J., Rampage, C., Ellman, B. & Halstead, K. 1988, *Feminist Family Therapy*, Penguin Books, Canada.

Hall, B. A. 1996, 'The Psychiatric Model: A critical analysis of its undermining effects on nursing in chronic mental illness', in *Advances in Nursing Science*, vol. 18, no. 3, pp. 16–26.

Keddy, B. 1996, 'A Feminist Critique of Psychiatric Nursing Discourse', in *Issues in Mental Health Nursing*, vol. 17, pp. 381–91.

Labonte R. 1997, 'Community and Public Health: an international perspective', *Health Visitor* , vol. 70, no. 2, pp. 64–7.

McLellan, B. 1995, *Beyond Psychoppression: A Feminist Alternative Therapy*, Spinifex Press, Australia.

Morgan, A. 1997, 'Expanding Possibilities: Women and Depression', in *Women's Health Statewide*, July.

Rosenau P. V. 1994, 'Health Politics Meets Post-Modernism: Its Meaning and Implications for Community Health Organizing', in *Journal of Health Politics, Policy and Law*, vol. 19, no. 2, Summer 1994, pp. 303–33.

Section 3

Affirming diversity

Introduction

Affirming diversity is a greater challenge in much of rural Australia than in the city. This is contributed to by considerable homogeneity of the people in many rural areas: a concentration on a very few industries, relatively few migrants, often no Aboriginal population, past institutionalising practices limiting the numbers of people with severe disabilities, homosexuality remaining concealed and therefore assumed to be non-existent, young people and old people assumed to be asexual. 'Deviance' in rural communities has traditionally been seen as extreme versions of known behaviours: drunkenness, infidelity, even poor housekeeping standards or poor farming practices. Many communities have not been exposed to diversity in cultural practices or sexual orientation, and they have not been required to renegotiate community values or develop inclusive behaviours beyond their existing comfort zones.

The chapters contributed by Alan Thorpe, and Lynne Hillier and Lyn Harrison, draw on their research in New South Wales and in Victoria, Tasmania and Queensland. These contributions demonstrate the way that lack of anonymity in the country differentially but negatively affects gay men and young women. When the sexual behaviour of young women becomes publicly known—seemingly inevitably because part of the value of sex for young men is to brag about it—they live with stigma and the discomfort of labelling. Alan discusses the exaggerated notions of heterosexism that pervade rural culture, and which serve to polarise views of sexuality and reinforce denial or scapegoating of homosexuality, increasing the vulnerability of young gay men to isolation, depression and self-harm. The stigma attached to these areas of sexual behaviours makes it both necessary and difficult to educate the community for change.

John Wilson, Judy Cue, and Garry Brian and Len Smith provide insights into delivering health services to and with Aboriginal communities in three very different settings. John examines the unique challenge of managing an organisation, in a cultural context within the Northern Territory that defies most of the known management literature. He challenges the political orthodoxies that he sees putting unnecessary burdens on workers expected to perform beyond the capacity of their role. Garry and Len critique a system, which in their experience inadequately serves its mandate. The lessons from Far North Queensland highlight a need to take a more holistic approach in addressing Aboriginal health. In analysing a Koorie women's health project in north-east Victoria, Judy Cue also defines the need for a holistic approach and one that gives women power over the direction of the program and their future engagement with health services.

The chapters of Hurriyet Babacan and Christopher Williams give complementary perspectives on issues affecting women of non-English speaking background (NESB) in rural areas. Hurriyet identifies the compounding disadvantages of being an immigrant, a woman and resident in a rural area, where there are barriers to accessing information and services, rural services are more monocultural and assimilationist, and hostile attitudes to migrants are being voiced because of the eclipsing of social justice perspectives. Hurriyet offers solutions through a brokerage approach which empowers women. Christopher identifies a range of unmet needs for ethnic elderly and their carers, and advocates the need for workers to have a critical awareness of the policy environment, and he identifies lobbying, organising and planning strategies that will develop a more equitable approach to addressing needs of NESB members of the community.

Chapters in this section demonstrate the benefits for rural communities in recognising and embracing the rich complexity of their diverse populations, and the responsibilities they share with the wider society in working towards inclusive policies and values.

15

Out in the bush
Rural health and homosexuality

Alan Thorpe

Introduction

Noel, 45: *If I did want to walk down the main street of Goulburn holding hands with another guy, it's just not on. I don't think I'll ever see that ... In time to come it will be quite acceptable. I'd love to try it.*

For gay and bisexual men coming to terms with their sexuality, there are many issues. Ostracism, isolation, confusion and fear are just some of these. Stereotyping in the media, a lack of useful role models and a socialisation process based on a presumption of heterosexuality all add to the difficulties men face in reconciling homosexual feelings with an often hostile environment. Such issues are probably compounded in rural communities where there may be an absence of role models and no access to sympathetic support services such as counselling. Many young men feel compelled to leave their small rural community for fear of what disclosure may bring, and to gain support from larger communities in city areas.

This is not, therefore, a chapter about identified good practice in service provision. Unfortunately, it highlights a major gap in the appropriate provision of health services to a significant proportion of the male population and is only able to outline early attempts to adequately redress the situation. It discusses the issues for gay men in rural communities and highlights their particular health service needs. These range from basic mainstream services being conducted sympathetically, to more urgent support in relation to mental health and suicide prevention.

Bryce, 21: *Tragic, small, conservative. If you were an individual you were basically stomped upon. I didn't really have a lot to do with the town as such.*

Clark, 36: (Keeping something in) *Well conscious of keeping my sexuality in ... That might have been kept in, being in a country town, you just couldn't, not that I'd go around and flaunt it these days but it would have, yeah, my sexuality would have been kept in. I was aware, seventeen ... Didn't come out until I was about twenty-three, within myself.*

Leon, 42: (To be anonymous?) *Sure, very difficult not to in a small town, everyone knows everyone else, which is not always bad ... not always good ... everybody knew what you were doing and stuff like that.*

Hugh, 18: *It was really small and everybody knew everybody. It was just, the only way to describe Oberon is something that Nick Cave would sing about. This is the guy who sings about electric chairs and kids being born with two heads. Well that kind of sums it up.*

Mike, 31: *In Sydney gay people do tend to be more openly accepted. If you're gay in Sydney you can just about be anonymous. If you're gay in Lithgow, with thirty thousand people you stick out a bit. Newcastle, more like Sydney but still that small town mentality. If you're gay in xxxx Creek, you get a girlfriend.*

Mal, 22: *Because in a country town it's isolation, Wagga, I know there are other people like this but how many ? what are they like? ... and because the media constantly had, even though they were somewhat derogatory ... they did have interviews with gay men and it was a topic that was at least being bandied around whereas a few years earlier you would have heard nothing about it, other than the bar-room jokes and stuff like that.*

In discussing these issues I draw on my own research (Thorpe 1996) conducted with men who have grown up in rural communities. All quotations, as with those above, are from this research and are based on interviews with men aged 18–59 who grew up in rural areas of New South Wales. I also draw on my work experience in the training of health care workers in South Eastern New South Wales, in establishing support groups for rural gay men and in providing individual support and counselling for gay men in rural communities.

The terms *sexual orientation* and *sexual identity* are used throughout this article and the following definitions have been adopted:

Sexual orientation is one's erotic, romantic and affectional attraction to the same gender (sex), to the opposite gender (sex) or both.

Sexual identity is an inner sense of oneself as a sexual being, including how one identifies in terms of gender and sexual orientation.

Sexual preference is a term once used to describe sexual orientation—bisexuality, homosexuality and heterosexuality—which is now outdated because sexual orientation is no longer commonly considered to be one's conscious individual preference or choice, but is instead thought to be formed by a complicated network of social, cultural, biological, economic and political factors (SIECUS 1996).

Coming out is another term that requires definition. Many gay men talk about coming out in terms of either accepting their homosexuality within themselves, or in revealing it to other people. Both these processes appear to be critical points in the life of a gay man (APA 1996). In this article I refer to coming out as a process, which could extend over a long period of time, whereby an individual comes to accept his homosexuality, and may share this with one or more others (Cass 1984, Troiden 1989).

Howells (1984), writing in *The Psychology of Sexual Diversity*, notes the cultural constructs of homosexuality, including influence of the church, law and medicine. He argues that in rural communities such influences are often very strong. A study by Rounds (1988) found that rural communities characteristically hold religion and church as important in the community, are more traditional in their moral values, expect greater conformity to community norms and are less tolerant of diversity. Little wonder that gay men assume low visibility. It is often a wise, if unfortunate, choice to stay in the closet. Many of the men I interviewed were very much aware of these constraints.

A little background

From my experience as a worker in rural communities I am aware of many inadequacies of service provision in relation to these issues, the difficulties of making contact with such men and the difficulties of developing a service that is clearly receptive and responsive to men's sexual health issues, especially around homosexuality. The epidemiology of HIV in Australia is such that gay men and other homosexually active men make up a high proportion of those infected. The figures continue to reflect that gay and homosexually active men account for over 80% of new infections As such, homosexually active men must be considered as a high risk category for HIV infection in particular, and Sexually Transmitted Disease (STD) infection generally. But beyond purely physical health needs there are other important issues.

Sexual health and sexuality encompasses sexual orientation, sexual identity and sexual behaviour. With sex between men, sexual health promotion, if it exists at all, is often focused purely on behaviour (i.e. condom use). Issues relating to orientation or identity, both of which impact on behaviour, are generally ignored in mainstream service delivery. Heterosexism (i.e. assuming everyone is heterosexual) tends to be pervasive and workers often provide nothing by way of support and acceptance for men exploring their sexual orientation or identity.

Cass (1984) contends that: 'All socialisation focuses on the heterosexual role. There is no anticipatory socialisation of the homosexual social type or role other than stereotype.' This lack of support or absence of homosexuality as an acceptable lifestyle can create a void for the individual which may be difficult to overcome. This clearly may lead to feelings of worthlessness, devaluing of self, fear of exposure, isolation and family conflict. It may also lead to risk behaviour ranging from unsafe sexual activity, drug abuse and even suicidal behaviour.

Coleman and Remafedi (1983, p. 69) assert that attempts to change sexual orientation are 'unscientific, unethical and psychologically scarring'. There is now a large body of literature that not only supports this but examines in detail the development of homosexual identity. For example, in reviewing a special edition of *Developmental Psychology* dealing with homosexuality, Strickland (1995, p. 13) says:

> *Sexual identity and orientation appears to be shaped by a complexity of biological, psychological, and social events. Gender identity and sexual orientation, at least for most people, especially gay men, occur early, are relatively fixed, and are difficult to change. The failure to consider diversity, the stigma and stresses associated with being a gay or lesbian person, and the 'closeted' conditions of the participants remain major problems and continue to limit investigations of gay, lesbian and bisexual issues.*

Also, McFarland (1993, p. 24) reviewing literature on homosexual identity development, points out:

> *A presumption of heterosexuality is one of the first issues gay and lesbian youth need assistance in challenging. The homosexual identity formation process involves moving from a heterosexual identity, given to a person in childhood, to a strong, positive, and accepting identity as gay or lesbian. Adopting this non-traditional identity involves restructuring the self-concept, reorganising a personal sense of history, and altering relations with others and with society.*

Against such views of homosexual identity formation there is debate about the extent to which our notion of homosexuality is constructed. Cass (1995a, 1995b) describes the essentialist approach that being gay is a real event, that heterosexuality is a default identity from which other orientations are differentiated. She notes, however, that many non-Western cultures take different viewpoints and in these, notions such as 'homosexual' may not exist. Thus the social constructionist approach argues that the notion of homosexual identity is specific to Western cultures. Social constructionist psychology, however, argues that while the concepts may be socially constructed, the experiences derived from them may be quite real for the individual and can't simply be rejected.

Lesbian, gay or bisexual identity formation is not a process of simply finding an inner sense of self. It is one in which people translate the everyday understanding of lesbian, gay or bisexual identity provided by Western indigenous psychologies into knowledge, behaviours, beliefs and experiences about themselves via the process of reciprocal interaction (Cass, 1995b, p. 8). The access of gay and bisexual men to mainstream services in relation to sexuality issues is therefore limited. Services do not show they are receptive and it is easier to ignore the issues, particularly in smaller communities. How does a health centre show that it is gay friendly ? Generally it does the opposite.
The range of issues not being adequately addressed include:

- younger men coming out, and having to hide their sexuality or perhaps move away from the local community;
- men who have sex with men but who may not identify as gay;
- unsafe sexual behaviour involving risk of HIV and other STD infection; and
- heterosexual young men straightjacketed into playing macho roles so they will not be thought effeminate, or worse still, gay.

The following are some services needed by gay men. Are they available and accessible from your local health service?

- relationship counselling (the ongoing SMASH survey (Prestage et al. 1995) reveals a significant number of seroconversions by men in relationships);
- sexuality (normalising, supporting, counselling);
- sexual health (STDs, AIDS);
- mental health (self-esteem, confidence).

If we accept health promotion principles as the underpinning of health services, then these are the sort of services that should form part of our overall strategies addressing men's health. Homophobia denies all men the full expression of feelings and actions. Homophobia is itself a plague on all men and so long as we have this dichotomy between gay and straight we will have a reluctance on both sides to access sexual health services. Restrictive role models of what it means to be a man are, I believe, one of the biggest barriers to accessing health services.

Gay men still have to come out because heterosexuals assume they are straight. Seeking a service when sexuality is not the issue can simply mean putting up with the assumptions. Seeking a service when sexuality is the issue can become problematic. Will I be accepted non-judgementally? Will the worker understand? Will they be able to deal with the issues?

We have seen in recent years what seems to be a greater general awareness and visibility of gay men and gay issues than there has ever been before. Take for example the spate of gay-themed films—from *Philadelphia, Four Weddings and a Funeral, Priscilla,* to *The Sum of Us.* There are gay characters on popular television shows like *Melrose Place.* The *Mardi Gras* is claimed to be the single biggest revenue generating event in Sydney, and is widely watched on television. It reaches into little rural places like Woolgoolga.

Bryce 21: I couldn't conceive that I could be gay and have a lifestyle. I don't know. Mainstream TV, all my aunts and uncles, all my friends, and everyone at my church, parents at school. There was nothing ever to suggest seeing a man and another man together. The only signs of gay culture I probably saw was on the news, a two-minute segment on Mardi Gras. To me it was just like a dream wrapped up in foil, all sparkling.

On the other hand we have seen in the last ten years or so a dramatic increase in the rate of rural male youth suicide in Australia. In a recent SBS documentary (*The Cutting Edge*, by film maker Con Anemogiannis), it was estimated that one third of youth suicide is gay related. That program listed causes as unemployment, drug use, sexual abuse, divorce, relationship break up and homosexuality. The film not only looks at loss of self-esteem, depression, loss of job and loss of male identity, but also such things as 'rural stoicism' and the 'ANZAC myth'.

Trends in rural youth suicide

A recent monograph compiled from existing published sources in English language journals and books over the past ten years, 'Youth Suicide in Australia', fails to mention sexuality issues. However, it does identify a number of groups with greater vulnerability including young males living in rural and remote areas who 'have a consistently higher rate of suicide than those in urban areas' (Dept Human Services and Health 1995, p. 4).

So, for young males 15–24, 'there has been an increase in completed suicide of almost fifty percent for this group from 1979 to 1993' (Dept. Human Services and Health 1995, p. 4), and it is estimated that there could be as many as 30 or 40 attempts for every completed suicide.

Despite the fact that sexuality is not listed as a suicide issue in this publication, some commentators have argued that sexuality issues are a significant factor in rural male suicide. A recent article in the American publication, *The Advocate,* (Bull 1994) discusses the concern in America about increases in youth suicide there since 1982. The author points to the contradictory nature of studies that explore the role of sexual orientation in youth suicide. Some studies were contradictory, some finding no evidence at all of gay-related issues. The author (Bull) questions the methodology of some of those studies. For example, he says about one question:

*The reluctance of family and friends to identify the sexual orientation of the victims may
have been exacerbated by the questions … including 'Did he ever say that he wished to
be a girl or insist that he was a girl?*

(Bull 1994, p. 38)

Obviously one of the big issues in identifying links between sexuality and
suicide is the frequent absence of evidence, or a failure to ask the right questions.

Whilst, as in Australia, official American guidelines regarding youth suicide
make no mention of sexual orientation, one study there found that nearly 30% of
the gay and lesbian youth surveyed had attempted suicide (Bull 1994, p. 37).

There is some recent Australian work that does discuss possible links
between youth suicide and sexuality issues. Dudley et al. (1992, 1995) report that
for suicide rates amongst young Australians, although 15–24-year male suicide
rates in metropolitan areas have risen two and a half times from 1964 to 1991, the
rates for Australian rural males aged 15–24 have increased fourfold in towns with
populations between 4000 and 25 000, and thirteenfold in towns with
populations less than 4000. The authors suggest that the mental health of
Australian rural adolescents may have worsened over the last dozen years, and
there is considerable indirect evidence that Australian rural youth are at risk from
a range of socioeconomic mental health and educational problems.

Dudley continues:

*More speculatively, students of Australian culture have observed that some of its
characteristics may be potentially psychopathogenic to young people, especially
adolescent males. These elements include a rigid secularism, populism and anti-
intellectualism, racism, xenophobia and homophobia, and a masculinist sexism, which
channels adolescent male identity into competition and aggressiveness, and teaches males
to devalue their emotional natures and feminine qualities. [There is a] myth of the
masculine virtues of toughness and emotional suppression in rural settings. More
conservative and isolated communities may perhaps tend to view mental distress and
illness as a moral failing. The predicament of gay males in these settings is also likely to
be acute.*

(Dudley 1995, p.6)

The description is of a culture where you are not really a man if you admit
to, discuss or seek services for, sexual health issues.

Plummer et al. (1995) also examine issues of masculinity in relation to rural
youth suicide. They contend that although mental illness has been established as
having a major link with suicide it is insufficient as an explanation. They
postulate that the social dimension of suicide may be related to problems with
our concept of masculinity.

Masculinity is an intense and powerful social process that is judged against
social standards and the pressures associated with masculinity may contribute to
failure to cope, isolation and patterns of mental illness. Even in 1995 it is harder

to imagine a more isolating experience during adolescence than gender non-conformity and dealing with an emerging homosexual identity (Plummer et al. 1995, p. 3). It is their conclusion that difficulties with masculinity, sexuality and homophobia play an important role in the suicide of young men.

The findings of my own research provide strong support for such a proposition:

Will, 27: *I felt very suicidal at that time and there was no-one to talk to so I just wanted to end it. It was very lonely. I was around twenty.*

Phillip, 33: *I thought about it a lot. I ... went and sat on the cliffs and contemplated jumping off, yet again.*

Peter, 27: *I felt so lonely I was suicidal at times. I thought about it a couple of times. Almost went through with it once. Around about sixteen. I thought of everything but the most painful way, hanging. I gave that idea up, then I thought about pills.*

Mike, 31: *Yeah, I tried to end it all a couple of times. But I thought, silly bastard what are you doing this for, leaving a mess for someone else to clean up ... Why has God done this to me? Why have I got all these feelings that I can't control and I've got to control it because I've got to go on living but what's the point and why do I feel the way I do? There must be something wrong with me to feel like this because you're not allowed to feel like this. It's a sin.*

Hugh, 18: *Oh yes, I envisaged the perfect way to do it. I was going to get a syringe, draw it up with battery acid then put it in my vein and just, there it was. Because I just thought fuck it ... there was nothing like the Mardi Gras that I'd seen when I wanted to move. I thought, I had to feel good about this. It wasn't just the fact that I was a faggot, there were other contributing factors as well. I got the syringe, but I didn't know how to unscrew batteries. That kind of fucked that up a bit.*

Steve, 21: *I loved to fantasise about it and just dream about it and see people's reactions seeing me, seeing them upset because that means they care, that's why ... the funeral, my family crying, missing me, me being wanted, and valued and felt sorry for, sometimes I'd like to just pick up a box of pills and see what would it be like to take these.*

Carl, 30: *To be honest I still get feelings like that (suicide). I've always found life incredibly difficult, I don't know why. Some people just seem to breeze through life, nothing seems to phase them very much. I've always found life a real hard slog. I don't know how much that's got to do with being gay, or issues of self-esteem but I've always found it incredibly difficult, still to this day. Many's the time I thought it wouldn't be bad if I went to sleep and didn't wake up.*

This then is the possible endpoint when appropriate support services are not available or are not accessed. This highlights the importance of developing and supporting local community gay groups in rural areas, like GLISTN in Goulburn,

Tropical Fruits on the North Coast; and Begay—where else but in Bega. Health Promotion and community development are about empowering individuals in the community and supporting them in their efforts to address their health issues. In this context it means support and development of such gay groups and affirmative action around homosexuality.

The need for and promotion of such groups, which offer local awareness and identity, and with which people can make contact is of vital importance. They may also offer a safer option to beats, as well as an acknowledgment, an affirmation, which is sorely needed, that it's okay to be gay. There are too few messages that say this, particularly in rural areas. And I believe that if we are serious about the health of all men then promoting that message is part of our responsibility.

Where is the bigger issue in health if it's not addressing the basic sexuality issues in young people? Where is the bigger risk in sexual health if our failure to address these issues may end in depression, desperation, isolation, or even suicide?

Other rural issues

There are a number of other issues for gay men that are distinctly rural. They provide some of the contributing framework to life in a rural community, and to the predicament of being gay in that community. There are five I would like to discuss here because they featured prominently in my research. They are: school; concepts of masculinity; heterosexism; role models; and rural culture.

School

The influence of the school environment may be more complex than the obvious and blatant homophobia, name calling and so on. The fact that such behaviour is often an accepted part of school culture makes it all the more powerful a message. These are some of the comments the men I interviewed shared with me:

Mike, 31: *You weren't allowed to talk about anything to do with sexuality because sex is a sin for the Catholic Church so as soon as you had thoughts like that you had to go and have cold showers.*

Andrew, 24: *From a small country town the teacher just has to mention that word and the class will say 'Oh, pooftas, they should be shot', or something like that.*

Hugh, 18: *The guy I broke up with got beaten up and I got warned that the same would happen to me so it was best I moved out.*

Bryce, 21: *The kids used to call me that at school [homosexual]. Yes. In primary school ... by then I think that everyone assumed, if I wasn't gay I was certainly different. Every* *now and then I would somehow get this abuse hurled upon me, being in the wrong place. That would just be standard. School was a painful ordeal that I had to go through. It was just like, I would close up, get on the school bus, go through the routine, get off the school bus, go back to my shelter. I was seven or eight ... went into my mum's bedroom and she was putting her make-up on, and asked her what a homosexual was. She just basically told me it was a man who was attracted to another man and God hates homosexuals and they're all going to die. Which was just great looking back on it now.*

Concepts of masculinity

Concepts of masculinity are often narrower and more rigid in country areas where there is less acceptance of diversity and less tolerance of someone who is different. This can have an impact on all young men, straight or gay, who may be restricted, often unconsciously, into narrow roles of what it means to be a man. Homophobia is as much about how heterosexuality is defined as it is about homosexuality.

Andrew, 24: *Coming from this town you either had to be a footballer, a surfer or on drugs and I was none of the three. I was the only male hairdresser.*

Clark, 36: *I suppose the outlook back in those days you weren't a man if you were gay.*

Bruce, 59: Because, I suppose the idols were men. Men who were men and certainly in that structure of the war and football, men were still men.

Glenn, 24: *My PE teacher he was incredibly homophobic, even to this day I see him. I can't even wave to him. Bastard. He often waves to me and I just can't do it. I just can't bring myself to be nice to him. He gave me a hell of a hard time. He was always like he was trying to toughen me up to be a man. I was just not interested in being a man.*

Hugh, 18: *When it comes to emotional stuff in small towns, it just gets forgotten. Men don't cry.*

Ivan, 28: *I used to dress up all the time. I was forever putting on dresses or whatever I could find, making it into a nice frock, and my mother used to scream at me about that: 'You're a boy, you're supposed to be wearing trousers'.*

Heterosexism

'Heterosexism' is the assumption that everyone is heterosexual. There are often some very subtle and not so subtle manifestations of this. How often do young men hear from a relative, 'When are you going to get married?' We know that there are many men who may do exactly that: get married, have children, and only realise or understand later, their attraction to men.

Phillip, 33: *I don't remember it as such, pressure to be heterosexual and straight either, it was almost as if, just naturally assumed that was the only way to be ... there was no* *other, there was no alternative anyway, there was no alternative to being straight and having a wife and three kids.*

Bill, 38: *I thought it was me. I thought it was wrong. I have two brothers, two sisters and each of those the people they were married to were from large families, very happy families and it was just naturally expected ... getting married.*

Will, 27: *My parents kept asking me when I was getting married, when was I going to settle down and get married, have kids, so they could have grandkids and all that.*

Steve, 21: *I thought about what I pretty much knew was never going to be, that was my wedding. My mother there, a bride, a white dress, just all the stuff that had been expected of me, and that I'd been hoping for years I could change and make happen. I was just crying because I knew it could never happen.*

Mike, 31: *I should be attracted to women because that's what I'm told and good Catholic boys should meet a girl and settle down and have six or seven kids and all these other thoughts, so it was very confusing for a while which is probably the reason I had three nervous breakdowns.*

Role models of gay men

I asked my interviewees about their early perceptions of what being gay meant, or how they pictured gay men and where these notions came from.

Clark, 36: *In those days, very effeminate, limp-wristed person. I think that's the way gay culture was looked on back in those days. They were fairies, you know. I think it was group pressure at school. If somebody was a little bit effeminate or something like that they'd get called poofta. You would if you weren't involved in sport, that sort of thing. If you were effeminate you were called a fairy.*

Hugh, 18: *From what I heard I thought they were all lipstick and high heels and stuff.*

Mike, 31: *I just understood it was guys who wanted to wear dresses and felt like they were females trapped in a male's body and they talked with a lisp and walked around with their hand up, limp wrists and platform shoes.*

Carl, 30: *Probably would have said the stereotypical screaming queen for want of a better term, super effeminate, very obviously gay person.*

Rural culture

There are often strong cultural and traditional expectations associated with living in the country which set up a range of pressures and expectations. Wotherspoon (1986) compiled a book in which nine men write about their experiences of growing up gay in Australia. He describes recurring themes, 'notably the sense of difference engendered in the writers' (1986, p. 7). The author points out that these stories not only refute the notion of a homosexual stereotype, but provide some needed material as to what that experience has been like. He cites common issues as isolation and a need for secrecy.

Wotherspoon also highlights the common migration of rural gay men to major cities because they offer privacy and anonymity and he chronicles the breaking of the 'wall of silence' after homosexuality being seen as a sin in religious terms, a crime under law, and an illness in terms of medicine. In rural communities such influences are often very strong. These may also relate to basic things like the size of the population, relative isolation, and stronger enforcement of commonly held views and beliefs. Coupled with this is the likelihood that your business is not your own.

Mal 20: *We had a very homophobic newspaper editor in town … He writes in his editorials quite amazing things because there's a lot of farmers around who are more than prepared to write in and support what he writes. 'Gays should all be burned or sent to Ireland.' That sort of thing, all these bizarre things. There was a big dance on and the story becomes 'Gay Sleaze Ball', with whips and chains and they're going to convert high school children and he goes on with the most right wing councillor in town who says things like 'Gays are all right if they pray for mercy on the steps of the church or turn straight'.*

Bryce, 21: *Elton John. I knew Elton John was gay. I think there was one or two other people. I knew Rock Hudson was gay, Cary Grant, James Dean. 'A sexual deviant'. I didn't identify with these people. I didn't really know what to do. I had no idea. At that time I was assuming … half way through high school I realised I probably was gay … I found it painful because I knew I couldn't do what I wanted to do.*

'I knew I couldn't do what I wanted to do.' For many gay men in smaller communities most of the change is 'out there', beyond their own community. And the more enticing 'out there' is, if they can't experience it themselves, then the more traumatic it may be. The increased visibility of gay men generally, if it has not been matched at the local level by local visibility and local support, may have served to emphasise the difficulties to be faced. It may have heightened the awareness of a gulf between the life of someone like Russell Crowe's character in Sydney in *The Sum of Us*, and the life for a young gay man like Bryce in Woolgoolga.

A key element may well be the local support. Local support and local visibility. This is one of the reasons why local support groups are so important. It reminds us that they need to be visible and need to be accessible.

Local events like film screenings, information and education stalls, involvement in and presence at mainstream community events can all play an important role. I point out, however, how valuable anything is that you do at a local level, because that has a greater likelihood of affecting the local environment in which rural young men are growing up.

Support in practice

I'd like to make five practical suggestions for health service delivery by health care workers, be they community nurses, sexual health staff, doctors, dentists. In doing so it may be useful to describe the successful model that was developed for the health districts in South Eastern New South Wales. Although organisational configurations have changed, the area at the time included major inland towns such as Goulburn, Young, Yass, Queanbeyan and Bega, and the coastal towns of Bateman's Bay, Moruya and Eden. An HIV support worker was allocated to each geographical health area of which there were three at the time. That worker was responsible for establishing a range of mechanisms that enlisted the support of other health workers and of community members. Volunteer AIDS Task Forces were established, comprising interested community members and health care personnel. People who wanted to work directly with people with HIV were trained for Volunteer Carers Support groups. Train the Trainer workshops were set up for health care workers and community workers. Training was offered to health care workers, which included needle exchange services and values clarification. With the support of volunteers, local gay support groups were also established.

So to the five suggestions.

Firstly, we need to be aware. Workers need to develop their awareness of the diversity of male sexual expression, of the diverse ways in which men perceive their sexual identity, of how homosexually active men may be gay or non-gay identified. We need to be aware of the health risks to these men and their partners, male and female. We need to be aware of the pressures placed on all young men to conform to stereotypes and how this impacts particularly adversely on young gay men. As a HIV Project Officer I conducted a range of training opportunities for health care workers which promoted discussion of these issues. The four-day Train the Trainer package included extensive values clarification around sexuality issues. A sexuality workshop was run a number of times and included a panel of gay men and lesbians.

Secondly, we need to be affirmative. Personal attitude and approach may be one of the biggest assets in effective sexual health promotion. Who is speaking out and speaking up on gay issues if health workers are not? Who is offering support if health workers are not? Where are the posters on our health centre walls that tell people that sexual health is also about accepting sexuality in its many forms?

The local AIDS Task Force held a charity screening of *Philadelphia* in Goulburn where a group of local people affirmed their support, where local gay men became ever so slightly more visible and this was of inestimable value. The task force also takes the lead each year for World AIDS Day activities, a key awareness-raising activity for the local community.

Thirdly, we need to be inclusive. Heterosexism is a big barrier to communication and access to services—we shouldn't assume that everyone is heterosexual. We shouldn't assume someone's sexuality, that they necessarily have a partner of the opposite sex. It is possible to talk about a partner in a gender neutral way. This can send a very big and positive signal to someone wondering whether they can trust us with their secrets and their health.

I once heard a nurse talk to a group of young people about their future and she focused solely on when they would all be ready to have a family. It was inappropriate to suggest that all of them would necessarily want to marry, or to have children, but how alienated would that make a young gay man feel?

Again our health worker training offered specific opportunities to critically appraise the capacity of services to be inclusive.

Fourthly, we need to be advocates. My first job in Yass was trying to get Needle Exchange stickers into public toilets. It took over six months and I felt, in talking to the council and local doctors about safe using and safe sex, that I was the only gay man in town. Certainly the doctors said they had never knowingly treated a gay man. But the process of those negotiations led to greater awareness and a greater exposure of the issues. We are all observed in our work, hopefully by some of the people who need us, and when you establish yourself as someone with sensitivity who can be trusted, contact may be made.

Fifthly, we need to encourage the young. We have to be able to tell young people it's okay to be gay or bisexual. There is a myth to be dispelled about converting impressionable youth. Supporting a young person's struggle to come to terms with their sexuality is not about conversion, and sometimes it's about saving lives.

On the New South Wales South Coast they've actually had Gay and Lesbian panels talking in schools. Students actually got to meet a gay man, and found that he actually looked and acted like anyone else.

Conclusion

Often as gay men we need nothing more than to know there are others like us. It may help much more to know there is someone down the street, not just someone in Sydney or even overseas. Unfortunately, all too often, for many gay men it may take a long time to find that out. If we, as health care workers, are not prepared to accept homosexuality and to publicly reflect this in our provision of health services, in what way can we possibly be coming near to responding appropriately to what are major sexual health issues—for men, gay or straight? I leave you with the words of one of the men:

Carl 30: *It's me, it's who I am. I sort of look at it this way. It took me probably half my life to understand what gay is about. Took me three-quarters of my life to accept it. After all that work and all the shit, this is who I am. I am normal.*

References

APA (American Psychological Association) 1996, *Answers to Your Questions About Sexual Orientation and Homosexuality*, Internet Factsheet: Lycos, 4.15 pm, July 19.

Bull, C. 1994, 'Suicidal Tendencies', *The Advocate*, April, 35–42.

Cass, V. 1979, 'Homosexual identity formation: A theoretical model', in *Journal of Homosexuality*, 4, 219–35.

Cass, V. 1984, 'Homosexual Identity: A Concept in Need of Definition', in *Journal of Homosexuality*, 7, pp. 31–43.

Cass, V. 1995a, *Sexual Orientation Identity Formation: A Western Phenomenon*, unpublished paper.

Cass, V. 1995b, 'Same Question—Different Answer: The Impact of Social Constructionist Psychology on the Study of Sexual Orientation', paper given to the 1995 Conference for the Scientific Study of Sexuality, Palm Springs, April 20–23.

Coleman, E. & Remafedi, G. 1989, 'Gay, Lesbian and Bisexual Adolescents: A Critical Challenge to Counselors', *Journal of Counselling and Development*, vol. 68, no. 1, pp. 36–40.

Commonwealth Department of Human Services and Health 1995, *Youth Suicide in Australia: a background monograph*, AGPS, Canberra.

Dudley, M. et al. 1991, 'Youth Suicide in New South Wales: urban-rural trends', *Medical Journal Of Australia*, vol. 156 pp. 83–8, Jan. 20.

Dudley, M. 1995, *Suicide among Young Australians, 1964–1991: Urban-Rural Trends*, private annotated copy, May.

Howells, K. (ed.) 1984, *The Psychology of Sexual Diversity*, Oxford, Basil Blackwell Publisher Ltd.

McFarland, W. P. 1993, 'A Developmental Approach to Gay and Lesbian Youth', in *Journal of Humanistic Education and Development*, vol. 32, no. 1, pp. 17–29.

Merton, R.K. 1990, *The Focussed Interview: A Manual of Problems and Procedures*, The Free Press, New York.

Plummer, D., Tawil, V. & Gow, A. 1995, 'Suicide and Sexual Health', paper presented to NSW Health Promotion Conference, Sydney, November.

Prestage, G., Noble, J., Kippax, S., Crawford, J., Baxter, D. & Cooper, D. 1995, *Sydney Men and Sexual Health: Methods and Sample in a study of Homosexually-active Men in Sydney*, Australia, HIV/AIDS and Society Publications, Sydney.

Rounds, K. A. 1988, 'AIDS in rural areas: challenges to providing care', *Social Work*, vol. 33, no. 3, pp. 257–61.

SIECUS (Sexuality Information and Education Council of the United States) 1996,

Sexual Orientation and Identity, Internet factsheet: Lycos, 4.00 pm, July 19.

Strickland, B. L. 1995, 'Research on Sexual Orientation and Human Development: A Commentary', in *Developmental Psychology*, vol. 31, no. 1, pp. 137–40.

Thorpe, A. 1996, *Sexuality and Straightjackets*, University of Canberra, unpublished thesis.

Troiden, R. R. 1979, 'Becoming Homosexual: A Model of Gay Identity Acquisition', in *Psychiatry*, 42, November, pp. 362–73.

Troiden, R. R. 1989, 'The Formation of Homosexual Identities', in *Journal of Homosexuality*, 17, pp. 43–73.

Wotherspoon, G. (ed.) 1986, *Being Different*, Hale and Iremonger, Sydney.

Further reading

Aldrich, R, & Wotherspoon, G., (eds) 1992, *Gay Perspectives: Essays in Australian Gay Culture*, University of Sydney.

Browne, R. & Fletcher, R. 1995, *Boys in Schools*, Finch Publishing, Sydney.

Connell, R.W., Dowsett, G.W., Rodden, P., Davis, M.D., Watson, L. & Baxter, D. 1991, 'Social Class, Gay Men and AIDS Prevention', in *Australian Journal of Public Health* , vol. 15, no. 3, pp. 178–89

Connell, R. W., Davis, M. D. & Dowsett, G. W. 1993, 'A Bastard of a Life: Homosexual Desire and Practice among Men in Working-class Milieux', in *ANZJS*, 29(1).

Dowsett, G. W. 1994, *Sexual Contexts and Homosexually Active men in Australia*, Sydney, Commonwealth Department of Human Services and Health.

Goggin, M. & Sotiropolous, J. 1994, 'Sex in Silence: A National Study of Young Gays', paper presented to the Xth International AIDS Conference, Japan.

Hinson, S. 1993, *An ethnography of teacher perceptions of cultural and institutional practices relating to sexual harassment in ACT High Schools*, MA Research Thesis, University of Canberra.

Hood, D. et al. 1994, *Report on the B.A.N.G.A.R. Project*, National Centre in HIV Epidemiology and Clinical Research, Sydney.

Mac an Ghaill, M. 1991, 'Schooling, Sexuality and Male Power: towards an emancipatory curriculum', in *Gender and Education*, vol. 3, no. 3, pp. 291–309.

McFarland, W. P. 1993, 'A Developmental Approach to Gay and Lesbian Youth', in *Journal of Humanistic Education and Development*, vol. 32, no. 1, pp. 17–29.

Merton, R. K. 1990, *The Focussed Interview: A Manual of Problems and Procedures*, The Free Press, New York.

Michael, R. T., Gagnon, J. H., Laumann, E. O. & Kolata, G. 1994, *Sex in America: A Definitive Study*, Little, Brown and Co., Boston.

Miranda, J. & Storms, M. 1989, 'Psychological Adjustment of Lesbians and Gay Men', in *Journal of Counseling and Development*, vol. 68, no. 1, pp. 41–5.

Newman, B. S. & Muzzonigro, P. G.1993, 'The Effects of Traditional Family Values on the Coming Out Process of Gay Male Adolescents', in *Adolescence* , 28(109), pp. 213–26.

Schneider, S. G., Farberow, N. L. & Kruks, G. N. 1989, 'Suicidal Behaviour in Adolescent and Young Adult Gay Men', in *Suicide and Life Threatening Behaviour*, vol. 19, no. 4, pp. 381–94.

Tremblay, P. J. 1995, 'The Homosexuality Factor in the Youth Suicide Problem', paper presented at the Sixth Annual Conference of the Canadian Association for Suicide Prevention, Banff, Alberta, October 11–14.

Vadasz, D. & Lipp, J. (eds) 1990, *Feeling Our Way*, Designer Publications, Melbourne.

Walker, J.C. 1988, *Louts and Legends*, Allen and Unwin, Sydney.

Wotherspoon, G. 1991, *City of the Plain: History of a Gay Sub-culture*, Hale and Iremonger, Sydney.

Zera, D. 1992, 'Coming of Age in a Heterosexist World: The Development of Gay and Lesbian Adolescents', in *Adolescence*, 27 (108), pp. 849–55.

16

The girls in our town
Sex, love, relationships and rural life

Lynne Hillier & Lyn Harrison

Introduction

Much has been written recently about young women's sexuality and the underlying barriers to their sexual health and sexual pleasure which come about in part through restrictive gendered expectations about their sexual behaviour (Holland et al. 1991; Lees 1993; Tolman 1994). Given the potential of a rural lifestyle to exacerbate and complicate these more general obstacles, it is surprising that we find little in the sexuality literature that explores this conjunction. In fact rural youth were labelled a forgotten group in a review of research on young people, sexuality and HIV several years ago (Rosenthal & Reichler 1994).

One of the most pervasive characteristics of life in a small town is the lack of privacy. In the case of young women for example, when age and gender are added to the mix, their private lives are rendered even more knowable. While young women in large urban centres are supervised by their parents and to a degree by their teachers and friends, this surveillance is limited by the anonymity of the city. In contrast, most young women who are born in a town where the population is small, and generations of families have lived in the same area, will be known to most of the townsfolk through the church community, service providers, health professionals (hospital, community health and medical centres), local businesses and sporting and social organisations. Particularly where the population is a stable one, surveillance of young people's activities overall is likely to be far greater than in the city where the range and numbers of services and sheer size of the urban area is likely to mitigate against such public knowledge.

The remoteness, which often accompanies rural living, together with the need for a critical population mass for health and other services to be viable, mean that the availability of sexual health counselling and medical and other support can be restricted or unavailable in some cases. Even where support services are available in the town, the ability to access them anonymously is likely to be compromised. Many small towns have only one chemist and one supermarket for filling prescriptions or buying condoms. Having the town's folk know that they are buying condoms or accessing sexual health services can create difficulties for rural young women who depend on the good-will of the community for their well-being. These factors are likely to have an effect on the ways that young women live out their sexual and romantic lives and the choices that they perceive are available to them.

In this chapter we will take a feminist social constructionist approach (Potter & Wetherell 1988) in examining the lives of Australian rural young women in the 1990s. This theoretical framework allows us to explore the ways in which the nature of small rural communities may mediate local understandings about the ways young women should behave in their sexual and social lives. Our focus is on the ways these young women understand what is expected of them and the ways in which they in turn negotiate these expectations. Rather than seeing sexual safety as based purely on an individual's rational decision making, a social constructionist perspective takes into account the importance of context and the interpersonal nature of sex in these young women's lives. According to this framework, it is not enough to just consider behavioural frequencies in research based on items from large numbers of surveys. Here it is the nature of the relations of power and social inequality within which the measured behaviour takes place, and also the cultural backdrop, that gives meaning to the behaviours (Parker 1991).

Our data come from a study with young people living in small towns with populations of 1500 to 10 000 in three Australian states (Tasmania, Victoria and Queensland). Participants in the study were 1168 year 8 and year 10 students (600 young women, 568 young men) from local secondary schools. The quantitative data were collected through a 45-minute survey that covered demographics, relationships, privacy, peer norms, sexual behaviours, knowledge of STDs, information sources, condom accessibility, access to services and open-ended items about the meanings of sex and safe sex. The qualitative data came from open-ended items in the survey and single sex group discussions with the students in each school in which we talked about country and social life, sexuality, relationships, privacy and other related issues (Hillier et al. 1996). In this chapter we will focus on the voices of the 600 young women who participated in the study. Information about the young men will be included for comparison or to highlight an issue of concern to young women's sexual health.

Living in a small town

Living in a small town was regarded positively by many students. In Queensland, young people talked about tropical pools and waterfalls and others lived close to, and enjoyed, the beach. The year 8s often alluded to the friendliness of their town and how they felt safe, secure and rarely lonely. One of them commented: 'We've got a lot of old people so it's really good. They all talk to you and everything and it's a really friendly town.' Another echoed this sentiment with: 'I think it's a warm, loving, caring sort of community thing, everyone cares about everyone else.' These positive comments were far less common in the senior discussion groups where the young women were more likely to find this care and attention intrusive.

There seemed to be a consensus among the young people that there was plenty to do in the town if you were male. Football and other sports, shooting rabbits, ferreting and riding motorbikes were among the many activities that boys enjoyed doing in their leisure time. The young women, however, often expressed concern that there was not the choice of activities for them, although guides, netball and church activities were mentioned. In one town the theatre had recently closed down. Young men who were not interested in those traditionally male activities were also obviously penalised.

One student remembered the time she tried to join the local football team:

> *They favour the boys more than the girls when it comes to sport in this town.*
> *Yeah, I asked if I could play football. They reckon it's too rough for me but I reckon I'd go all right.*
> *They think it's too rough but like it's not like we can't look after ourselves.*
> *They play netball but we're not allowed to play football.*
>
> (young women's discussion group, Tasmania)

There was also the often expressed feeling that there was little in terms of a future available to young women in the town. Boys talked about taking over the farm and getting apprenticeships and while it was clear that a job was not always assured, there seemed to be even less future there for the young women, one of whom said: 'You don't have much choice about leaving unless you want to be a checkout girl.' To support this contention, we were told by a school principal that the best job available for the brightest girls in the town was in the chemist shop.

Partly as a result of this, 80% of the young women and 65% of the young men said that they would leave the town at the end of school. Most of them gave university and career as the reason, but others mentioned boredom and travel as their reasons for leaving.

There's no secrets in a small town

Notwithstanding the anxieties that all parents express about their adolescents' sexual lives, and the lengths that parents and parent figures will go to to regulate young people's sexual activity, there is a parallel assumption on the part of young people that their sexual lives are, and should be, a private matter. This was, however, difficult for them to achieve.

An important finding of this research was that the majority of the group felt that they were under constant surveillance by the townsfolk that they knew, and this was of particular concern in areas of their lives that they wanted to keep private from their parents (Warr & Hillier 1997). More germane to the theme of this chapter, young women's perceptions of surveillance were significantly stronger than young men's. In general terms, well over half of the girls felt that where they lived it was not easy to do things without others knowing, and this forced them to look for strategies to maintain secrecy. In regard to seeking advice from doctors on sexual health issues, over half the young women believed they could not see a doctor without everyone knowing and, for 21%, that they could not trust a doctor to maintain their confidentiality. In the discussion groups these concerns were further elucidated:

> … in the country it's like you can't be real discreet about it, like if you go to the doctor's clinic then you know like a hundred people there and everyone knows you … someone that's going to tell someone else … gossip… and then it'll get back.
>
> (young women's discussion group, Victoria)

Others talked about the staff at health services, including one girl's mother who worked at the hospital, and the likelihood that they would betray confidences. One girl's description of the town's hospital as 'a big gossip factory' typified concerns about being noticed and talked about when accessing medical help.

There was particular concern in regard to privacy, where prescriptions for contraceptives were required or where there were concerns about pregnancy. Unfortunately, a trip to another town did not guarantee confidentiality either. As one young woman commented about going elsewhere for health services:

> And people at school, people talk. Oh I saw such and such and they were going down to [the city] but they wouldn't say [what they were going for] and I reckon she was doing this or I reckon she was doing that. And that's how rumours start.
>
> (young women's discussion group, Tasmania)

Condom access and use

Dominant constructions of heterosexuality privilege penetrative sex (Hillier et al. 1998) and the promotion of consistent condom use has been an important strategy in the prevention of STDs and pregnancy. However, buying condoms at a local chemist or supermarket in these small communities presented similar problems for young people to those experienced when accessing health services. This seemed to be a problem which weighed more heavily on the young women. In response to survey items about the difficulty and comfort of obtaining condoms, many young people reported finding it difficult and this was partly to do with the response of the salespeople. One fellow was asked: 'What would your mother think'? when he attempted to buy them. Another young woman said: 'It wouldn't just be between you and your partner, it would be between you and the whole town.' Notwithstanding some of the young men's problems with accessing condoms, the young women consistently found it more difficult and were more uncomfortable with accessing them. This can partly be explained by gender differences in expectations of behaviours. As one young woman explained:

> Well if a guy goes in and buys condoms it's like they're just checking it out or maybe they're just being curious, just being boys. But if a girl goes in then they're having sex.
>
> (young women's discussion group, Queensland)

Victorian girls echoed the Queensland girls' concerns:

> It's nerve-racking, you basically know everyone in the shop.
> It's like … Are they going to tell my mum?
>
> (young women's discussion group, Victoria)

Given the obvious problems that many of the young men and women had with accessing condoms, and the young women's ambivalence about sex, it was pleasing to note that 70% of young people used a condom at last sex. Not surprisingly, fewer of these were young women (young men 76%, young women 64%).

It was clear also in many of the focus groups and meanings of safe sex responses that pregnancy was regarded by the young women as a more pressing danger than STDs, and so it was often easier to take a contraceptive pill than go through the motions of buying a condom.

'Sluts' and 'studs': reproducing gender differences

The young women had many concerns about people in the town, including their friends and parents, knowing that they were having sex and this was related to the difficulty of including sexual intercourse as a behaviour that fits dominant ideas of what constitutes 'the good feminine'. Basically 'good girls' do not have sex and there are punishments awaiting those who transgress which centre around gaining a 'reputation'. Given that their sexual partners rarely had similar fears, and in many cases felt that their reputations would be enhanced by people knowing that they had had sex, the young women's concerns about people finding out were justified. As one boy said: 'You do it for the feeling and to brag about it afterwards.'

The importance of a good reputation and the damaging effects of a bad one for young women in small rural towns were described over and over again in discussion groups. As one year 10 student said:

They [boys] have a one night stand and nothing happens. We're more in fear of getting labelled like a tart or a slut or something. Whereas the boys if they have it, they don't get labelled ... and we're more ashamed of it if we do.

(young women's discussion group, Queensland)

The young men were also aware of the double standard exemplified in the slut/stud dichotomy. On many occasions, boys who had lots of sex were described as 'lucky' and 'a hero'. When this discrepancy was pointed out to them, one young man noted: 'It's not fair but it happens.' The consequences for the young women of having a bad reputation could take the form of exclusion from the other peer groups, discrimination by friends' parents and sexual harassment from other young men. One young woman described graphically what happened to a friend who had gained a bad reputation in her town:

Well sometimes like if you have lots of boyfriends and stuff ... like I know someone that got a song made up about them because of it. And it was just horrible, and like they don't, the boys, well the boys made it up about the girl and they just don't care about what the girl was feeling. She was just so upset and it was really bad.

(young women's discussion group, Victoria)

Others demonstrated the ways in which they had internalised beliefs about 'good girls' and 'bad girls'.

You'd feel dirty and stuff because you've got all these rumours going around.
You might lose your friends.
And you just feel left out.
And your mum would find out.

(young women's discussion group, Victoria)

The problem of a damaged reputation is vastly magnified in a small town where there is one school and everyone knows everyone else. Young women can choose to stay within the acceptable boundaries and not have sex, or have sex with a partner and try to keep it quiet. Accessing health services and buying condoms—two of the main strategies recommended for achieving sexual safety—

left rural young women exposed to the risk of a sullied reputation and its attendant consequences.

The pros and cons of having a relationship

Not surprisingly, given the double standards in the peer culture and the general culture of the town, there were many gender differences in ideas about 'relationships'. In general, young men saw more reasons to have a relationship than did the young women who described more reasons for not having a relationship. Boys were more likely to endorse 'so I can have sex' as a reason for a relationship whereas girls were more likely to endorse 'because I will be expected to have sex' as a reason for not wanting a relationship. As a young woman in year 10 said: 'You just go for the not too hot ones.' Indeed, concerns about the role of sex in relationships reverberated throughout all of the young women's discussions about relationships, for example: 'I don't want someone who's just going to want to sleep with you, have sex all the time.'

Given the restrictive nature of dominant views of the good feminine, and the dangers that young women perceived to be inherent in having sex, these differences are not surprising. Apart from sex, young women were more likely to want a relationship for hugs, closeness and friendship and young men were more likely to want a girlfriend for outer appearances and because everyone else had one. Young women tended to believe that they had more to lose from being in a relationship than did young men, including being taken away from their studies and not having time with their other friends. If one adds to this expressed concerns around surveillance and reputation in the context of the small town, it is clear that girls were aware of the price that they had to pay for having a boyfriend, but especially for having sex. It was surprising, therefore, to find that there were no gender differences in those who had experienced sexual intercourse (39% year 10, 17% year 8). However, there were marked gender differences in their understandings of what sex means.

Meanings of sex

Overwhelmingly this group understood sex as heterosexual intercourse. However, for many of the young women (and a smaller number of young men) this was understood within the context of a loving relationship, and sex was seen as an investment in a future with their partner.

> *It means commitment, love. A true love, an undying love, a never ending love!*
>
> (young woman 0870)

> *It means that you are committed to your partner.*
>
> (young woman 0975)

Perhaps the most stark difference in the meanings of sex was the lack of a sense of embodiment in the young women's responses. Orgasm, clitoris, breasts and physical pleasure were mentioned by no-one. The vagina was mentioned only in relation to the penis and it was always disembodied. Whereas the young men were able to describe their own physical pleasure in their bodies, for example 'a good heady and a good growl' or 'injecting your penis into her vagina until you blow your load', this was never the case for the young women whose pleasure was described only in relation to the relationship and never in relation to physical pleasure.

Possibly the most telling indication of the emotional toll on these young women as they negotiate the difficult terrain of their sexual lives was in their answers to an item (only given to senior students):' How did you feel after the last time you had intercourse'? The responses were coded as positive or negative. More than half of the responses were positive; however, out of the 31 negative responses, 27 were from girls. In their recent research, Donald et al. (1995) found that the young men and women in their study had very different emotional reactions to sexual intercourse. The young women in their sample had more negative feelings after sex than did the young men, in particular, when their behaviour sat outside what they perceived to be the confines of the acceptable feminine. Young women reported feeling much happier after sexual intercourse if the sexual encounter occurred within the context of a steady relationship, if there was no alcohol involved and if they thought their peers were also sexually active. Young women were clearly walking a fine line between acceptable sex and unacceptable sex, and the delineation seemed in part to be controlled by contextual factors rather than the sexual act per se.

Sex and alcohol

The abuse of alcohol by young people and the link with other self-harming behaviours is of widespread concern in the community. A recent article in *The Australian Magazine* (Wynhausen 1998) examined this issue as it relates to rural young people's mental health. Previous research has indicated that the use of drugs and alcohol is correlated with increased sexual activity and a greater likelihood of engaging in high-risk sexual behaviour (Rotheram-Borus et al. 1995). A recent national survey of young people and sexual health has confirmed these findings pointing to the prevalence of binge drinking and its connection to unsafe sex (Lindsay et al. 1998). It is not clear from our study that alcohol use is higher among rural youth than it is in the general population, but discussions in focus groups do indicate that it has a central place in the social life of rural young people (Hillier et al. 1996).

It is often thought that alcohol abuse is more common among young men but in our study there were no sex differences in answer to the question: 'In the past year when you had sex, how often were you under the influence of alcohol'?

Twenty four per cent of the sexually active senior students (n=114) reported that they occasionally, often or always combined alcohol and sex and 17% of these same students reported being drunk the last time they had sex. The young women exercised a number of strategies to circumvent restrictions around sexual behaviour, one of which was the use of alcohol. Although they expressed regrets about their sexual behaviours while under the influence of alcohol its disinhibiting effects also allowed them to engage in sexual activities they would have felt constrained to do otherwise. For young people in general, but particularly for young women, this is a totally unsatisfactory and dangerous technique for exploring their sexuality

Some concluding comments on implications for service provision

Though many students in this study were enthusiastic about what a small town could offer them in terms of idyllic surroundings and a sense of community, it was clear that, like most things, what is good can also be bad. Our findings suggest that small towns can be less than supportive when it comes to promoting the sexual health of young people, particularly young women. Geographical isolation and inadequate funding for appropriate youth specific services are significant barriers to promoting sexual health in small towns and will continue to act as limits on what can be achieved. However, our findings do suggest some areas where health professionals and educators can make improvements.

Adults still have difficulty accepting that many young people are sexually active. The age at which young people become sexually active is decreasing with each generation (Dunne et al. 1994; Hillier et al. 1996) and rural youth do not stand outside these trends. Denying that young people are sexual human beings is therefore self-defeating and dangerous. Research indicates that abstinence only approaches do not work and, likewise, sexual health education that concentrates only on plumbing and what not to do has little effect on young people's sexual health practices.

Schools are still seen as the primary site for sexual health interventions and there are some initiatives in Departments of Education (Harrison & Hay 1997; Harrison & Dempsey 1998) that seek to investigate contextual factors in sexual decision-making, focusing for example on gender power relations and their effects on decision-making. These approaches, however, are still in their infancy and are yet to be adopted in all schools. Given the connections between alcohol abuse and unsafe sex there also appears to be a need to make programmatic links between drug and alcohol education and sexuality education. Teachers in rural schools have an important role to play here, but so do health professionals in rural areas. These professionals are often asked to take supplementary sessions on STD and/or pregnancy prevention in schools and the most successful programs see both teachers and agencies working together to integrate teaching and learning in this area. These collaborations build trust and increase the likelihood that young people will access local services for information and referrals.

Young people often spoke disparagingly about their local medical practitioners and their apparent inability to maintain confidentiality. Our data indicate that young people trust the information that they gain from practitioners and other health professionals but that they rarely feel comfortable accessing this information (Hillier et al. 1996). The continuing medical education development project which offers one way of informing doctors of these issues is an effort to improve doctor/patient relationships.

Health Centres are also under-utilised by rural young people and there is evidence to suggest that generic health services often do not provide an environment in which young people feel comfortable talking about their sexual health needs. Nurses situated within Community Health Centres need to think about ways of maximising opportunities for young people to access them. This can be done within or outside the school system. For example, one way schools can provide easy access to advice and referral on sexual matters is via the school nurse who can ostensibly be approached for ailments such as headaches and then in the privacy of the consulting room be used for sexual information, support and referral. We have also seen successful partnerships between school and community where, for example, local community health educators have facilitated a young women's group which meets at the school once a week to discuss issues around sexual health and well-being. This process is not only valuable for young people but allows community health educators to reflect on their own values and practices and to question gender and power in relationships. We have written elsewhere about the problems young people may experience in accessing services located close to shops or businesses with only one prominent entrance. Appropriate methods of payment for young people also need to be considered if their confidentiality is to be maintained (Warr & Hillier 1997). Health services can also consider more effective means of condom distribution, given the embarrassment young people suffer when trying to access condoms in public spaces.

Finally, there is a need to educate parents about young people's sexual health issues and the problems they have in accessing and operationalising information. A health educator in one rural town who participated in the study has had some success in conducting information nights for parents which she initiated in response to our research findings. Parents are an accessible and generally trusted source of information for young people, and bringing them into the sexual health education arena, especially where resources are scarce, can only enhance parent child communication around sexual health and is one way of breaking down sexist attitudes.

References

Donald, M., Lucke, J., Dunne, M. & Raphael, B. 1995, 'Gender differences associated with young people's emotional reactions to sexual intercourse' in *Journal of Youth and Adolescence*, 24(4), pp. 453–64.

Dunne, M., Donald, M., Lucke, J., Nilsson, R. & Raphael. B. 1993, *1992 HIV risk and sexual behaviour survey in Australian secondary schools*, Brisbane: National centre in HIV Social Research.

Harrison, L. & Dempsey, D. 1998, '*Everything else is just like school' Evaluation report from the trial of 'Catching On': A sexual health curriculum for Years 9 and 10*, National Centre in HIV Social Research, Centre for the Study of Sexually Transmissible Diseases, La Trobe University, Melbourne.

Harrison, L. & Hay, M. 1997, *Minimising risk, maximising choice: An evaluation of the pilot phase of the STD/AIDS Prevention Education Project*, Research report, National Centre in HIV Social Research, Centre for the Study of Sexually Transmissible Diseases, La Trobe University, Melbourne.

Hillier, L., Harrison, L. & Warr, D. 1998, '"When you carry condoms all the boys think you want it": Negotiating competing discourses about safe sex,' in *Journal of Adolescence*, 21, pp. 15–29.

Hillier, L., Warr, D. & Haste, B. 1996, *The rural mural: Sexuality and diversity in rural youth*. A report to the community, National Centre in HIV Social Research, Centre for the Study of Sexually Transmissible Diseases, La Trobe University, Melbourne.

Holland, J., Ramazanoglu, C., Scott, S., Sharpe, S. & Thompson, R. 1991, *Pressure, resistance, empowerment: Young women and the negotiation of safer sex*, Tufnell Press, London:.

Lees, S. 1993, *Sugar and spice: Sexuality and adolescent girls*, Penguin, London.

Lindsay, J., Smith, AMA & Rosenthal, D. (1997). *Secondary students, HIV/AIDS and sexual health*. Melbourne: Centre for the Study of STDs, La Trobe University.

Parker, I. 1991, *Discourse dynamics: critical analysis for social and individual psychology*, Routledge, New York.

Potter, J. & Wetherell, M. 1988, *Discourse and social psychology*, Sage, London.

Rosenthal, D. & Reichler, H. 1994, *Young heterosexuals, HIV/AIDS and STDs*, Department of Human Services, Canberra.

Rotheram-Borus, M., Mahler, K. & Rosario, M. 1995, 'AIDS prevention with adolescents', in *AIDS Education and Prevention*, 7, pp. 320–26.

Tolman, D. 1994, 'Doing desire: Adolescent girls' struggles for/with sexuality', in *Gender and Society*, 8(3), pp. 324–42.

Warr, D. & Hillier, L. 1997, '"That's the problem with living in a small town": Privacy and sexual health issues for young rural people', in *Australian Journal of Rural Health*, 5, pp. 132–9.

Wynhausen, E. 1998, 'End of the Road'?, in *The Australian Magazine*, June 20–21, pp. 14–21.

17

Managing Aboriginal health

A view from the north

John Wilson

Introduction

This chapter offers the reader some personal reflections upon my experience over the past three years as manager of Nganampa Health Council in remote central Australia. After outlining the service delivery and organisational context, several key fields of tension experienced in my remote area management practice are identified and discussed. It is not presumed that these are necessarily generic and dialogue with a view to developing relevant and useful theory to better inform remote area health management practice would be welcomed. The views expressed in this chapter are my own and do not necessarily represent those of the Health Council or its employees.

Background: The service delivery context

Nganampa (a Pitjantjatjara word meaning 'our') Health Council (NHC) is an Aboriginal community-controlled health organisation. and is the sole provider of health care services on the Anangu Pitjantjatjara (AP) Lands in the far north west of South Australia.

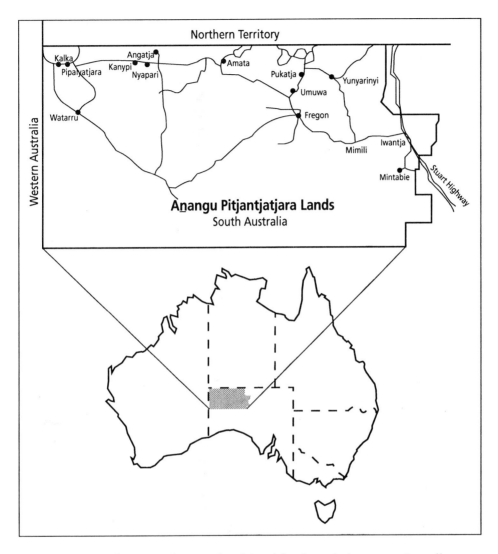

Incorporated in 1983, the membership of the Association comprises all Anangu (Pitjantjatjara word for Aboriginal people) resident on the AP Lands (population 3000 approx).

The population is clustered in six main communities, several smaller but developing communities organised around extended family groups and many smaller family group housing clusters referred to as 'homelands', these being intermittently occupied as people move between traditional land and the stores, schools, clinics and other services located in larger communities.

The health service is governed by a Health Committee of 20 Anangu members, with broad representation from communities and other stakeholders. The area of operations is remote and vast, covering in excess of 100 000 square kilometres of semi-arid country with no permanent above ground water supply. Anangu have experienced a relatively recent process of colonisation marked by the influence of progressive missionaries so that English remains a second language and many people still live a semi-traditional lifestyle. Decision making, social roles and resource allocation are essentially determined by family relationships and traditionally conferred status. The land was returned under freehold title to its traditional owners in landmark land rights legislation in 1982 and Anangu Pitjantjatjara was constituted as the formal land-holding body. Travel is on unsealed roads, which can be dangerous or impassable in wet weather, yet people travel extensively and frequently throughout and beyond the AP Lands for work, social, family, recreational or ceremonial reasons.

The economy relies heavily on employment opportunities in the public sector in services such as health and education since there are few developed natural resources. Net disposable income is less than two thirds the national average (South Australian Centre for Economic Studies 1994). The Health Council is the largest Anangu employer on the AP Lands, injecting very significant levels of revenue into the local economy via salary payments and the purchase of goods and services. Whilst future options for economic development are in all likelihood limited, Anangu are interested in pursuing tourism, cattle and mining enterprises if these can be undertaken in genuine partnership with traditional owners. Formal educational levels remain low with most people possessing limited English literacy skills although many people possess substantial bilingual skills.

Environmental conditions are harsh and adequate housing is not yet available for all. Early housing was inadequately designed and constructed and has poorly or intermittently functioning health hardware.[1] Morbidity patterns are closely related to living conditions and lifestyle considerations and whilst Anangu on the AP Lands have retained their land, language and culture there are still major impediments to achieving secure water supplies, and adequate housing and waste disposal systems (Pholeros, Rainow & Torzillo 1993). Morbidity is characterised by very high attack rates of preventable infectious disease in young children with accompanying high rates of hospitalisation, a chronological spectrum of nutritional disorders (Gracey 1991) and a disproportionate burden of chronic disease (in particular diabetes, hypertension and renal disease) in adults (Miller & Torzillo 1996). Life expectancy at birth for Indigenous men is nearly twenty years less than that for non-Indigenous men, with the difference being nearly eighteen years for women (Australian Bureau of Statistics 1993).

Nganampa Health Council

Purposes

According to its constitution, the first three purposes of the Council are:

- (a) to operate an independent Anangu controlled primary health care service;

- (b) to provide accessible and effective primary and preventative health care to its members and those assisting them;
- (c) to run health programs and deliver services that are sustainable, comprehensive and regional.

Paraphrasing the National Aboriginal Health Strategy Working Party (NAHSWP) (1989) definition, primary health care contains the following key features:

- offers universally required essential health care;
- is culturally acceptable, affordable and accessible to all;
- is preventative and educational as well as ameliorative;
- is participatory in its processes;
- promotes self-determination and self-reliance.

Core services

The Health Council provides a comprehensive service incorporating the essential core elements of primary health care: 24-hour primary clinical care; population and public health programs and preventative care; access to specialist and ancillary health services; a comprehensive health information and medical records system; standard staff selection/orientation/development/ support systems; professional management, outcome and activity measures; and processes for review and evaluation.

At the time of writing there are 112 employees, 88 of these full time with the majority being Anangu. The staff complement includes 35 Aboriginal health workers, 16 community health nurses, 3 medical officers and a number of public health program staff. Clinical services are located at nine clinic sites across the area of operations. Standard treatment protocols are utilised and these are common to health care services across central Australia. Close clinical links are maintained with Alice Springs Hospital 450 kilometres distant, this being the closest centre for referral and evacuation.

Centre of excellence

Nganampa Health Council is a centre of excellence in the provision of remote area health care, achieving best practice in the delivery of clinical services such as immunisation, antenatal care and growth monitoring. The Environmental Health and HIV/STD Prevention and Control programs are nationally regarded as at the cutting edge of program design and delivery.

Retention rates for non-Anangu professional and clinical staff are unequalled elsewhere in remote Australia and a key strength of the organisation has been its capacity to retain a group of highly skilled and committed key staff over a decade or so, thus ensuring a critical mass of corporate knowledge and competency so essential for sustained program development, and for avoiding past mistakes or 'reinventing wheels'.

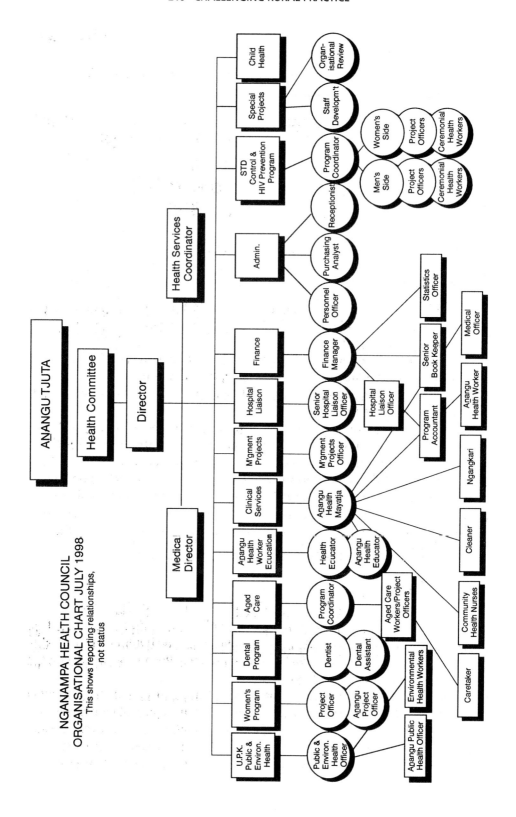

NGANAMPA HEALTH COUNCIL
ORGANISATIONAL CHART JULY 1998
This shows reporting relationships,
not status

Management structure

The Health Committee (see organisational chart opposite) is the governing body, taking all of the key decisions in relation to resource allocation, program direction and staffing. Working as an administrative team supporting and advising the committee are an Anangu Director, a medical director who has administrative responsibility for the delivery of clinical services, and myself as manager who has administrative responsibility for the day-to-day operational requirements.

The Health Committee meets monthly and operates from an administrative base at Umuwa which is centrally located on the AP Lands. The membership structure of the committee provides for direct representation from the main communities across the AP Lands, Aboriginal health workers, the peak women's advocacy organisation and the Anangu Health Mayatjas (managers) administratively responsible for the health clinics located in each of the six largest communities. In this way a pragmatic and effective balance of members is struck, representing the key interest groups and maximising the potential contribution of Anangu stakeholders from within and outside the staff group. Additionally, four community representatives are elected at each annual general meeting and these may come from any constituency. The management role presents a unique set of contextual challenges fashioned by a combination of the following factors:

- remoteness of the service;
- climatic and environmental conditions;
- the cross cultural context;
- the absence of social and human services infrastructure taken as given in urban settings;
- the low political priority historically given to Aboriginal health issues in Australia and consequent underfunding of services and inadequate level of physical and human resources and health infrastructure;
- the difficulties associated with recruiting and retaining skilled staff; and
- the absence of contextually appropriate theory to inform management practice.

It is to the last of these factors that I now wish to turn my attention.

Key tensions in management practice

There is a bewildering plethora of management theory texts and 'how to do it' guides on the market. Bookshelves groan with these many and often weighty tomes—the snappier 'pop-management' titles to be found gracing the shelves in airport bookshops and newsagents. I have, of course, been seduced on occasions by promising titles, alluring covers and glowing claims or testimonies found on their covers and purchased a number of these—only to find them singularly unhelpful. I have taken management courses with similar results. The management text is yet to be written, or the course devised, to which the remote area health services manager can confidently refer as a guide to daily practice. This should not be taken as a claim on my part that management is little more than an art form (as distinct from a 'science' if you will !) or that insights from mainstream management theory and experience are not useful to an extent in a remote health practice setting. The point is overstated simply to make that point.

Management can be described as a process of achieving goals through and with people and involves securing and applying resources in a planned and directed fashion. As manager, my roles include the provision of advice and information to the Health Committee in the setting of goals and program directions, the support and direction of staff, the securing and allocation of resources, and focused leadership through representing the organisation's interests beyond its boundaries, and promoting/affirming the organisation's vision and goals.

My experience suggests that the management practice context is unique, not least of all because of fields of tensions inherent to the setting which continuously demand management responses at the level of daily decision making and action. Several of these fields of tension will now be described and some implications for management practice discussed.

1 Ideology/implementation: The heavy burden of ideology

In my practice, I frequently experience a tension between ideology (the way things 'ought' to be done or the way things 'ought' to be) and implementation (the way things happen or the way things are). This is not the place to enter into a detailed discussion of the meaning of the term 'ideology' (many books have been written about this too!) but rather to suggest that in the arena that is Aboriginal health care the dominant ideology is represented by several key organising concepts, especially 'self determination', 'community control' and 'holistic health care'. Transforming these concepts into programs, which in turn illustrate, reinforce or justify the ideology in a self-fulfilling fashion, is problematic, however. At the level of program design, implementation and development, this tension might better be described as a struggle between rhetoric and reality. Two illustrations follow:

(a) The roles of Aboriginal health workers

Health workers have been described repeatedly as the 'lynchpin' or 'cornerstone' of Aboriginal health services, as the 'main deliverers of primary health care' or as 'agents of social change'. This rhetoric does not match the reality on the ground in remote area health services (Tregenza & Abbott 1995). Rather than seeing this disjunction as an indication that the rhetoric is misplaced, ideology continues to prescribe the rhetoric as the ideal to which health service managers and staff and health workers themselves should aspire.

There are many reasons for the gap that exists between the rhetoric about health workers and the reality of their practice and many of these are so obvious that the question must be asked about what purposes are served through the continuing pervasive propagation of the rhetoric. Health workers with little formal education or limited English literacy, for example, cannot be expected to perform many of the clinical assessment or treatment tasks undertaken by nursing or medical staff. Community members may quite reasonably prefer to be examined by or discuss their medical history with a clinician other than a health worker for reasons of confidentiality. Egalitarian relationships in clinical teams are a nonsense where relative industrial and employment conditions and other severe structural inequalities exist.

The rhetoric in effect has a number of severely deleterious consequences for health workers at the practice level. It can place impossible expectations and burdens of responsibility upon them, require of them behaviours that may bring them into direct conflict with other family members, obfuscate the real and important contributions that they do make, and leave them feeling as if these contributions are inadequate or do not measure up to some ideal standard.

At a structural level, the rhetoric blocks progress towards genuinely collaborative dialogue between health workers, other health professionals and managers about health worker role definition whilst promoting 'blaming' and 'scapegoat' attitudes. Importantly, it also masks structural career limitations such as inadequate salary levels and advancement pathways, the absence of effective industrial advocacy, poor employment conditions or inadequate staff development and upskilling opportunities for health workers.

A way through this disjuncture is to abandon the rhetoric as 'ideal' and encourage definition of role and identification of contribution at the actual workface, reinforcing the valuable contributions health workers do make and encouraging genuinely collaborative efforts by work teams to amplify and extend these contributions. In comparison with other professional groups within the organisation, health workers have relatively ineffective avenues for pursuing industrial claims, wage parity or workplace reform—a cynic might claim that health workers certainly make for a relatively inexpensive and industrially compliant 'cornerstone/lynchpin' for remote area health services!

The management challenge here is to work with staff to develop increasingly collegial workplaces, and to promote an industrial relations and organisational policy framework that promotes this.

(b) Holistic health care

The ideology and associated rhetoric of holistic health care is as pervasive as that pertaining to health worker roles. The NAHSWP (1989) defines health as 'not just the well-being of the individual but the social, emotional and cultural well-being of the whole community. This is a whole-of-life view and it also includes the cyclical concept of life-death-after'. The challenge as a manager is to assist the

Health Committee and staff to translate this often quoted motherhood statement into effective and sustainable program activity on the ground.

Certainly a comprehensive primary health care service requires a raft of preventative and educative community health programs. Of particular importance are sustained public health initiatives that ensure the provision of essential services, adequate housing and functioning health hardware without which community health standards cannot be improved or preventable infectious or lifestyle disease reduced. Also important is the provision of a raft of social and community services taken for granted in urban settings, such as mental health assessment and treatment services, aged and disability care services, child care, sporting and other recreational infrastructure, public transport and access to a full affordable range of consumables, especially food, fuel and clothing.

Since the Health Council operates in an environment where most of the above requirements for making healthy lifestyle choices are absent, directing scarce resources into community health education programs needs to be weighed carefully in terms of relative impact if the diversion of resources away from provision of first line clinical assessment, treatment and care is a consequence.

An appropriate management response to this difficult question of priorities is to adopt a public health perspective focused on outcomes rather than ideology. Definitional and boundary issues concerning so-called 'new' and 'old' public health make for neat academic debates without being particularly useful on the ground. (Kirke 1992) argues that none of the perspectives hailed as 'the new public health' provide an adequate basis for public health practice. Rather, at the level of management practice, a range of strategies and interventions that requires support and choices about the allocation of scarce resources will be heavily dependent on the context (Baum 1995).

For example, in relation to antenatal health care, considerations about the proportion of women offered the choice of a home or 'traditional' birthing experience should be secondary to that of improving the population's mean birthweight. Or to take another example, the provision of programs aimed at maintaining or re-establishing traditional food gathering practices should be a lesser priority than effective and early nutritional rescue of children failing to thrive.

This is not to suggest that a range of approaches to public health issues is not required; only that it is spurious to proceed on the basis that all approaches have an equal claim on scarce resources, and even that certain approaches should enjoy priority by virtue of their perceived ideological superiority. The morbidity patterns and living conditions experienced by Anangu means that the first priority for health services delivery involves the provision of basic clinical assessment and treatment services to high risk populations and thereby necessarily places high value on the central role that health care professionals and 'experts' must play in the effective delivery of those services (Somers 1995, pp. 314–15).

Once again, as with the earlier discussion of health worker roles, community development initiatives that ignore a public health perspective tend to have a 'push down' effect at the same time as they espouse a 'bottom up' approach. They place unrealistic expectations on Aboriginal people who themselves may be struggling to survive in circumstances where basic community services and infrastructure are absent. Yet such circumstances would never be tolerated by their non-Aboriginal advisers in their own urban environments of origin (to where they nearly always return) since they rightly regard the provision of such services and infrastructure as fundamental citizenship rights.

A public health approach to management starts from an understanding of the illness profile associated with the population being serviced, an incremental approach to problem management and program development and affording priority to the provision of public health infrastructure (including clinical assessment and care) at a level expected and enjoyed by citizens nationally.

Programs need to be sustainable, have associated activity and outcome measures, incorporate surveillance and research activities and deliver demonstrable health benefits that directly impact on the illness profile of the population serviced.

A key skill for managers is a capacity to remain pragmatic, to stay focused on achievable goals and to be able to distinguish between short-term and longer-term objectives whilst articulating the links between these. Short-term objectives may at times appear to be at odds with, or running in contradiction to, longer-term and broader goals. Pragmatic compromise or 'next best' alternatives are often necessary in the achievement of desired ends. Encouragement of incremental program development and sustainable activity is vital in the face of what can appear to staff as intractable or overwhelming long-term problems. Staff and management committees require goals that have the following key characteristics:

- have relevance and immediacy;
- are achievable;
- provide direction and suggest priorities;
- deliver outcomes that have demonstrable benefits;
- promote a sense of achievement and progress; and
- provide a springboard/framework for further action.

A public health perspective recognises that people need to be informed and have opportunities to participate if they so wish in the development and provision of services.

It is around this question of process that a second field of tension for remote area health service managers is identified and discussed.

2 Process/progress: Making 'planning' work

The ideologically prescribed process for attaining 'self determination' is that of 'community development'. The term is, however, a politically contested and emotively charged one. Conveniently, as with the term 'community', it represents a powerful idea that has been captured as a rallying post by ideological forces on both the political left and right. The concept of 'community' has been extensively critiqued in the social sciences literature and is aptly termed by Bryson and Mowbray (1981) the 'spray-on solution' to social problems for policy makers.

On the AP Lands, the communities were established as colonial constructs, imposed by missionaries and bureaucracies as convenient strategies for delivering services and relating through 'rational' bureaucratic processes with Anangu. These communities have no foundation in traditional Anangu society, which remains essentially kinship and family based in its decision making and resource allocation structures. Being politically sophisticated and astute, Anangu have readily adapted to negotiating within these structures whilst remaining culturally unincorporated into their underlying belief systems.

For example, many Anangu remain unconvinced about the value, relevance or efficacy of decision making structures based upon the notion of representative democracy since traditionally negotiation processes are family and kin based. This fundamental difference in belief systems has important process implications for management since planning, imagined in the management literature as a linear, rational, narrowing/focusing and representative process, simply does not occur in this way in Anangu culture.

Meetings of all kinds are viewed by Anangu as essentially discrete events where the particular interests dominant in the membership attendance at that particular meeting frequently hold sway. For cultural reasons, avoidance relationships and kinship obligations may determine public patterns of interaction and influence. Meetings are occasions for important public posturing and rhetoric. The real business is often done elsewhere. Of course, much of this is true of meetings in non-Aboriginal organisations and structures but the political negotiating is frequently more complex, less transparent, more embedded in familial social obligations and relationships, and more unpredictable in Anangu organisations

In addition, the remote area context means that planning processes are frequently interrupted or diverted by unanticipated events such as heavy rains that make roads impassable, unanticipated family, ceremonial or sorry business that can involve large population movements, the breakdown or unavailability of vehicles, technical communication disruptions, ill health requiring referral or evacuation to a distant location, or the sudden imposition of unanticipated demands by external funding or service delivery agencies.

Necessary management responses in such a context include the ability to distinguish between advice or guidance that management may offer and those processes that remain essentially Anangu business—key decisions about resource allocation, appointments, policy direction and allocation of formal organisational status and power are Anangu business; non-Anangu managers should advise and even on occasions entreat, but need at the end of the day to defer to Anangu decision making structures and resultant decisions. These may not always be palatable or comfortable for the manager. An acknowledgment of the limitations of one's role and influence is necessary.

In my experience, a tension is frequently experienced between the need to 'go with' culturally acceptable processes and the urge to progress certain programs, agendas or ideas. The pressures on managers to demonstrate progress can be intense and arises both from within the organisation (for example skilled and motivated staff who have a particular view about what needs to be done) and from without (for example funding agencies who wish to see monies spent and outcome reports written).

The key here is to work closely alongside the Health Committee to ensure that program development fits within the organisational mission and agreed constitutional and service delivery goals and that organisational structures agreed and supported by Anangu are in place and actualised.

For example, the health service has developed organisational structures that require consultation with and active involvement from Anangu in all areas of program planning and development. Anangu Health Mayatjas have administrative responsibility for clinic teams; Anangu co-ordinators are appointed to work alongside non-Anangu program co-ordinators; key program staff work with Anangu 'malpas' (advisers). Program co-ordinators report to Anangu committees and meet frequently with the Anangu director and with the chairperson of the Health Committee.

These structures, of course, do not work perfectly and practice dilemmas and conflicts inevitably arise. Nevertheless, the structures have been sustained over time and are strongly supported by, and reflect the wishes of, Anangu. A fundamental management responsibility and task is therefore to actively support and use these structures and continually reinforce for all staff the central importance of these (and the people occupying the associated roles) in the life of the organisation.

The history of colonisation and development of associated funding, service provision and reporting (accountability) structures on the AP Lands has focused on communities as the sites for 'doing business'. In relation to policy and program development within the health service, the provision of standard regional services is a particularly important consideration. Clinical services must conform to an agreed minimum standard and be delivered according to agreed standard treatment protocols at each clinic location, for example.

A particular strength of the health service has been its capacity to manage service development and delivery from a regional perspective. To do this consistently requires discipline on the part of the Health Committee members whose cultural frame of reference is oriented towards family and kinship relations and whose historical framework for negotiating with bureaucracies such as housing or essential services authorities has been the local community.

The management task here is to assist the Health Committee in its deliberations from a regional perspective through building and reinforcing a shared organisational vision, reinforcing and retelling the organisation's history of success, and developing programs that have a regional architecture in relation to their auspice, ownership, goals, staffing, service delivery reach, consumer access and outcomes.

A sense of organisational history and pride in achievement is especially important for building a shared vision and regional approach to the Health Council's management processes. Anangu have much to be proud of in relation to their health service, which is at the leading edge of health services provision in remote Australia. Nganampa Health Council has made major gains in health service provision in remote Australia. Success has been achieved for many reasons, not the least of these being the Health Committee's determination to prioritise sustainable regional program development and their experience has shown that sustainable development requires all of the following in a remote area context:

- clear straightforward goals that have measurable targets;
- strategies that are feasible and acceptable;
- adequate resources applied as a priority over time;
- skilled consistent leadership and management.

Conclusion

It is the last of these ingredients listed immediately above that has been discussed in this chapter by drawing upon personal management practice experience. Several key fields of tension in relation to my practice as manager of Nganampa Health Council have been identified and examined, and some wider implications for management practice in remote health services are considered. It is hoped that this contribution will be useful for others in reflecting on their own practice and in contributing to the development of theory for practice for remote area health services managers.

Notes

1   'Health hardware' is defined as the physical equipment necessary for healthy, hygienic living in remote areas. The equipment must have design and installation characteristics that allow it to function and to maintain or improve health status. In a water supply system, for example, this will include both the bore and basin plug (ref. Pholeros, P., Rainow, S. & Torzillo, P. 1993, *Housing For Health*, Alice Springs: Health Habitat).

References

Australian Bureau of Statistics 1994, *Deaths, Australia 1993*. ABS Catalogue no. 3302.0, Australian Government Publishing Service, Canberra.

Baum, F. 1995, 'The Way Forward' in *Health For All: The South Australian Experience*, Baum F. (ed.), Wakefield Press, Kent Town.

Bryson, L. & Mowbray, M. 1981, 'Community: The spray-on solution', in *Australian Journal of Social Issues*, 16, pp. 255–67.

Gracey, M. 1991, 'Nutritional problems in remote Aboriginal Communities', in *Report from the National Conference on Aboriginal nutrition in remote and rural communities*, April, 1991, 17–18, Alice Springs, NT Government Printer.

Kirke, K. 1995, 'A State Public and Environmental Health Authority' in *Health For All: The South Australian Experience*, Baum F. (ed.), Wakefield Press, Kent Town

Miller, P. & Torzillo, P. 1996, 'Health, an indigenous right: a review of Aboriginal health in Australia', in *Australian Journal of Medical Science*, 17, pp. 3–12.

National Aboriginal Health Strategy Working Party 1989, *A National Aboriginal Health Strategy*, AGPS, Canberra.

Pholeros, P., Rainow, S. & Torzillo, P. 1993, *Housing For Health: Towards a Healthy Living Environment for Aboriginal Australia*, Health Habitat, Alice Springs.

Somers, R.L. 1995, 'Injury Prevention', in *Health For All: The South Australian Experience*, Baum F. (ed.), Wakefield Press, Kent Town

South Australian Centre For Economic Studies 1994, *Economic Study of the Anangu Pitjantjatjara Lands*, S.A.C.E.S., Adelaide.

Tregenza, J. & Abbott, K. 1995, *Rhetoric and Reality. Perceptions of the roles of Aboriginal Health Workers in Central Australia*, Central Australian Aboriginal Congress, Alice Springs.

18

Koorie well women

Judy Cue

Introduction

The Koori Well Women's project in rural Victoria was the start of the acknowledgment and identification of the health needs of Aboriginal women who live in semi-rural communities in the Upper North East of Victoria.

The funding for the project came from the Public Health Branch of the Department of Human services under the Victorian Program for the Prevention of Cancer of the Cervix. North Eastern Women's Health Service, (NEWomen) auspiced this project in consultation with local Aboriginal women and Aboriginal organisations. The objectives of the project were to inform and educate women about cancer of the cervix and to encourage and support Aboriginal women to undertake regular cervical cancer screening.

The Koori Well Women's Project took a holistic approach to informing and educating Aboriginal women about cervical cancer. It brought Aboriginal women together from diverse backgrounds and also allowed for identification of other health issues within the community.

The paper describes the process and the outcomes of the project. It will show how the knowledge of the Aboriginal women in the community was developed to a point where understanding the importance of women's health issues began to be owned.

The Koori Well Women's Project was a joint venture between a mainstream rural women's health service (NEWomen) and the Aboriginal women in the Wodonga district.

NEWomen invited three Koori women (two were health workers) from the Wodonga area to take part in the initial stages of the project. This initial stage of the project was to create a job description to employ a project worker who would develop a project to identify health needs, to hold a number of health information sessions and to raise the women's awareness to the health services that are available in the Albury/Wodonga area.

The project

I began in the position as a project worker and I was based in Wodonga. The Koori women involved with the initial stage of the project were now part of the project reference group along with my supervisor and a community worker for NEWomen. Throughout the project the reference group met on a monthly basis to monitor the project, provide valuable support and share ideas.

Prior to this project there had been no study or needs analysis conducted for Koori women in the North East of Victoria. So it was very important to plan, develop and implement a project that was going to meet the health needs of Koori women who live in semi-rural and isolated rural areas in the North East of Victoria.

I designed the project into five phases that incorporated the objectives identified by the project reference group. The five phases of the project were developed to be flexible enough to change direction if it was required. During the first phase of the project I identified many different aspects amongst the women who live within the project's geographical area.

For example, the Koori women who live in this area came from different parts of Australia which meant that the women may have internalised different cultural values and beliefs and may have experienced different government policies, directly or indirectly. Another aspect that needed to be recognised was that the women in this area either worked, attended school, stayed at home or had to travel some distance to services.

When developing the plan for this project I developed a framework to assist with the different phases that had to be visited throughout the life span of the project, keeping in line with the funding service agreement.

Phase one: Reaching out

Phase one was to introduce the women and the agencies in the geographical area to the project and to inform them about the objectives of the project and about the role I played as a worker and how they could be involved in determining the direction of the project. It was also to promote the project on a local regional and state level so relevant information could be exchanged and shared.

A mailing list of Koori women who live in the district was developed through word of mouth and with the assistance of the women in the reference group. However, the women first gave permission to be placed on the mailing list. It consisted of the names of 40 Koori women who were sent a promotion letter. From the mail-out 23 responded, saying they would be interested in the project. Many of the women could identify their concerns, interests or needs in relation to specific health issues/topics or were just expressing interest in participating in the project. Besides the mail-out conducted there was also individual contact and group consultation. From the 34 promotional letters sent to agencies on a local level, five were interested in finding out about the project.

Phase two: Getting together

The second phase of the project was to offer two informal discussion sessions for the women to participate in the planning of the information sessions. The first informal discussion was held during mid-afternoon and the second one was offered in the evening. From the 42 invitations sent out to all the women on the mailing list, 29 women responded and a total of 21 women attended the discussions.

During the discussions two non-Aboriginal women, with the permission of the Aboriginal women, mind-mapped the concerns, interests or topics the women wanted delivered through the information sessions to be held at the later dates. They discussed the times that would suit and the venue in which the sessions would be held. Some of the issues or concerns the women raised were: children's health, stress, diet/eating/nutrition, diseases, time, childcare, addictions, assertiveness, parenting and women's health in general.

Phase three: Processing, sorting and organising

Phase three was to collate the information and identify themes, for example, the women raised issues around stress, management of stress, causes of stress, etc. Therefore an information session was offered on stress management, aromatherapy and massage.

To plan, develop and implement the information sessions took some time to organise, requiring appropriate dates, times, venues and facilitators. To have all components corresponding sometimes was a miracle. However, perseverance and patience are a good recipe for getting what the women wanted, when they wanted it and how they wanted it. Letting the women know about the information session required a mail-out and promotional work on an individual, group and community level. This also gave a sense of how many women were interested and an indication of those who would be coming to the information sessions.

Phase four: Providing, sharing and receiving

Five information sessions were offered to the women. The first was on stress management, aromatherapy and massage. Three non-Aboriginal women presented the information session and it was also an introduction to the Albury/ Wodonga Women's Centre to many of the women who attended. Many found the evening a time to relax and to learn about alternative ways to relieve stresses that we face in our everyday lives.

The second information session was held in conjunction with Albury's Woomera Aboriginal Corporation's health screening program, and a survey on pap smears was also conducted. One session was held during the day and one in the evening. The night session allowed the women who worked or attended school an opportunity to come along to Woomera to discuss concerns or issues relating to their health. The session allowed the women to support each other, and provided a place to talk freely about what they wanted to share without feeling threatened or shamed. The community nurse who runs the Well Women's clinic at Woomera conducted the session.

The third session, 'Bridging the Gap', was for young women and caregivers, including mothers, aunties, and grandmothers, or important people identified by the young women, to develop effective ways of communicating with each another about topics that are hard to talk about at times. The session enabled the participants themselves to be actively involved by introducing creative ways to discuss issue or concerns.

The fourth session was on family violence and drug and alcohol abuse. This session was held both in the afternoon and in the evening. The presenter for these two sessions came from an Aboriginal women's rehabilitation program. Both sessions were well attended and the women supported each other through talking about experiences and the concerns that were raised about our community issues.

The last session was on HIV/AIDS and STDs. This was held out of town and conducted by the Aboriginal Health Unit. The exchange of information was very valuable to all the women who attended, and the sharing of stories raised awareness about preventive measures and an understanding about HIV/AIDS.

There was evaluation of the information sessions at the end of each session and also on an ongoing basis, directly with the women, or by discussing the progress of the project with the reference group.Evaluation involved filling out an evaluation sheet as well as discussions with individual women and small groups.

Phase five: Where have we been?

The last phase was to document the project and the outcomes and the experiences we had through this journey. The women in our community now have a stronger bond and aim to form a support group that plans to meet informally on a regular basis. The project had many spin-offs from the information sessions. For example, the first information session was held at a women's centre, which introduced the women to the agency that may offer programs or workshops in the future to meet our needs. It also gave a true indication of the health issues/concerns affecting the women in this area. The project dismissed assumptions made about the failure of Koori women to have regular pap smears. The pap smear survey indicated that the majority of the women who participated in the survey had undertaken a pap smear in the last two years. However, young women under the age of twenty who were sexually active were not having pap smears. This clearly identified the need for an educational program to be developed to promote the importance of regular pap smears and health checks from the age of thirteen years, not eighteen years as promoted in the mainstream.

A health focus poster group was also developed during the project. It enabled women to get together to express the health issues in our area through painting. Five posters were developed focusing on the themes:

1   Pap smears and breast checks
2   Stress
3.   Domestic violence
4   AIDS and STDs
5   Support for pregnant women

The posters are seen in our community services and also mainstream health services in our area.

The project needed a unique and creative way to express and reflect its process. It was put forward to the reference group that the project should be documented in a visual form which may be used in the future as a community development tool. The women who participated in the project were invited and encouraged to be part of the video.

Conclusion

In conclusion, the women in our community were consulted throughout the project on the direction that this written account should take. The project was designed to be flexible enough to change direction if the women identified a necessary change. The project was also designed to take a holistic approach to women's health and not just to focus on one aspect.

19

Indigenous Australian ill health
Time to rethink?

Garry Brian & Len Smith

Introduction

Of the many challenges facing rural and remote health services, none is of greater magnitude or greater urgency than the need to find creative and effective solutions to the problems of Indigenous ill health. As if the medical, public health and health system problems are not enough of a challenge, we now find ourselves in an era when the politics of race have been quite deliberately brought to the surface in Australia, when the very need for special services for Indigenous people is being questioned, and when some political leaders seem to be prepared to implicitly legitimise racism in the name of rejecting political correctness. In this environment it is probably more important than ever to find practical ways of addressing the problem of Indigenous health, and to avoid pointless and potentially counterproductive political and ideological posturing.

The challenge

The Australian Institute of Health and Welfare (1998) has just released the most recent of a long series of reports documenting the extent of Indigenous ill health in Australia. As we have pointed out elsewhere (Smith & Douglas 1995, Brian & Smith 1996, Gray & Smith 1996), Indigenous Australians have a combination of health disadvantages that places them in a position like no other group in the world. Unlike almost the entire world, apart from the populations of Russia, some of its former satellites, and a small number of desperate states in Africa, the health of Indigenous Australians is not getting any better over time, and may be getting worse. And in contrast to the Indigenous people in the other Anglo settler societies—New Zealand, the United States and Canada—Indigenous Australians have not shared at all in the substantial health gains that have been occurring in the rest of the population, and as a consequence the gap between their health and that of the majority society has been getting wider.

It is not that nothing is being done. The problem is that despite good intentions, extensive programs and substantial expenditure, nothing that has been done has resulted in any measurable improvement in Aboriginal health, whether we look at it in terms of disease, disability or death.

Overall, the commonwealth spends over $1 billion a year on identified Indigenous welfare and development programs, and a recent report commissioned by the Department of Family Services and Health has estimated that in 1995–96 over $800 million was spent on health services for Indigenous people—about the same per capita as was spent on non-Indigenous people (Deeble et al. 1998). The state and federal governments provided the bulk of the funding. The study found that use of Medicare and the Pharmaceutical Benefits scheme was at only about a quarter the rate of the general population, and that this rate was even lower in remote areas, but this low use was counterbalanced by greater use of hospitals and community health services, including special Aboriginal health services. But no matter how much governments spend and how much effort is made by particular individuals or organisations, it is obviously insufficient or misdirected, since it is not producing the desired outcome of a demonstrated improvement in health.

In the face of the failure of existing policies and programs to yield measurable improvements in health, a detached observer might conclude that a radical rethink is required at both the strategic and the programmatic level. Yet there is no sign of this occurring. The lack of success of existing programs is generally attributed to inadequacies in the resources available rather than in the basic approach, and even among Indigenous groups the solution proposed for improving health appears to be, essentially, more of the same. Part of the reason for this conservatism is political. There are a bewildering number of players and interest groups involved in Indigenous health and the field is highly charged politically. In too many instances there seems to be an unwillingness to disturb existing institutional arrangements, which almost give the appearance of having been designed to ensure that no one is forced to accept ultimate responsibility. This includes in particular the often unsatisfactory division of responsibilities between the commonwealth and the states and territories, where gaps and overlaps in responsibilities may, conveniently to all parties, allow action and responsibility to be avoided. The politics of the Indigenous health organisations are also complex, and custodians or gatekeepers both in and outside the organisations may have a vested interest in the continuation of the existing distribution of resources, influence and responsibility.

A second aspect of this conservative environment is a shortage of intellectual inputs. This requires explanation, because it has not always been the case. Between 1970 and the early 1980s our colleagues Gordon Briscoe and the late Fred Hollows were associated with three significant intellectual contributions to the development of Indigenous health services—the community controlled medical services, the National Trachoma and Eye Health Program, and the Public Health Improvement Program. All three were characterised by innovative thinking and a willingness to confront existing interest groups and power structures in order to achieve specific health and health service outcomes. But the difficulty of turning new ideas and insights like these—valid as they may be— into effective action and improved outcomes, and the risk of failure, may be reason for the cautious approach that prevails today. The community controlled medical services have spread far and wide across the country, but this proliferation has been based on the right of people to have access to services rather than on any particular evidence of their effectiveness. The two national programs, the Trachoma Program and the Public Health Improvement Program, were particularly targeted at rural and remote communities, and were also characterised by a possibly naïve willingness to be held accountable for the achievement of particular outcomes that were not in fact achieved. The Trachoma Program was only partially successful in achieving its national objective of eliminating trachoma and its sequelae, although it did spawn a number of successful related local projects. The Trachoma Program also identified the overwhelming importance to Indigenous health in rural and remote communities of upgrading the physical environment and health hardware (RACO 1978). It was on this basis that then prime minister Malcolm Fraser was persuaded to set up the Public Health Improvement Program, which had as its objective the remediation of community infrastructure across the nation. This was quite radical at the time, since this is generally regarded as the province of state, territory and local government, but unfortunately, the program was never adequately resourced; it was succeeded by a variety of largely unsuccessful programs culminating in the current use of army engineers in a range of construction and training projects, including dust abatement, airstrip construction, water reticulation, waste disposal and so on, aimed at upgrading the health hardware in particularly disadvantaged remote communities.

These army projects are probably the most innovative development in Indigenous health undertaken in recent times, and they have gained wide acceptance in the communities involved, despite widespread criticism initially for being unsustainable and paternalistic.

There have also been successful local non-government projects addressing the nexus between the physical environment and health. The best known is probably that in the Anangu Pitjantjatjara Lands (Pholeros et al. 1993). These authors stress the need to carefully survey the adequacy of the health hardware in individual dwellings and communities, and to provide sustainable solutions to the problems identified. They report successful results from a ten-year project in the region involved, but the challenge of expanding such intensive local projects to national programs across the remainder of Australia remains to be met. It is difficult to see how this could be done without the task force approach being used by the army.

Primary health care

Currently the main thrust of national Indigenous health policy appears to be to extend access to primary care to the entire population. This is being done by extending the network of community controlled medical services, which have become the central component of Australian government Indigenous health policy and program funding. The provision of primary care through a community controlled service that people can relate to and identify with was initially a response to the indifference, hostility and cost of mainstream Australian service providers. It was a uniquely Australian innovation, which has since found a broader rationale within the framework of the Alma-Ata Declaration of Health for All by the Year 2000 (WHO/UNICEF 1978). However, in the Australian context some of the key elements of the WHO paradigm have been missing, particularly the focus on maternal and child health and on the comprehensive provision of basic services to an entire client population.

The fact that the community controlled medical services are pivotal to commonwealth government policy makes it difficult for alternative paradigms to be contemplated, even though evidence is so far lacking that this strategy has produced significant improvement in Indigenous health. Of course it may be argued that the lead time required for improvements to filter through to the national statistics is so long that any positive effects are yet to be seen. Or perhaps it may be argued that the hundred or so services currently in existence are too few in number to even impact on those statistics. At the local level questions about the efficiency and effectiveness or otherwise of the services could be addressed by an examination of data on interventions and outcomes, but in general there appears to have been a reluctance to establish evaluation procedures of this kind.

Aboriginal health workers

The Chinese communal health system of the 1960s was one source of inspiration for the development of the Aboriginal community controlled health services. The

Aboriginal health worker concept, which developed mostly out of the community controlled services, was based in part on the model of the Chinese barefoot doctor. But today, in both the community controlled and state/territory health sectors, the Aboriginal health workers face a severe identity crisis.

Aboriginal health worker training has traditionally been in basic clinical methods. However, from a follow-up questionnaire (Brian & Hollows n.d.) circulated to health workers who had previously attended ophthalmic skills transfer workshops (Brian et al. 1990), and from discussions with other Aboriginal health workers, it seems that it is rare for them to be able to function effectively in that role. The greatest advocates for the Aboriginal health worker concept seem to be those with an interest in continuing involvement in health worker training.

As the least well trained health professionals, with limited competency, a poorly developed career structure, low pay, and little respect from fellow workers and from communities, Aboriginal health workers often find themselves with a job description that includes expected failure. In the rural and remote practice setting, we have encountered a number of common problems with Aboriginal health workers.

In many cases, the use of Aboriginal health workers appears to be primarily a job creation strategy, perhaps aimed at individual and community development. Given the disadvantage of rural and remote Indigenous communities, this might be a reasonable objective, although it could be better executed. However, if the use of Aboriginal health workers is really a strategy to improve Aboriginal health, then, on the whole, it is woefully unsuccessful. Health workers are not nurses or general practitioners and do not have their skills. They have no counterpart in non-Aboriginal communities, and if it is unacceptable in urban and rural white communities to use semi-skilled or unskilled family and community members to provide a lesser health service than an Australian community is entitled to, then it is surely unacceptable to do so in an Indigenous community where the need is so much greater. If the situation demands nurses and medical officers, then conditions and remuneration in rural/remote locales must be made sufficient to attract and retain these health professionals.

There seems to be little future for the Aboriginal health workers in their current role. At present, they represent a confused and generally disappointing attempt to substitute third world solutions for first world responsibilities. If health workers are interested in providing clinical care, then they should be given every opportunity to train to become nurses or doctors. This would need to involve more than just providing study grants. It could mean the temporary relocation of an entire family to university accommodation, or the provision of frequent travel to and from university, and there would be no guarantee or expectation that an individual so supported would then return to their community of origin.

The paradox is that at the same time as Indigenous health workers are struggling to fill their current role, the most urgent gap in the staffing of Indigenous health services—service planning—remains largely unfilled. The role of Aboriginal health workers needs to be radically redefined, and rather than being trained as providers of clinical services, they should be trained as planners and managers of health services. They should occupy a unique position, controlling the planning and the process of service delivery, and liaising between health service providers and community members. In this role, they ought to be well schooled, skilled, and remunerated. While recognising the necessity of modification for the Indigenous cultural milieu in which they will work, it is important that their training be mainstream, so that workers are free to take their marketable skills and move beyond their own community if they so wish.

Health workers should have the major voice in enunciating community preferences and priorities in health care. Negotiation with service delivery professionals would ensure these are known and observed. Medical services provided must be of the highest quality, as measured against what is available in metropolitan areas. This cannot be a matter of negotiation, and they must be provided by trained medical professionals, whether general practitioners or specialists. Medical professionalism is in some quarters regarded as synonymous with paternalism, but no apology should be necessary for attempting to provide the highest service quality across urban and rural Australia.

Unfortunately there is unlikely to be ready acceptance of the need for a re-examination or modification of the role of community controlled health services, of the priority of primary health care, or of the role of Aboriginal health workers, despite the evidence that what is being done does not seem to be working. The ideas that were breakthroughs in the 1970s are now so thoroughly embedded in the current arrangements for Indigenous health services that they have the status of accepted wisdom, and they have a capacity to stifle debate and to defy scrutiny and change.

Delivering specialist services in rural and remote areas

Although the National Trachoma and Eye Health Program did not fulfil all its medical aims, it accomplished much on the wider agenda of Indigenous health, and led to the establishment of many community controlled health services in remote areas. It was a project for its time, in contrast for instance to a recent project in which the army provided ophthalmic surgery in tents pitched in the grounds of a public hospital, basically relieving the health authorities of the need to provide a sustained accessible service. There is a consensus now that there is no longer a place for one-off medical specialist and hospital extravaganzas, and that services must be provided on a continuing or regularly repeated basis, in or close to communities.

In addition to its core ophthalmic staff, the Trachoma Program enlisted the help of 80 volunteer ophthalmologists who each spent up to three weeks in the field, receiving travelling expenses only. They were mainly concerned with medically treating active trachoma, with prescribing spectacles to those who needed them, and with the provision of cataract and trachoma surgery. For this, a task force approach can be successful. Today, however, with the emergence of lifestyle diseases such as diabetes, which affects up to 40% of those over 40 years of age in some Indigenous communities, patient surveillance and treatment require an ongoing commitment, as exemplified particularly in the treatment of diabetic retinopathy. This sort of commitment cannot reasonably be expected of volunteers, and nor should rural and remote communities be expected to receive such services as charity, when it is so obviously a right enjoyed by all other Australians.

Specialist medical services need to be delivered in or near to rural and remote communities, improving patient access and increasing uptake, and where possible they should be integrated with primary health care services. The quality of the service provided should be no less than that expected by urban Australians. It should also be as comprehensive and as medically appropriate and possible. Such a service may, of necessity, be limited, but it should deal well with the more prevalent problems occurring in the target population. It must also act as a conduit into available tertiary medical care as needed. Initially, the service should be able to identify and handle the backlog of diagnostic and therapeutic intervention required. Then, either continuously or on a regular cycle, it should settle to a sustainable level of activity, as determined by population need and resource availability. When services are delivered to Indigenous communities, there is a need, in addition, for local people to be trained and used as service managers and liaison personnel. This will increase the likelihood that the service will be responsive to local needs, aspirations, and sensitivities.

There is a paucity of health data for Indigenous communities, and what is available is not necessarily of good quality. Specialist medical service delivery needs to be accompanied by data collection. Such health databases ought to be used in the evaluation of service performance and medical intervention outcome measures, and in setting the priorities of an ongoing needs-based health service.

For all this to occur, resources controlled by disparate authorities and organisations must be co-ordinated, so that the service may be sustained by mainstream funding in the long term. With rural and remote medical specialist service delivery, the difficulty is in bringing patients, service providers, and resources together. Innovation is required not in the medical treatments, but in the organising and financing of the service. Successful service delivery must offer the opportunity for legitimate non-resident service providers to engage in long-term service provision to rural and remote Australians presently disadvantaged by lack of access or opportunity.

For reasons of insufficient workload, lack of professional contact and support, lack of ancillary staff, and family and social considerations, the provision of specialist services in small rural and remote communities by resident specialists is unlikely to occur in any sustained widespread manner. The alternatives of coercion and conscription of non-resident service providers have no place if there is to be interest, commitment, and service quality. This is all the more so since such service involves the difficulties of travel, spending time away from home and urban practice, and dealing with the sometimes inhospitable conditions of remote Australia and its communities.

In eye health, the specialist service providers are the optometrist and ophthalmologist. Each must be prepared to provide a regular ongoing in-community service, but they cannot be expected to do so in a context which is to their financial and professional detriment. It is important that these professionals not view this undertaking as charity work, but that the rural or remote service unit[1] is a constituent of their regular practice, and is remunerated in the same way. The same standards and commitment would be expected as for other parts of their practice. As part of the professional commitment that is then established they should be available for telephone advice to other health professionals committed to the locality, and to facilitate referral of patients with urgent needs between visits.

The overall objective is to encourage metropolitan and large provincial city specialist service providers interested in rural/remote service to incorporate a community, group of communities, or region into their urban-based practices. For ophthalmology, this arrangement allows for the satisfactory handling of the leading causes of ocular morbidity, cataract and trauma, and the emerging catastrophe of Indigenous diabetic retinopathy.

Professional development and support, and innovative funding arrangements will need to be organised to promote this approach. Funding strategies could involve government financing of the transport, accommodation, facility, equipment, and ancillary staff costs for the service, covering the overhead costs of the specialist's metropolitan base practice, or creating an arrangement whereby this work attracts a Medicare fee for service rebate at some multiple of the rate for a comparable service provided to an urban-based patient.

In 1995, the Fred Hollows Foundation began a two-year project in Far North Queensland which incorporated aspects of ophthalmic and optometric service delivery to Torres Strait and Cape York communities, along the lines outlined above. Toward the end of 1996, with a service developed and functioning, the Foundation approached the Federal Minister of Health and Family Services with an invitation to audit the model, and examine its applicability for delivery of eye and other specialist services across Australia. The Minister commissioned a review of eye health and service delivery in Aboriginal and Torres Strait Islander communities (Taylor 1997), which found that the Fred Hollows Foundation model was an appropriate method of delivering rural and remote eye services.

However, 18 months after the acceptance of the report, and despite well-intentioned commonwealth endeavours at implementation, there is yet to be any identifiable outcome in terms of on the ground service provision across Australia. It seems that this report may well succumb to the inertia typical in other aspects of Indigenous ill-health.

Unfortunately, the delivery of specialist medical services to rural and remote Indigenous communities will make only a minor contribution to health improvement. If real changes are to be achieved in Indigenous health in Australia, development strategies will need to focus not only on improved health services and upgrading the physical environment, but also on achieving and maintaining a healthy social environment, and developing the will and capacity on the part of individuals to take control of their own health. Philosophically and intellectually, the Indigenous health debate needs to move on from the mantras of the 1970s. We need to find ways to break out of what have become familiar and comfortable ways of thinking, to question conventional wisdom, and to mobilise the intellectual, professional and political resources needed to take a fresh look at the problem. This will require a commitment to the highest professional standards, a freeing of the debate from the constraints of the status quo, and the development of evidence-based policies and programs based on scientific principles and orientation towards action and outcomes.

Note

1   A geographic region may have one or more service units. A service unit comprises one or smaller, less resourced, peripheral communities with a larger, better resourced, hub community, in close proximity, which anchors the service. The hub community may act as such for several service units.

References

Australian Institute of Health and Welfare 1995, *Australia's health*, AIHW, Canberra.

Brian, G. 1997, *Medical specialist service delivery to rural and remote Australian communities: a demonstration project*, Report to the Fred Hollows Foundation.

Brian, G. & Hollows, F., Unpublished data.

Brian, G., Dalzell, J., Nangala, S., & Hollows, F. 1990, 'Basic ophthalmic assessment and care workshops for rural health workers', in *Australian and NZ Journal of Ophthalmology*, vol. 18, no.1, pp. 99–102.

Brian, G. & Smith, L. 1986, 'Indigenous health services: improving delivery in rural and remote areas', in *Current therapeutics*, May 1996, pp. 11–13.

Deeble, J., Mathers, C., Smith, L., Goss, J., Webb, R. & Smith, V. 1998, *Expenditures on health services for Aboriginal and Torres Strait Islander people*, Department of Health and Family Services, Canberra.

Gray, A. & Smith, L. 1996, 'Is there a low road to Aboriginal health?' in Robinson, G. (1996), *Aboriginal health: social and cultural transitions*, NTU Press, Darwin.

Royal Australian College of Ophthalmologists 1980, *The National Trachoma and Eye Health Program*, RACO, Sydney.

Pholeros, P., Rainbow, S. & Torzillo, P. 1993, *Housing for health: towards a healthy living environment for Aboriginal Australia*, Healthhabitat, Newport Beach, NSW.

Smith, L. R., & Douglas, R. M. 1995, 'High and low roads to Aboriginal health', in *Medical Journal of Australia*, vol. 163, no. 2, pp. 97–9.

Taylor, H. R. 1997, *Eye Health in Aboriginal and Torres Strait Islander Communities*, Commonwealth of Australia, Canberra.

WHO/UNICEF 1978, *Primary health care. Report of the International Conference on Primary Health Care, Alma-Ata, USSR, 6–12 September*, WHO, Geneva.

20

Do I belong here?

An exploration of the issues facing women of non-English speaking background

Hurriyet Babacan

Introduction

This chapter is based on work I undertook in a number of rural and remote areas in New South Wales, Victoria and Queensland. I was involved in a range of projects with non-English speaking background (NESB)* communities in Shepparton, Mildura, Albury-Wodonga, Griffith, Robinvale, Mt Isa, Townsville, Coffs Harbour, Mareeba, Goondawindi and Wide-Bay Burnett area from 1990–97. The areas of research covered training, employment, ethnic ageing, NESB women and community resourcing and structures (Babacan & Doyle 1995, Babacan 1996, Babacan 1997, Babacan 1998). The chapter will examine the issues facing NESB women in rural areas, in the context of the current debates on immigration, settlement and service delivery.

---

* A terminology vacuum has been created by the abandonment of the term NESB (non-English speaking background) by the government and the community sector. In this chapter the terms migrant, immigrant, newly arrived, ethnic communities and NESB will be used interchangeably.

Debates on immigration and settlement of ethnic communities have generated considerable discussion in the public arena, including in rural areas. Rural Australia is still highly monocultural, and there is an unequal distribution of resources to ethnic communities in those areas. Furthermore, ethnic communities are confronted with fragile institutional structures and inadequate support services.

Ethnic communities, in the main, do not constitute a critical mass in terms of community size and therefore are unable to effectively exercise their citizenship rights. This means they are not adequately consulted or represented, and are unable to influence policy and to secure an adequate share of social resources. There is a continual decline in the support for NESB communities in rural locations, and the cycle is a vicious one. This decline is aggravated by greater assimilationist pressures, and monocultural population environments of rural communities. This impacts in a greater way on NESB women who are isolated and without support. The overall result for NESB women is deprivation, lack of empowerment and a continued practice of 'out of sight, out of mind ...'.

Demography of rural Australia

Australia is a multicultural country with approximately 23% of the population being born overseas. When the children of overseas born are included this figure is over 40% (Australian Bureau of Statistics 1996). This is a significant number of people to have the immigration experience or to be the child of someone who is an immigrant or a refugee. The 1996 Census identifies that immigrants from a non-English speaking country and their children make up over 20% of the total population of Australia. Significantly, approximately 14% of the population spoke a language other than English at home.

The number of immigrants entering Australia are mainly concentrated on the eastern coast in Australia and mainly in large cities and regional towns (Hugo 1996). The proportions of people in Australia from non-English speaking backgrounds are not reflected in their settlement in rural areas of Australia. Governments in recent years have attempted to locate newly arrived immigrants to rural areas due to pressure on cities. In 1996 approximately 12% of overseas-born persons were living outside a major urban centre compared to approximately 35% of Australian-born persons. Approximately 8% were NESB women.

The distribution of NESB people across rural areas varies considerably within and between states and territories. For example, some areas such as Morwell, Shepparton, Griffith, Mareeba have approximately 11% of their population of NESB origins, while others are as low as 0.5%. The mining town of Coober Pedy in South Australia has a NESB population of 25% although this is a rare reflection of population composition of Australia (Conner & Heilpern 1991). This presents a picture of rural Australia with varied distribution of ethnic communities and differing patterns of settlement (Gray et al. 1991).

An important consideration that is often overlooked is the immigration category of people who have arrived in rural areas. The categories of immigration are critical in the determination of types of services and support needed for those community groups. There are very few studies of specific patterns of immigration to rural ares. Three main categories of immigration were noted by Gray et al. (1991) : family reunion (54%), refugee and humanitarian programs (25%) and employer nomination(5%)

The majority of women come to Australia under either the family or refugee category. The immigration program is a gender-biased program since it places emphasis on skill. Skill is a gendered concept, resulting in a concentration of women in particular types of industries which are often not valued by the immigration intake policy. The skills of these women are often not assessed prior to their arrival. While there are no studies that examine the immigration status and skill base of NESB women in rural areas, my own experience and research in rural areas indicates that most of these women have arrived as dependants on spouses or other family members (Babacan & Doyle 1995, Babacan 1997).

Settlement issues of NESB communities in rural areas

Settlement is defined as:

The process by which an immigrant establishes economic viability and social networks following immigration in order to contribute to, and make full use of, opportunities generally available in the receiving society.

(The National Population Council 1988)

Successful settlement has depended on a number of factors. These determinants have been identified by Cox (1989) as the nature of the ethnic group, the nature of welfare developments, the nature of attitudes in the host country towards immigrants and, generally, the political and economic climate. Length of time has also played a role in how well an individual or a community settles, although this shows considerable variation within and between groups.

There has been a large number of theories put forward as to why immigrants settle in rural areas. These are linked directly to why immigrants migrate and why Australia hosts an intake program. Collins (1988) has identified that immigration programs are directly linked to the process of capitalism and global shifts of funds and people. This is similar to the concept of 'ethnoscapes' as defined by Appadurai (1990). Following this analysis Stilwell (1992) explores the condition leading to rural settlement and argues that these centres create spatial constellations conducive to capitalist accumulation. One of the key conditions to meet the requirements of accumulation is the availability of adequate quantities of labour. Immigrants have traditionally fulfilled labour shortages in Australia and the post-Second World War settlement in rural areas can be seen from this economic perspective. There are numerous examples of immigrants being settled (either by government policy or voluntarily) in regional or rural centres, such as working on the Snowy Mountain Scheme, in the mining industry, in particular agricultural industries and as seasonal labourers. Immigrant women have traditionally fulfilled roles in supporting men and their labour or productivity (on farms, in packing industries) has not been counted or included.

At the individual or community level a number of studies have been conducted to identify the location decisions of immigrants. Maher and Stimson (1994) distinguished between natural attractors (climate and physiographic factors such as the beach) and constructed attractors. Constructed attractors can be economic—areas with good employment prospects—or social cultural—social networks, social cohesion, availability of housing, existence of social infrastructure. Social networks were found to be important for immigrants as they provided sources of valuable information and cultural and linguistic support.

The reasons why immigrants settle in rural locations were often linked to their reasons for arrival in Australia, such as escape from persecution, joining family or for lifestyle reasons. Murphy (1997) studied the initial location of immigrants and identified the settlement patterns related to a number of factors: (in order of importance) location of spouse, location of family, location of friends, job opportunities, lifestyle/climate, housing, information flows, links to and distance from country of origin, and previous visits to Australia/region. In addition to the above factors Hazebroek et al. (1994) pointed to other factors such as proximity to workplace, transferability of occupational skills, access to places of worship, extent of cross-cultural marriages, number of dependent aged, previous socioeconomic background, location of arrival base and length of time in Australia.

The settlement patterns of NESB communities in rural and remote areas have not been adequately studied. For example, we do not know the process by which certain ethnic communities settle in particular areas such as Italians and Turks in Mildura in grape growing, the Sikhs in Coffs Harbour in banana growing, the Italians in Mareeba and coastal Far North Queensland in tobacco and sugar cane, just to name a few.

NESB women in the main have settled in rural areas following the decision of their spouses or families, sponsorship patterns (where men marry women from overseas) or in search of better life opportunities. For example, many Filipina women in rural Queensland have settled there due to their spouses living there. In the words of one Filipina respondent:

> *I did not know where I came to. I had no say in it. My husband had a farm here and so I came to live with him. It was a shock to come here at first, but now I am used to it.*

> (Townsville 1997)

Settlement issues for NESB women in rural areas

The needs of immigrants settling in rural areas are basically similar to those of people who settle in cities, but social structures and relations entered during settlement are different, as are conditions affecting service delivery. In particular, immigrants who choose to settle in rural areas are likely to be isolated from large urban concentrations of ethnic groups and to be offered few or no services aimed at meeting their specific needs (Gray et al., p. xiii)

Stilwell's notion of disarticulation is useful in understanding why there are problems and barriers. The process of capital accumulation is one that produces disproportionalities or structural imbalance. Forward and backward linkages between various aspects of production do not exist. This manifests in the form of sectoral disarticulation where there are no linkages between productive sectors, social disarticulation which is an inequality in the distribution of social resources and political disarticulation. The overall effect is one of imbalance, conflict and structural fragmentation (Stilwell 1992). It is in the process of this disarticulation and fragmentation where immigrants settling in rural areas fall in between the gaps. The fragmentation manifests itself in many aspects of social life. A number of studies have confirmed this (Allbrook Catalini 1991, Doyle 1992, Kickett & Allbrook 1992, Conner & Heilpern 1991).

There are some serious issues, barriers and problems for NESB women in rural areas which are emerging or have existed for a long time. Eliadis et al. (1988) emphasise that immigrant women 'grapple daily with the dialectic between ethnicity and gender'. For rural immigrant women Mageean (1988) points out that the factors of being an immigrant, a woman and being in a rural area do not simply add to each other, they have a multiplying effect. Studies indicate that NESB women carry out the burden of the dual shifts, isolation, significant barriers to participation and information. Lack of culturally relevant support services, breakdown of family networks due to immigration, lack of child care and transport difficulties are factors that contribute to the isolation of women in rural areas (Reeve 1994, Andreoni 1989, ANTA 1996).

A number of barriers or issues exist in rural areas for immigrant women. My own work revealed that many NESB women did not understand ways to access services in rural areas and did not understand the way government and other institutions operated. Barriers existed in terms of a monocultural service delivery framework, greater assimilationist approaches, lack of concentration of communities, lack of specialist services, lack of language services, lack of access to information and more general issues of isolation and lack of access to transport (Jupp & McRobbie 1992, Allbrook Catalini 1991). One respondent stated that she 'did not know where to go to get help in looking after her disabled husband'.

Many authors have pointed to a general lack of resources in rural areas. However, the resources allocated to NESB communities in rural areas were significantly lower. Immigrant women are affected by the lack of resources as they are often isolated and have most of the family responsibilities. The lack of a critical size and distances made it difficult to secure additional resources (Riley 1995, Gray et al. 1992).

The older and more established NESB communities in rural Australia are experiencing significant changes to the composition of their communities. The younger members of the community are increasingly being attracted to urban centres in search of employment and educational opportunities or for change of lifestyle. The increasingly ageing established communities are in decline and new communities are emerging as minorities in a scattered manner. Often a gender imbalance has occurred since the men have died earlier and older women are left alone. This leaves the NESB communities without cohesion and community (Babacan 1996a).

The findings of my research in all rural areas confirmed that there is a lack of infrastructure for ethnic communities in rural areas, especially in areas where there are only small pockets of particular groups. What exists is often fragile and not well resourced. There is an over-reliance on a small number of agencies which are often under resourced. Small and newly emerging groups often do not have their own organisations and cannot access the mainstream ones (Jupp & McRobbie 1992, Mageean 1990). Immigrant women have raised concerns about not being able to access community services, language classes and information technologies, and about a lack of community space. Where structures do exist they have not been supportive of NESB women's participation in terms of language, transport and childcare. One respondent pointing to a gender imbalance in some ethnic agencies stated that 'all the men go there, no women come. So I do not feel right to go by myself'.

Mainstreaming is a term that refers to a general provision of services where program service delivery and design is established to suit the totality of the community. It is concerned with generic service delivery. In the last decade, respective governments have emphasised mainstreaming and the provision of services for migrants within the generic structure. Unfortunately, many of the mainstream services have not been able to provide culturally and linguistically relevant services to ethnic communities, especially women. The thrust for mainstreaming has been accompanied by a declining funding base to ethno-specific services.

Many immigrant women utilise ethno-specific services much more than men, since often women will use a service or attend a program if another woman from the same background is attending (Babacan 1998). Where mainstreaming has taken place, this has impacted on immigrant women in a drastic way since there are often few agencies providing services. With the abolition of such programs there has been a vacuum created in terms of the needs of older and newly emerging communities (Jupp & McRobbie, Mageean 1990). Gray et al. (1995) point out that service delivery has taken place in a void of information, where service providers just did not know the extent and nature of the needs of immigrants.

Access to information is a major problem in immigrant settlement generally. This is intensified in rural areas for immigrant communities due to language barriers, lack of access to interpreters and translated materials, lack of access to bilingual staff and general isolation. Some attempts have been made to address information strategies through use of technologies and specific models of information delivery. Little documentation is available on what has been successful. There is generally a problem in accessing information technologies for NESB communities, especially older NESB adults and women (Mageean 1990, Gray et al. 1991, Conner & Heilpern 1991). It was also noted that many immigrant women tended to have literacy problems (in their own language and in English) thereby rendering most forms of written information useless. Kickett and Allbrook identified that the best method of information dissemination was 'word of mouth' but due to large distances and isolation this method also had severe limitations.

Isolation is a major difficulty for rural communities generally. Marginalisation in rural areas is greater due to the monocultural nature of such environments and the slower tendencies for change generally. This is exacerbated for NESB communities especially for older adults and women. Reeve (1994) found that lack of English language skills preclude women from using the telephone and the car, the two main resources in overcoming isolation. Many women from newly emerging communities expressed as a priority a need to obtain their driver's licence (Reeve 1994, ANTA 1996).

Ageing is manifesting itself as a serious problem amongst longer established immigrants in rural areas. The decline of communities, the lack of appropriate care structures and the tyranny of distance has caused anxiety in many ageing NESB communities. The Department of Health and Family Services has identified ageing communities as the Italian, Greek, former Yugoslavian, Dutch, German, Polish and Russian. The Department has forecast that by the year 2010 there will be other NESB communities with ageing emerging as a major issue. These communities are Spanish speaking, Arabic speaking, Vietnamese and Filipino (DHFS, 1996, unpublished planning data). Many of the studies on ageing for NESB communities have identified that age care services are monocultural and residential care facilities do not provide culturally appropriate care. Considerable pressure is placed upon families and carers to look after their older family members in the absence of relevant care and supportive networks. In many situations family networks are broken due to immigration and internal migration of family members which compounds the isolation of NESB older adults. This is aggravated further by a loss of English language skills and reverting to the original language. This situation is worse for older NESB women whose husbands have died. These women have traditionally not had the opportunity to learn English or to use social systems. There are major difficulties in surviving and learning these skills at an older age (Babacan 1995, Rowland 1991).

Lack of participation is a major issue for rural NESB women. Many women in my research confirmed the absence of participation in activities, training and information programs and in decision making structures that impact on their lives. Consultation by government and non-government was deemed to be tokenistic with no real avenue for input. Communities complained of the rhetoric not matching the reality in terms of participation and being able to affect change to improve their reality (Allbrook Catalini Research 1991, Doyle 1992, Jupp & McRobbie 1992, Gray et al. 1991).

As the medium of communication and information, language problems in rural areas have been widely studied. Problems in relation to language are deep and some are related to structural issues. Firstly, there is the major issue of access to interpreters and translated material. Many NESB women are not able to use the Telephone Interpreter Service. There have been instances where the translated materials available in urban areas are not disseminated to rural areas or are not relevant to those settings (Hazebroek 1994, Jupp & McRobbie 1992, Gray et al.).

Another key issue in language is access to English language and literacy classes. The Human Rights and Equal Opportunity Commission (1994) pointed to a narrowing of focus of government subsidised lessons to what is termed 'survival English' and vocational English. This disadvantages other groups such as women, people in the workforce and older adults. The issue of loss of acquired language with ageing has not been validated and solutions sought. Many women did not have literacy skills in their own language prior to immigration. The rationalisation in English classes has a multiplier effect in rural areas, especially when coupled with lack of other language support services. The Adult Literacy National Project (1995/96) pointed to difficulties in adequately providing for the needs of people in rural and remote areas. Some of the issues include the lack of adequate resources, lack of teachers with specialist qualifications, difficulties in access to classes and lack of appropriate pathways.

Maintenance of language and culture is extremely difficult to maintain in rural and isolated areas. Carman (1990) found that cultural maintenance was not being encouraged in the school environment and that many students were experiencing conflicts in relation to their cultural identity. These findings were confirmed by Elliott (1993) in her study of children in Wagga Wagga. There is anecdotal evidence to suggest problems with religious practice such as access to suitable places of worship, dress codes and behaviour. Allbrook Catalini Research identified that many communities were critical of the dominance of 'white Anglo Saxon Protestant values' in the delivery of services in all levels of government.

The research I undertook in rural areas identified employment, training and qualifications as very significant issues. Lack of access to vocational training, inappropriate course design and delivery, user pays principles for many courses, limited career pathways, non-recognition of overseas qualifications, limited access to English language learning and limited opportunities to access technologies in use are some of the problems being experienced by immigrant communities, including women. The changing economic and political climate is causing extreme hardship for people in rural environments. Anecdotal evidence suggests that the general thrust of restrictions to social welfare, user pays principles and mainstreaming have significantly impacted on the lives of rural NESB communities. Many older communities, who have often worked toward establishing industries in particular regions, are experiencing major changes to the economic structures and are not able to understand the nature of and reasons for the change. In the settlement phase newly emerging immigrants need greater amounts of funds to establish themselves in a new country and often the high levels of unemployment, inability to upgrade skills and lack of eligibility for certain welfare services is emerging as a major pressure point for rural NESB community agencies (Babacan 1997a, Grace et al. 1997, Mageean 1990, Conner & Heilpern 1991, Allbrook Catalini Research 1991).

While it is not possible to generalise about attitudes towards NESB communities in rural areas a number of studies have identified significant problems with monocultural approaches to service delivery, lack of sensitivity to cross-cultural issues and outright racist attitudes. The abandoning of political correctness current in Australia has granted permission for expression of hostile and even racist attitudes towards people who are different. The attitudes and racism that exists is both at a personal and institutional level. Conner and Heilpern provide instances of hostile attitudes at the individual level, such as abusive behaviour from neighbours. Many of the studies have focused on the institutional level and its covert nature. The Access and Equity programs until the change of government pointed to the need for further training of staff of government and non-government agencies. With the policy of mainstreaming, it is critical that racist or hostile attitudes do not become entrenched or reflected in rural institutions. Some of the ways in which this occurs is not necessarily linked to direct discrimination, but indirect discrimination, such as treating everyone as the same when they are not, not seeing differences and special needs, or stereotyping of certain groups or homogenising communities (HREOC 1994, Azra 1996, Conner & Heilpern 1991, Mageean 1990, Jupp & McRobbie 1992).

A respondent in rural Queensland who was admitted to hospital talked of her experiences of racism. A Filipina (1996) stated:

> *I was admitted to hospital and was very ill and in terrible pain. The nurse at the hospital said 'I should let you die you black witch but unfortunately you count as a person and I will get into trouble.'*

There are other issues such as access to housing, employment and transport. While these are issues generally relevant to many in the rural areas regardless of their ethnic background, the immigrant status of individuals coupled with barriers of gender tends to compound the problem further.

What emerges is a situation of dominance and fragmentation of NESB communities, with women in extremely vulnerable and isolated positions. It is a situation of groups of NESB women with less status, less bargaining power than others, less knowledge of Western systems, lack of community development structures, little experience in promoting or advocating their demands and few opportunities to develop these skills. This is not to state that there are no success stories within rural Australia—there are many. However, these success stories can be multiplied if the structural and social barriers are removed.

Future directions

The issues facing immigrant women in rural areas cannot be seen in isolation from economic, social and political issues affecting the whole of the rural sector. The decline of some industries, impact of economic rationalism, mainstreaming, globalisation, and market competition are major structural issues that go to the heart of the problems faced by rural communities generally. These factors impact on rural women differently and yet very few studies have been undertaken to identify experiences and coping strategies women have adopted.

The following suggestion on future directions, with emphasis on a brokerage model, is not in any way aimed at resolving some of these macro structural problems. The intention is, however, to assist in the development of strategies that will enhance NESB women's support and coping mechanisms in very isolated communities.

A brokerage model

A brokerage model of service delivery works well for marginalised groups. Such a model empowers and skills women to advocate on their own behalf. Appropriate methods of participation by NESB women are an essential component of its success.

A brokerage model is essentially where an existing organisation in the mainstream acts as a *broker* between the community and other services, other organisations and government. A good example of this is found in the Home and Community Care (HACC) project in Townsville, where a multicultural broker works with mainstream agencies to provide HACC services to older immigrant women.

The advantages of a brokerage model are:

- there is a minimum requirement of resources;
- there is a merging of mainstream and ethno-specific or multicultural services;
- it provides an agency that can provide support to isolated communities;
- it ensures expertise, support and advocacy for otherwise unheard voices;
- it empowers women with skills and works towards self-sufficiency;
- it provides linkages and networks with other agencies;

- it acts as an agent of change by creating awareness of special needs and issues in the mainstream;
- there is a holistic approach to the needs of immigrant women;
- it ensures participation and provides for visibility;
- it can lead to further development or provision of services;
- it places responsibility of problems and social needs on the general community and not just immigrant women.

This model works best when an agency in the mainstream exists, with the sensitivity and resources to provide the brokering role. In instances where such an organisation does not exist, it can be created through the work of sensitive individuals or through a network of organisations collectively. A brokerage model in rural areas for immigrant women can exist on an issue basis (for example education) or generally across a range of service areas.

The needs of immigrant women in rural areas are multi-dimensional and cannot be reduced to simple solutions. The brokerage model offers one approach to tackle complex social, political and economic factors that impact on the lives of immigrant women living in rural Australia.

References

Appadurai, A. 1990, 'Disjuncture and Difference in the Global Cultural Economy', in *Theory, Culture and Society*, vol. 7, pp. 295–310, Sage.

Adult Literacy National Project 1996, *Unmet Need and Unmet Demand for Adult English Language and Literacy Services*, National Centre for English Language Teaching and Research, Macquarie University, Sydney.

Allbrook Catalini Research 1991, *Government Service Delivery to People of Non-English Speaking Background Living in Rural and Remote Areas*, Working Papers on Multiculturalism, no. 5, OMA, AGPS, Canberra.

Andreoni, H. 1989, 'Immigrant Women in an Isolated Rural Community', in *Women in Rural Australia*, James, K. (ed.), University of Queensland Press, Brisbane, pp. 96–115.

ANTA 1996, *The Skill and Delivery Needs of Rural and Regionally Isolated Queensland Women*, TAFE Qld, Brisbane.

Australian Bureau of Statistics 1996, *The Australian Census of Population and Housing*, AGPS, Canberra.

Babacan, H., 1998, *Muslim Elderly in Queensland*, Islamic Women's Association of Qld, Brisbane.

Babacan, H. 1997b, *NESB Unemployment and Case Management*, Migrant Employment Network, Brisbane.

Babacan, H. 1997b, *Access and Equity Issues in Residential Care*, Department of Health and Family Services, Canberra.

Babacan, H. 1996a, *From Here to Where: Issues Facing Older Adults in Queensland*, Council on the Ageing Conference, Brisbane.

Babacan, H. 1996b, *How are We Caring... Report of the Evaluation of Multicultural Residential Age Care Support Program*, Ethnic Communities Council of Qld, Brisbane.

Babacan, H. & Doyle, R. 1995, 'It is too Hard to Grow Old in This Country', in *Rural Social Work*, vol. 2.

BIMPR 1996, *Community Profiles 1991 Census: Overseas Born*, AGPS, Canberra.

Carman, K. 1990, *Meeting the Needs of People from Non-English Speaking Backgrounds in Wagga Wagga*, Wagga Wagga.

Collins, J. 1988, *Migrant Hands in a Distant Land: Australia's Post-War Immigration*, 2nd ed., Pluto Press, Leichardt.

Conner, N. & Heilpern, S. 1991, *Focused Study on Non-English Speaking Backgrounds in Remote/Rural Areas of Australia*, The Centre for Multicultural Studies, University of Wollongong, Wollongong.

Cox, D.1989, *Welfare Practice in a Multicultural Society*, Prentice Hall, Sydney.

Doyle, R. 1992, 'Case Studies of Access and Equity in Selected Localities', in *Access and Equity Evaluation Research*, McRobbie, J. & A. (eds), AGPS, Canberra, p. 39.

Eliadis, M., Colanur, R. & Roussos, P. 1988, *Issues for Non-English Speaking Background Women in Multicultural Australia*, AGPS, Canberra.

Elliott, M. 1993, ' Non-English Background Children in Wagga Wagga Schools', in *Rural Education Issues*, Boylan, C. & Alston, M. (eds), Charles Sturt University, Wagga Wagga.

Grace, M., Lennie, J., Daws, L., Simpson, L. & Lundin, R. 1997, *Enhancing Rural Women's Access to Interactive Communication Technologies*, QUT, Brisbane.

Gray, I. W., Dunn, P. F., Kelly, B. M. & Williams, C. J. 1991, *Immigrant Settlement in Country Areas*, BIR, AGPS, Canberra.

Hazebroek, A., Stewart, K., Gaston, G., Holton, R. & Hai Tan, Z. 1994, *Planning Criteria for the Provision of Immigrant Services in New Areas*, BIMPR, AGPS, Canberra.

Hugo, G., Maher, C. & Jackson, R. (eds) 1996, *Atlas of the Australian People—1991 Census*, BIMPR, AGPS, Canberra.

Human Rights and Equal Opportunity Commission 1994, *State of the Nation: A report on the People of Non English Speaking Background*, AGPS, Canberra.

Jupp, J. & McRobbie, A. (eds) 1992, *Access and Equity Evaluation Research*, AGPS, Canberra.

Kickett, D. & Allbrook, M. 1992, 'Access and Equity in Geraldton and Midland', in Jupp, J. & McRobbie, A. (eds), *Access and Equity Evaluation Research*, AGPS, Canberra.

Maher, C. A. & Stimson, R. J. 1994, *Regional Population Growth in Australia*, AGPS, Canberra.

Mageean, P. 1988, *Overcoming Distance: Isolated Rural Women's Access to TAFE Across Australia*, TAFE National Centre for Research and Development, Adelaide.

Mageean, P. 1990, 'Pathways to Participation: the Vocational and Further Education Needs of Adult Immigrants in Rural Australia', BIR, AGPS, Canberra.

Murphy, J. 1997, *Initial Location Decisions of Immigrants: Results of the Longitudinal Survey of Immigrants to Australia*, Joint Commonwealth/State/Territory Population, Immigration and Multicultural Research Program, DIMA, AGPS, Canberra.

Reeve, C. 1994, ' Migrant Women in the North West Mining Towns of Western Australia', in Franklin, M., Short, L. M. & Teather, E. K. (eds), *Country Women at the Crossroads: Perspectives on the Lives of Rural Women in the 1990s* , University of New England Press, Armidale.

Riley, D. 1995, *Lifelong Learning in Rural Areas: Between a Rock and a Hard Place*, Proceedings of the 11th National Conference, SPERA, University of Ballarat, Ballarat.

Rowland, D. T. 1991, *Pioneers Again: Immigrants and Ageing in Australia*, AGPS, Canberra.

Scarvelis, N. 1995, 'The Rural Equity and Access Program: Catering to the Settlement Needs of Decentralised Migrants', Conference Proceedings, 3rd National Immigration and Population Outlook Conference, Adelaide.

South Australia Ethnic Affairs Commission 1985, *Riverlands Consultation*, Adelaide.

Stilwell, F. 1992, *Understanding Cities and Regions*, Pluto Press, Leichhardt.

21

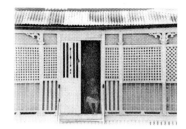

Older migrants and their carers in rural Australia

Christopher Williams

Introduction

In 1993, I was involved in a study of the human service needs of the elderly and their carers in nine local government areas in Far North Queensland. The study, commissioned by the then Department of Human Services and Health, aimed to:

- identify and describe the human service needs and preferences of the ethnic elderly and their carers in the nine local government areas;
- evaluate the effectiveness of existing ways of meeting these needs in the above locations; and
- make recommendations on the future development of services for the ethnic elderly.

Though we both had had previous experience of working with ethnic communities, my colleague, Jo Lampert, and I realised that this was no easy task, especially if we were to undertake this in a culturally sensitive and appropriate manner. Who would we talk to, how would we contact them? There was much more than language difficulties at stake, and plenty of room for misunderstanding. Concepts that may have one meaning in one culture might have a completely different or possibly no meaning at all in another.

Was it even possible to generalise about a group known as the 'migrant' or 'ethnic' elderly? Could we ask older people and their carers about the difficulties they might experience? We knew that many ethnic elderly are suspicious of strangers asking questions, and some of the issues around which the research was conducted (caring, personal care) were matters that, culturally, would not normally be discussed with strangers. We knew too that, in some cultures, to say that you are not coping with a situation is to compromise your honour. If you would not admit this to your closest family, why would you tell a stranger?

There were a number of other difficulties. 'Everybody knows what the needs of the ethnic elderly are.' We heard this a lot. Many different people (whether ethnic groups or mainstream service providers) claimed to know these needs, yet there seemed to be all kinds of barriers to enabling older people and carers to speak for themselves. Access to them was sometimes jealously guarded by community leaders who might have reason to be suspicious or cynical about government and about authority or of the possible motives of the researchers. We also came across a number of 'no go' areas. For example, in many cultures, you just can't talk about mental health issues.

Although all too conscious of these and other possible difficulties in the study, Jo and I went ahead and hired and trained a team of eleven research assistants, most of whom spoke the language of at least one major ethnic group and many of whom spoke several.

Although acutely conscious of the pitfalls of cross-cultural research throughout the study, our findings nevertheless revealed enormous levels of unknown and unmet needs in the various communities. Some of these are detailed below.

Case study: The findings

The following broad findings are summarised from the report *Growing Older in a New Home*. The quantitative material is supplemented with some of the many poignant statements made by the elderly or their carers during the course of the study.

Ethnic elderly

In the survey of the ethnic elderly themselves, 150 people (aged 60 or more) of 40 different nationalities were interviewed, roughly half men, half women. Of these, 69% were aged 70 or more.

As expected, family relations were of overwhelming importance. Whilst many had relatives who lived nearby and whom they saw regularly, it did not necessarily follow that they enjoyed supportive environments. Some elderly with relatives nearby experienced extreme isolation and other difficulties.

> *I feel like I'm a burden for my own children. I'd rather stay in my own home, but I can't manage any more. I like to be near my family, but can't someone help my daughter when she needs it? (Indian—Mulgrave)*

> *I am blind and need constant care, but I feel terrible that I put all this extra pressure on my daughter, who cannot leave me. (Greek—Innisfail)*

Approximately 33% lived alone (20% of males, 45% of females). Moreover, about 20% had no relatives nearby. Likewise, although many had close friends in the neighbourhood, they did not necessarily see them often and 30% had no close friends. In all, 21% knew nobody of the same ethnic background in their areas.

> *I'll just cope. Don't worry about me. I'll just keeping taking care of myself. (Polish—Atherton)*

> *I'm afraid if I ask for help, I'll be put in a home. (Italian—Tully)*

> *I'd like to meet my old friends, but we're all too old and sick now. Where would I meet people? At their funerals? (Italian—Gordonvale)*

> *Nobody visits. Now that my husband is gone I could die and nobody would notice. (German—Cairns)*

> *None of my neighbours have ever visited. I'm too proud to ask them any more. (Dutch—Mareeba)*

Many found their living situation very difficult, for reasons of loneliness (particularly amongst women), isolation, lack of transport and family conflict. The majority experienced one, or more, disabling health problem and many were concerned about the effect these had on their autonomy and independence. For 41%, financial insecurity was a major concern. About half, mostly women, said they had difficulty with English. Many said they wanted more company, more financial security, more transport, more assistance for their carers, more information about services, more independence and the desire to be shown greater respect. Most of them received little assistance with daily tasks and indicated that they would like more help, particularly with transport, housework, and gardening. Many neither knew about nor used any community services at all. When asked about the kind of barriers they experienced to having their needs met, the most frequent responses related to financial problems, hostile community attitudes and government indifference. Other responses included family difficulties, lack of transport and information.

> *I feel scared and lost. I don't even know how much money I have in the bank, since I have never done my own accounts. (Italian—Mulgrave)*

> *Is there anybody to help me with housekeeping? If there is, I don't know about it. Besides, I can't afford anybody. (Italian—Gordonvale)*

Overall, the most important finding was that a significant proportion of the ethnic elderly were extremely isolated and many had little knowledge and made little use of services that might have been able to assist them.

Carers

The study also surveyed 59 carers. Most were daughters or daughters-in-law. Of these, 36% were over the age of 60. Many carers said that their caring was full-time work. Most said that they would like more assistance in caring, with 60% saying that they received no assistance at all, either from service providers or other family. Most carers would prefer help to come from within their families. Over half the carers neither knew of nor used any available services. Even when services were known, they were often seen as inaccessible—either because of distance, cultural inappropriateness or because old people would not use them.

What do you mean what do I feel? It's my duty. I have to do it. Who cares what I feel? (Italian—Innisfail)

What is there to feel about? I am resigned to it. I gave up my being to care for her. (Italian husband)

As a Muslim, I believe it is God's will. I do my duty and keep smiling. (Albanian daughter)

Whilst many carers felt it was their duty and responsibility to continue caring, high levels of stress, guilt and frustration were experienced by many. Some felt trapped by cultural expectations and could not expect any respite acceptable to the person cared for. Many felt shame about asking for help and/or a fear of strangers, despite often a desperate sense that they had no life of their own.

I am widowed, have three children and my elderly father to care for. At night when they've all gone to bed, I weep out of loneliness. I'm a young man. When will I ever find time to learn English, and find a life for myself here in Australia? (Timorese son)

I have never had a girlfriend because I care for my mother. I have had a lonely life. (Maltese man, 39 years old)

My husband doesn't understand my duty, so I feel constantly guilty. I'm always neglecting someone. (Yugoslav daughter)

Service providers

A total of 67 service providers were also surveyed. Most reported that they had little contact with ethnic communities and cited the following possible reasons for this: the importance of family care in ethnic communities, cultural and language barriers, ignorance of available services, suspicion, cost, lack of transport.

Many providers believed that their services were appropriate for use by the ethnic elderly but assumed that their needs were being met within their own communities. Some agencies believed that the ethnic elderly have no specific or different needs to anybody else. Very few agencies provided information about their services in languages other than English, or had any special interpreting arrangements, bilingual staff or training to deal with cross-cultural issues.

In general, there was little understanding and knowledge of ethnic minorities amongst the service providers. Many of these agencies were already under strain in providing mainstream services and had little energy or resources for attempting to meet the needs of minorities.

To investigate further would have required time and resources far beyond those that were available to the project.

Who are the ethnic elderly and what are their needs?

Acknowledging some of the difficulties mentioned earlier, it is fair to say that this study has touched only the surface of the extent of need amongst the ethnic elderly and their carers in the rural communities surveyed. Yet they confirmed nevertheless that the ethnic elderly and their carers are amongst the most vulnerable and potentially needy groups in Australia's multicultural society.

This situation is likely to be exacerbated in the coming decades. Amongst some culturally and linguistically diverse groups, the proportion of elderly is growing much faster than in the general elderly population, and by the year 2001, the elderly of NESB will represent almost 25% of population 65 years and over (Rowland 1997, p. 75).

It is widely believed, however, that ethnic families and communities are more 'integrated' and self-sufficient than those of Anglo-Australia and that therefore they do not 'need' as many services. Whilst fewer ethnic elderly live alone and more live with families than is the case amongst other Australians, many ethnic elderly nevertheless may enjoy far fewer family resources than the Australian- born (Rowland, 1991, p. 153). Moreover, since they are significantly less likely to use community services than the other Australian elderly, the pressures on a smaller pool of carers are greater than is the case amongst the Australian-born population (ACOTA 1985, pp. 131–37). This situation may be greatly exacerbated in rural areas, where access to human services may not be so readily accessible (Williams and Lampert 1994, p. 53).

The ethnic elderly in rural areas: The prognosis

In the circumstances described in our findings, what hope is there of being able to provide culturally sensitive and appropriate services in rural areas for both the ethnic elderly and their carers, many of whom are leading stressful, disappointed lives with little prospect of respite? What prospects are there for improving the understanding of service providers, especially in a situation in which resources are scarce?

Overall, the prospects do not seem to be very good. It is well known that there are a number of very specific barriers to the development of effective and efficient human services in rural areas (for example lack of critical mass, lack of infrastructure, lack of collateral services, distance, dispersed demand, transport, etc. (Collingridge 1991, p. 2; NCIYF 1994, p.145). There are, in addition, more general problems such as overlapping and inconsistent planning regions, the inappropriateness of urban mainstream models of service delivery for application in rural areas, lack of flexibility in funding arrangements, insufficient co-ordination, insufficient training, poor research and inadequate needs assessment, etc. (DHHLGCS 1991, p. 2).

For all of these kinds of reasons, people in rural and remote areas (including the ethnic elderly) look set to continue bearing greater costs associated either with gaining access to or with being denied access to human services.

Since the study, the situation has almost certainly deteriorated even further. The retreat from the traditional welfare state, now being taken further and faster by the Howard federal government, has continued to involve a reduction in the role of government in the provision, subsidy and regulation of human services as well as a shift in the 'mix' or 'balance' of human service provision between government, non-government or voluntary, for-profit and informal (generally family) providers of care.

Particular features of this trend are the extension of markets and quasi-markets, the purchaser-provider split and compulsory competitive tendering (CCT) (Healy 1998, pp. 32–42). Economic rationalism and managerialism appear to predominate in both the private and public sectors. In addition to the now well-known loss of essential infrastructure in rural areas (for example banks, shops), we see human services being increasingly rationalised, downsized and outsourced. In this situation, the welfare of vulnerable groups such as the ethnic elderly and their carers is increasingly threatened. Inequalities are increasing. Opportunities for citizen participation are reduced and the capacity for community development undermined (Hoatson et al. 1996, pp. 128–30; Falk, 1997, p. 15)

Despite all the rhetoric of choice and empowerment, consumers appear to be becoming increasingly disempowered. Competition policies set the interests of various stakeholders in opposition to one another, and the most vulnerable come off worst. Questions of cost and 'value for money' have become the primary criterion of decision making (Davis in Considine & Painter 1997, pp. 208–22). 'Efficiencies' achieved as a result of economic rationalism (downsizing, rationalisation of services) may be absorbed as hidden social or personal costs by the weakest players in the new welfare marketplace—consumers, carers or community organisations (Muetzelfeldt in Rees & Rodley 1995.) Arguably, much of the 'rationalisation' that has been undertaken in rural areas involves such a displacement of costs.

Accessible services for the rural ethnic elderly

For reasons such as these, it appears unlikely that additional resources will be readily available for the development of new services for already marginalised groups in rural areas. Practitioners in rural areas can expect to have 'to do more with less'. Except where there are large numbers of one ethnic group, it is unlikely that there will be sufficient critical mass for ethno-specific services to develop (Barnett 1988, p. 15).

Extrapolating from our findings, the critical task facing rural practitioners is to figure out how to use existing rural resources more effectively, in ways that enable such mainstream services as there are to become more sensitive and responsive to the needs of the ethnic elderly and their carers. In other words, we need to develop policies that will deliver linguistically and culturally appropriate services, information targeted to the ethnic aged, appropriate consultative and participatory processes and appropriate training (Ethnic Aged Working Party 1987).

But how will this be done? Clearly new methods of organisation, service delivery and funding need to be developed (Reid & Soloman 1992, pp. 14–15) and there are many (though not equally desirable) ways of 'doing more with less' in rural areas. These may include such processes as resource-sharing, collocation of services, multi-purpose centres, co-operative or multi-funding arrangements, brokerage and outsourcing mechanisms, user pays arrangements and the use of new technologies areas (Victoria, Office of Rural Affairs 1991, pp. 5–6).

Some of these arrangements might be relatively easily applied to enable culturally appropriate and sensitive services to be targeted towards the ethnic elderly in situations that could otherwise not be operated because of a lack of critical mass. Brokerage approaches, such as the Community Options approach trialled under the Home and Community Care (HACC) Program, which enable services to be tailor-made to the needs of individuals, is particularly applicable and suitable for use in rural areas (House of Representatives 1994, p. 72).

The success of such possibilities depends on strong co-ordination and planning at a regional level as well as upon strong local community development activity. Local practitioners have a pivotal role as catalysts for change, as advocates, mediators, lobbyists, etc. especially in situations in which available services may be inaccessible because the elderly (or their carers) either do not know about them or consider them unsuitable.

Practice in such a context will involve a range of planning, policy, organisational and community development skills.

Human service planning in rural areas

Whilst the rural human service worker may need a formidable range of skills to address some of the problems considered here, there is arguably no greater barrier to the development of human services in rural areas than the lack of a coherent local planning process.

At present, the ability of local communities to respond to local needs is severely constrained by the centralism of the funding and decision-making processes and there is little appreciation of the composite needs of local communities and of the differences between them (ALGA 1993, p. 1). There is little opportunity for local community interests (such as those of the ethnic elderly or their carers) to be heard or represented in planning services such as HACC (House of Representatives 1994, pp. 54–7). Indeed planning for local communities often takes place in a confused nightmare of overlapping or conflicting jurisdictions. Effective delivery of human services in non-metropolitan areas requires a greater emphasis on decentralisation, localisation and decompartmentalisation and more imaginative approaches to community management (Collingridge 1991, p. 6). There is a need for local provision and ownership of services, the use of local knowledge, local decision making and co-operative co-ordination arrangements at the local level, especially arrangements that can overcome critical mass problems. Since each community is unique, new methods of organisation, service delivery and funding must be developed on the basis of locality-specific information and participation (Reid & Soloman 1992, pp. 6–10).

To become widely applicable such approaches require a much higher degree of multi-sectoral planning and co-operation than presently exists and there needs to be a much greater degree of imagination and flexibility on the part of planners and funding bodies, allowing greater autonomy and decision making at the local level. There needs to be a more appropriate balance between 'top-down' and 'bottom-up' planning processes and a much greater degree of flexibility amongst state and federal funding organisations to enable a greater degree of local decision-making about priorities and needs, even if within a framework of central policy direction (Collingridge 1991, p. 6; O'Toole, 1993, pp. 8–13).

Such an approach suggests a pivotal role for local governments and community-based organisations in influencing and co-ordinating the planning process at the local level. Initiatives such as Integrated Local Area Planning (ILAP) offer a holistic view of local area planning, emphasising the need for partnership between the three levels of government, the community and the private sector and for establishing long-term processes for decision-making and resource allocation (ALGA 1993, pp. 1–9).

Such proposals offer the prospect of a complement or balance to 'urbocentric' and centralist (top-down) planning approaches that tend to disempower local rural communities. They help to create a forum in which it is more likely that the needs of groups such as the ethnic elderly and their carers can be articulated. Programs such as ILAP also facilitate the development of possibilities such as collocation of services, cross-funding, resource sharing and brokerage models mentioned earlier.

Implications for practice in rural areas

In the kind of planning context described above, the rural practitioner may feel particularly disempowered. In addition to a knowledge and awareness of their own communities, rural human services workers need to have a critical understanding of the policy environment in which they are working.

This requires a range of policy, planning, organisational and community development skills. As informers, connectors, mediators, front-liners and generalists (Cheers 1992, pp. 5–6), workers need a wide range of policy-practice community development skills, for example in such areas as personal communication, working in groups and meetings, community education, resourcing community structures and processes, conflict resolution, negotiation and mediation, to name but a few (Ife 1995, pp. 237–46).

It is important that rural practitioners guard against a false dichotomy between policy and practice. The term 'policy-practice' is useful. Particularly in rural areas, it is vital that human service practitioners regard influencing policy as a major part of their practice, whether at the organisational or community development level. This involves taking a critical and empowering approach to practice (Ife 1997, p. 166).

Such practice requires a critical understanding and awareness of the current policy environment, generally hostile to the development of generous and socially just policy (Rees & Rodley 1995, pp. 23–5) as well as a range of contextual knowledge and analytical skills such as: knowledge of the community, its needs and aspirations; knowledge of and ability to participate in both intra-and extra-community networks; organisational knowledge and skills. Policy practice and analysis skills involve understanding the nature of the policy environment, how policy-making occurs, as well as the political skills required to get issues onto the local or regional policy agenda (Dalton 1996, pp. 91 et seq.).

Thus ideally, the practice of the rural human service worker is grounded in a range of interactive, political and organisational literacy skills (Rees, 1990, pp. 113 et seq.) leading them to an increased awareness, a more sophisticated analysis and a new vocabulary to empower them for working in an essentially hostile environment (Ife, 1997, p. 170). Thus important contextual knowledge and skills in the current hostile policy environment would include an ability to understand and use the language of economic rationalism and managerialism without becoming seduced by it and without colluding with the injustices that underlie it (Jones & May, 1992 pp. 385 et seq.; Rees 1994, pp. 291 et seq.).

Other important contextual knowledge requires practitioners to become familiar with the kinds of structural difficulties facing the local community, with the local politics, with the existing resources, networks and processes (Kenny 1994, p. 169). Indeed, rural workers need to be 'steeped in' a knowledge and sense of belonging to their communities (Cheers 1992, p. 8). In working with ethnic groups, important contextual knowledge would include such things as the ability to recognise how and why human services programs may be inaccessible to migrants or how certain structures and processes may discourage their participation (Kenny 1994, p. 169).

Such a critical understanding and awareness provides the basis for a critical empowerment approach to policy-practice, whether at an organisational, community development or regional planning level. Since most policy-practice occurs within an organisational context, most policy-practice skills are skills practised at the organisational level. Organisational policy-practice skills are aimed at enabling practitioners (and consumers) to be more empowered within their environment, more able to influence organisational direction and policy. Such skills involve having a good understanding of power, influence and authority structures both inside and outside the organisation. They involve being able to use strategically the organisational environment, its goals, structure, culture, etc. either to bring about or to resist changes affecting the welfare of clients. Such work cannot be undertaken in isolation and requires political and analytical skills that foster collective action—for example, networking, coalition building, etc. (Jones and May 1992; Ife, 1997, pp. 202–4).

For rural practitioners, policy-practice involves community development, yet this is scarcely valued in the current climate of economic rationalism. Community development capacity is being severely eroded (Hoatson et al., 1996, p. 130; Kenny 1996, pp. 108–10) and even the discourse of community development seems to have died (Onynx 1996, p.101). Discourses about 'bottom-up' processes of change and action, about the rights of people to have a say in decisions that affect them, about participation, mutual, collective action and the demand for resources have all been displaced by the harder discourses of economic rationalism and managerialism (Onynx 1996, p.100; Falk 1997, p. 15). Insofar as community development practice can occur at all, it is itself caught on the horns of a dilemma—between a small, localist and conservative self-help rhetoric, which it may be all too easy to adopt when governments are withdrawing resources, and the more radical, community empowerment and partnership approaches that demand greater government accountability and responsibility. Community development today is bedevilled by considerable struggle over questions of how to retain and reclaim integrity, how far to compromise and how to reassert community development principles, at a time when it is increasingly forced to work within an instrumentalist idiom in which the rhetoric of social justice is displaced by a concern with professionalism and industry, competencies, service agreements and competitive tendering (Kenny 1994, pp. 236–7; Kenny 1996, pp. 110–11).

Whatever the ideological underpinnings of practice, at least two elements of traditional community practice should still be possible in rural areas, albeit in an environment with scant resources and requiring therefore a high level of commitment on the part of the worker. These are to work with local communities to help identify needs and to engage in lobbying, advocacy and social action to influence policy and improve service delivery (ACOSS 1992, p. 4).

Needs identification is a critical basis for social justice and should be linked directly to policy development and change in organisational practice (ACOSS 1992, pp. 43–7) as well as sharing and valuing the expertise, wisdom and experience of clients (Ife 1997, p. 189).

Some practical suggestions for working with the ethnic elderly in rural areas

To become a strong catalyst and advocate for the development and/or improvement of services for the ethnic elderly requires that rural practitioners adopt a strong policy-practice/community development focus for all their activities. Organisational and political literacy forms the basis of their knowledge and skills.

But what, in practical terms, are the kinds of activities that rural human service workers might perform in relation to the ethnic elderly and their carers? Since every rural community is unique, the following is a very tentative list of possible activities that may help to address the kinds of issues faced by older migrants, carers and service providers discussed earlier. These are based on some of the recommendations in *Growing Older in a New Home*.

In coalition with other workers and organisations, the practitioner could:

- lobby government departments and funding agencies: for more funding for services for the ethnic elderly in general and/or for enabling mainstream organisations to offer more culturally appropriate services; for the development of appropriate language, training and other policies to increase the sensitivity of mainstream service providers to the needs of the ethnic elderly; for more flexible funding to allow the possibility of more interorganisational and intercommunity resource sharing and collocation of services;

- participate actively in interagency groups interested in improving service accessibility for the ethnic elderly;

- act as a broker, advocate and catalyst for ethnic organisations and clubs to help them become more self-sufficient or enable them to obtain funds to provide support to their own ethnic communities;

- advocate on behalf of local ethnic groups to gain access to mainstream media so they can educate their communities about services;

- work co-operatively with other local organisations or act as a clearinghouse to collect and disseminate information relevant to ethnic communities and to the elderly;

- organise information packages in community languages;

- organise carer support groups;

- organise a forum on ethnic elderly for local service providers and funding bodies;
- form an Ethnic Elderly Action Group;
- investigate and promote the possibilities for local planning embodied in such proposals as Integrated Local Area Planning (ILAP);
- pressure organisations to adopt in mission statements and objectives a commitment to making services culturally and linguistically appropriate, especially with regard to recruitment and training of staff;
- invite members of ethnic community organisations to talk to staff about the needs of the ethnic elderly;
- lobby organisations to increase training for staff in cross-cultural communication skills;
- make provisions for local ethnic communities to participate in discussions and decisions affecting their communities;
- consider how such interests may be represented on management committees or boards;
- consider outreach possibilities such as advertising in languages other than English, in ethnic newsletters, on ethnic radio and television, with fliers posted in appropriate places;
- recruit and train volunteers from ethnic communities to support the elderly for example, visiting services, support groups, interpreting;
- develop culturally appropriate assessment of needs for use in ethnic communities;
- organise social opportunities for ethnic elderly to meet with members of their own ethnic group, including outings, teas, etc.;
- work with other organisations (including professional associations) to build solidarity, networks and coalitions concerning human service needs in the area or region.

Conclusion

This chapter has attempted to highlight some important issues likely to face the ethnic elderly, their carers and service providers in rural areas. The analysis has been premised upon the assumption that, in the current political and economic climate, resources are going to be harder to come by in rural areas. Rural practitioners will be expected 'to do more with less'.

Much of the organisational, policy practice and community development work that might be undertaken to support the ethnic elderly and their carers focuses on ways of making better use of resources that may already exist within the community. This is not to say that rural practitioners should allow governments off the hook too readily. Although much can be done at the community level, governments have a continuing responsibility to meet the needs of minorities. But governments may not fulfil this responsibility (or will do so only sparingly) unless they are subjected to political pressure. Such pressure can be brought to bear from the community level—from the bottom—and be pushed upwards.

Such developmental work, however, cannot be undertaken alone (by the practitioner) or even by a single organisation. Indeed, developing the power base of rural communities is an essential basis for attracting resources (Collingridge 1991, 9; Saw 1994, p. 38). Local communities need to be freed of the constraints and lack of imagination that is the legacy of too great a degree of control from the centre. They need to seek and be offered the opportunities to develop their creativity, imagination and enterprise.

The rural human service practitioner has a key policy-practice/community development role in building such networks and coalitions. No one could pretend it is an easy path, especially in the current human services environment. As the Buddhist sage has it with regard to enlightenment: 'A journey of a thousand miles begins with one step.'

References

Australian Council of Social Service 1992, *Improving Service Delivery to Migrants: the Role of Community Development*, Proceedings of conferences held in Sydney, Melbourne, Perth and Hobart.

Australian Local Government Association 1993, *A Guide to Integrated Local Area Planning*, Canberra: ALGA.

Barnett, K. 1988, 'Aged Care Policy for a Multicultural Society', in *Australian Journal on Ageing*, vol. 7, no. 4.

Borowski, A., Encel, S. & Ozanne, E. (eds) 1997, *Ageing and Social Policy in Australia*, Cambridge University Press, Melbourne.

Cheers, B. 1992, 'Some thoughts on Multiskilled Rural Welfare Practitioners', in *Rural Society*, vol. 2 no. 1

Collingridge, M. 1991, 'What is wrong with Rural Social and Community Services' in *Rural Society*, vol 1, no. 2.

Dalton, T., Draper, M., Weeks, W. & Wiseman, J. 1996, *Making Social Policy in Australia*, Allen and Unwin, Sydney.

Davis, G. 1997, 'Towards a Hollow State: Managerialism and Its Critics' in Considine, M. & Painter, M. (eds), *Managerialism: The Great Debate*, Melbourne University Press, Melbourne.

Department of Community Services 1987, *Strategies for Change: Report of the Ethnic Aged Working Party*, AGPS, Canberra.

Department of Health, Housing and Community Services 1991, *Innovative Service Models in Rural and Remote Areas*, Rural and Remote Areas Unit.

Department of Health, Housing and Community Services, October 1991, *Barriers to Effective Service Delivery in Rural and Remote Areas*, Rural and Remote Areas Unit.

Dunn, P. 1990, 'Successful Aging in a Non-Metropolitan Area', in *Rural Welfare Research Bulletin*,

Falk, I. 1997, 'A Learning Community', in *Community Quarterly*, no. 43.

Healy, J. 1998, *Welfare Options*, Allen and Unwin, Sydney.

Hoatson, L., Dixon, J. & Sloman, D. 1996, 'Community Development and the Contract State', in *Community Development Journal*, vol. 31, no. 2.

House of Representatives Standing Committee on Community Affairs, 1994, *Home but not Alone: Report on the Home and Community Care Program*, AGPS, Canberra.

Ife, J. 1997, *Rethinking Social Work*, Allen and Unwin, Sydney.

Ife, J. 1995, *Community Development*, Longman, Melbourne.

Jones, A. & May, J. 1992, *Working in Human Service Organisations: A Critical Introduction*, Longman Cheshire, Melbourne.

Kenny, S. 1994, *Developing Communities for the Future: Community Development in Australia*, Nelson, Melbourne.

Kenny, S. 1996, 'Contestations of Community Development in Australia', in *Community Development Journal*, vol. 31 no. 2.

Muetzelfeldt, M. 1995, 'Contrived Control of Budgets' in Rees, S. & Rodley, G., *The Human Costs of Managerialism*, Pluto, Sydney.

National Council for the International Year of the Family 1994, *Creating the Links: Families and Social Responsibility*, AGPS, Canberra.

Onyx, J. 1996, Community Development Trends in Australia: trends and tensions', in *Community Development Journal*, vol. 31 no. 2.

O'Toole, K. 1993, 'Replacing Rurality with Human Services in Victorian Local Government', in *Rural Society*, vol. 3, no. 3.

Rees, S. & Rodley, G. 1995, *The Human Costs of Managerialism*, Pluto, Sydney.

Rees, S. 1990, *Achieving Power: Practice and Policy in Social Welfare*, Allen & Unwin, Sydney.

Rees, S., Rodley, G. & Stilwell, F. 1993, *Beyond the Market: Alternatives to Economic Rationalism*, Pluto, Sydney.

Reid, M. & Soloman, S. 1992, *Improving Australia's Rural Health and Aged Care Services*, National Health Strategy, Background Paper, No. 11.

Rowland, D.T 1997, 'Ethnicity and Ageing', in *Ageing and Social Policy in Australia*, Borowski, A., Encel S. & Ozanne, E. (eds), Cambridge University Press, Melbourne.

Rowland, D.T. 1991, *Ageing in Australia*, Longman Cheshire, Melbourne.

Saw, C. 1994, 'Replacing Rurality with Human services in Victorian Local Government: A further response', in *Rural Society*, vol. 4, no. 3/4.

Victoria, Office of Rural Affairs 1991, *Study of Government Service Delivery to Rural Communities*, Victorian State Government, Melbourne.

Williams, C.J. & Lampert, J. 1994, *Growing Older in a New Home*, James Cook University: Centre for Social and Welfare Research, Townsville.